The Devil behind the Surplice

The Devil behind the Surplice

Matthias Flacius and John Hooper on Adiaphora

Wade Johnston

PICKWICK *Publications* · Eugene, Oregon

THE DEVIL BEHIND THE SURPLICE
Matthias Flacius and John Hooper on Adiaphora

Pickwick Publications
An Imprint of Wipf and Stock Publishers
199 W. 8th Ave., Suite 3
Eugene, OR 97401

www.wipfandstock.com

PAPERBACK ISBN: 978-1-5326-1772-0
HARDCOVER ISBN: 978-1-4982-4262-2
EBOOK ISBN: 978-1-4982-4261-5

Cataloguing-in-Publication data:

Names: Johnston, Wade, author.

Title: The devil behind the surplice : Matthias Flacius and John Hooper on adiaphora / Wade Johnston.

Description: Eugene, OR : Pickwick Publications, 2018 | Includes bibliographical references and index.

Identifiers: ISBN 978-1-5326-1772-0 (paperback) | ISBN 978-1-4982-4262-2 (hardcover) | ISBN 978-1-4982-4261-5 (ebook)

Subjects: LCSH: Flacius Illyricus, Matthias, 1520–1575. | Hooper, John, –1555. | Church history—16th century. | Reformation—Germany. | Great Britain—Church history—16th century.

Classification: BR305.3 .J72 2018 (print) | BR305.3 .J72 (ebook)

Manufactured in the U.S.A.   01/10/18

To my wife, Tricia; my children, Magdalen, Nicholas, Isaiah, Augustana, and Sophia; my parents, Jocelynn and John; my former parish, Christ Evangelical Lutheran Church; and the institution at which I now serve, Wisconsin Lutheran College.

Contents

Acknowledgments

FIRST AND FOREMOST, I thank Carrie Euler for her accessibility, advice, and refining of my capabilities as a student and author. I also thank Robert von Friedeburg for his instruction and for expanding my intellectual and research horizons. I owe a debt of gratitude to David Rutherford for his encouragement, counsel and support when questions or obstacles arose during the process of writing this book. Gregory Smith has taught me to ask bigger questions and to wrestle with possible answers. I thank Steven D. Paulson for his writings, which have so shaped my theology, and for his graciousness in agreeing to serve as a reader and improver of this book and what I have written subsequently.

None of this would have been possible without my family. I thank my wife, Tricia Johnston, indubitably my better half, a faithful proofreader, and an ever-patient spouse. I thank my children: Magdalen, Nicholas, Isaiah, Augustana, and Sophia. Too many times this endeavor has taken my attention from them. My parents, John and Jocelynn Johnston, worked tirelessly to provide me with an opportunity to undertake a work like this. I will never be able to repay them. Christ Evangelical Lutheran Church in Saginaw, Michigan graciously permitted me time, including an extended sabbatical, and the benefit of the doubt that such a study could prove worthwhile for others beyond our parish boundaries. Many others deserve acknowledgement for their reassurance and discernment. Though there are too many to mention, I owe special gratitude to Karl Vertz, John Bortulin, Aaron Moldenhauer, Phil Hirsch, John Seifert, Marko Schubert, and the late Herbert Kuske, who urged and facilitated my continued study.

Abbreviations and Translations

ESV   *The English Standard Version Bible.* New York: Oxford University Press, 2009.

KW   Robert Kolb and Timothy J. Wengert, eds. *The Book of Concord: The Confessions of the Evangelical Lutheran Church.* Minneapolis: Fortress Press, 2000.

LW   *Luther's Works.* 55 vols. Edited by Jaroslav Pelikan and Helmut T. Lehman. American ed. Philadelphia: Fortress; St. Louis: Concordia, 1955–1986.

All translations of passages from Latin and German manuscripts are my own, unless otherwise noted.

Introduction

THE YEARS 1546 AND 1547 shook German Lutheranism to its core. Cataclysmic shifts plunged Luther's disciples into a crisis of identity and confession. In the span of fourteen months, the great reformer died and the Schmalkaldic League of evangelical territories and cities suffered a crushing defeat in the Battle of Mühlberg. The grave silenced Luther's prophetic voice. Imperial forces rendered Protestantism's political protectors nearly impotent. Philipp Melanchthon, Luther's treasured colleague and the author of the foundational confession of evangelical Christianity in Germany, the *Augsburg Confession*, found himself the reticent and frightened purported theological head of the German Reformation. Duke Moritz of Saxony now stood as German evangelicalism's most prominent prince, having gained that distinction only recently through what many Lutherans considered blatant treachery. Aligning with the emperor with the promise of a hefty titular and territorial reward, Moritz had attacked his cousin's forces, dividing Elector John Frederick's attention between the imperial forces and his own. The future of the Reformation loomed precariously in the balance and had never seemed darker.

Emperor Charles V was determined to seize the window of opportunity afforded him. He enjoyed peace with France, a lull in the Turkish threat, and significant momentum from his decisive victory over the Schmalkaldic League. This was his chance to address once and for all the long-festering and unresolved religious question in Germany. That was the purpose of the *Augsburg Interim*, which sought to reintroduce Roman Catholic ceremonies and doctrine with the ultimate aim of a complete reunion of the Roman Catholic and Lutheran territories in Germany under the papacy. The *Interim* was not to take the place of a church council. Rather, the emperor intended it to function as a stopgap measure, template, and impetus for later conciliar reform. The evangelical churches in Germany protested the measures included in the *Interim* vociferously. The only meaningful implementation without conflict took place in the southwest of Germany under the threatening watch of Spanish occupying forces, although some advances were made elsewhere as well, usually with the employment or serious threat of military force. So confident indeed were the victorious imperial forces that Cardinal Granvella warned, "You are going to learn Spanish."[1] The persecution was severe. Hundreds of pastors were deposed or fled, many living in forests. The loss of their clergy, many long established in their parishes, only exacerbated popular animosity toward the new measures.

Moritz of Saxony, recognizing the impossibility of implementing the *Augsburg Interim* in his new realm, charged his theologians, including Melanchthon, with constructing a compromise formula. It primarily treated ceremonies, but also included ambiguous doctrinal statements, even on the chief doctrine of justification. The controversy that resulted showed the first fault lines along which Lutheranism would crack in the next few decades (Crypto-Calvinistic, Majoristic, Synergistic, etc.), differences of orientation and spirit that had likely long festered beneath the surface.[2] This evidenced a "coincidence of the content of the Wittenberg message with its method," as Robert Kolb has aptly described it.[3] Kolb with this phrase means to emphasize that students of Phillip Melanchthon entered the contest on both sides, with even his opponents often employing his own method as they strove to set his theology in contrast to Luther's. In this struggle, the Adiaphoristic party, like many Philippists in subsequent controversies, which consisted of many of the same players, were largely centered in Wittenberg and Leipzig. The Gnesio-Lutherans, of whom Flacius was a prominent representative, established an early stronghold at Magdeburg and later in Jena, where John Frederick founded a new university after losing his electoral title and lands.[4]

Into the breach, in the midst of this identity, confessional, and political crisis, stepped a foreigner who likely never preached a sermon in German and lacked full proficiency in that language. Matthias Flacius, denounced by his one-time friend and mentor, the usually moderate Philipp Melanchthon, as the "Illyrian viper" and "runaway slav"—a racial slur utilizing a clever play on words because Latin does not distinguish the word Slav from slave—would become perhaps the most divisive figure in German

1. Olson, *Matthias Flacius and the Survival of Luther's Reform*, 124.

2. For more on Kaufmann's argument regarding the anachronism of speaking of Gnesio-Lutherans at this time, see Kaufmann, *Das Ende der Reformation*, 74. For a similar assessment of the implications of the Adiaphoristic Controversy, see Kaufmann, "Matthias Flacius Illyricus. Lutherischer Theologe und Magdeburger Publizist," 184.

3. Kolb, *Bound Choice, Election, and Wittenberg Theological Method*, 5.

4. Schmauk and Benze, *The Confessional Principle and the Confessions of the Lutheran Church*, 597.

Lutheranism well beyond the time of the publication of the Formula of Concord.[5] Twenty-seven years of age, a gifted and promising Hebrew instructor at the University of Wittenberg, a student of Melanchthon and Luther, he became the most prolific author in Germany for the next five years. This Illyrian upstart framed the debate, delineated the boundaries of true Lutheranism, and led the resistance of the last holdout of the Schmalkaldic League, the city of Magdeburg, popularly known during this period as "our Lord God's chancery."[6]

Meanwhile, in England, Henry VIII had died and his son, trained by evangelical tutors and very favorable to Reformed Christianity, came to the throne. English reformers prayed that he would be England's Josiah, the king who would bring the English Reformation to completion. For the small circle of ecclesiastical leaders close to Thomas Cranmer, this meant reformation along the lines of the Swiss Reformation, especially the reformation in Zurich, initiated by Ulrich Zwingli and now guided by his successor, Heinrich Bullinger. John Hooper, a Henrician exile, returned to England from Zurich with the encouragement of Bullinger, his theological and pastoral mentor and the godfather of one of his children. Hooper seemed a promising theologian, preacher, and teacher in the mold of what the evangelical ecclesiastical elite thought England needed. By all accounts indefatigable and scrupulous in his pastoral responsibilities and a phenomenal preacher, Hooper was invited to preach before the king and his councilors during the Lenten season of 1550, the solemn, penitential season of the church year.

Never one to pass up an opportunity to advance the evangelical cause as he had imbibed it in Zurich, Hooper preached a series of seven sermons on the Book of Jonah. In these sermons he called for quick and thorough reform of the Church of England along Zwinglian lines. He advocated a top-down reformation of English Christianity, led by the king, through example, good laws, and the appointment of faithful bishops, pastors, and university professors, as well as the removal of unfaithful ones, especially those who refused to make a clean break with every aspect of the old religion. Edward was impressed, but not everyone was sold on Hooper's message. Thomas Cranmer was livid and Bishop Nicholas Ridley of London worried that Hooper was undermining the slow, yet effective, progress of reform already underway. Eventually won over by Ridley, the Privy Council also had concerns. The chief point of contention arose when Hooper questioned the retention of vestments in the English Church, particularly in the rite of

5. Olson, *Matthias Flacius and the Survival of Luther's Reform*, 129.

6. Rein's recent monograph on Magdeburg propaganda in the Interim crisis takes its title from this popular moniker for the city: *The Chancery of God: Protestant Print, Polemic and Propaganda against the Empire, Magdeburg 1546–1551*.

episcopal consecration. This was part of a broader objection to traditional aspects of congregational worship that had been retained in general use.

Surprisingly, given the displeasure of Cranmer and the others, on Easter of 1550 Hooper received news that he was to be awarded the bishopric of Gloucester by King Edward VI. Hooper refused to accept the appointment, however, unless consecrated without the prescribed vestments and oaths, which made mention of the saints. This was likely illegal, but his request was initially granted. When Ridley refused to perform the rite under such conditions, however, Cranmer, stung by Hooper's attack, sided with him, and the Council eventually placed Hooper under house arrest and then in the Fleet prison in London. Hooper finally conceded, was consecrated in the prescribed vestments and according to the prescribed rite, and served faithfully as a bishop until his death under Edward VI.

Through examination of the arguments of Matthias Flacius Illyricus and John Hooper, as well as the conditions in and under which they made them, this book will argue, first, that adiaphora served as a lens for the larger theological frameworks within which both men operated, one intentionally Lutheran and one just as intentionally Zwinglian. Adiaphora also provided a glimpse into what each man held to be the key doctrine of the Reformation and its chief threat. For Flacius, this was justification by grace through faith, *sola gratia* and *sola fide*; for Hooper it was another sola, *sola scriptura*, or Scripture alone. Second, while both men wrote contemporaneously and raised objections regarding the same doctrinal topic, their arguments cannot be divorced from the very different political climates, military conditions, and constitutional arrangements within which they were made. In fact, while Hooper certainly would have objected to vestments no matter the setting, given his theology, Flacius would not have objected to the surplice had it not been for the circumstances. While Flacius articulated a doctrine of adiaphora, his objections were largely a factor of circumstances; they were contextual. The surplice, for instance, was unacceptable because of the conditions under which it was reintroduced and not in and of itself. Hooper's objections, however, were grounded in his doctrine of adiaphora alone. He saw the vestments in question as inherently unacceptable. Third, although resistance theories have traditionally been associated with the Reformed and not Lutherans, it was the Lutheran, Flacius, and his Magdeburg colleagues who made a case for resistance to the emperor through lesser magistrates, while Hooper taught near absolute obedience to the monarch, a view much closer to that usually attributed to the Lutherans of the time. Finally, each man made extensive use of the Old Testament, but the passages, patterns, and paragons they selected are telling. Their choices in this regard shed light on the nature of their individual controversies, their hopes for their respective reformation movements, their conceptions of what the church should look like, how its reform should be organized, and what its relationship with the state should be.

More generally, this work will argue that Flacius viewed and framed the controversies of his day through the lens of those of Luther's time. Moreover, like the later Luther, he operated with a pronounced apocalyptic sense. While he established doctrines with the New Testament, he most often illustrated them with the Old Testament. Moreover, whenever possible, he appealed to Luther and the confessional statements of the Lutheran Reformation, as well as the earlier writings of Wittenberg theologians, especially Philipp Melanchthon. This study will also demonstrate that Flacius, with Luther, viewed doctrine as one single entity and not as a collection of doctrines, which is why he saw in the proposed compromises and changes of the *Leipzig Interim* a threat, not only to certain teachings of Luther and the Scriptures, but to the entirety of the teachings of Luther and the Scriptures, and especially the chief article of justification. Finally, through his appeals to earlier periods of persecution, both biblical and subsequent, Flacius' conception of the true church as a remnant faced with the necessity of confession and martyrdom will become evident. For Flacius, this emphasis on a suffering and persecuted church militant, engaged in a quest for doctrinal and practical fidelity to the Word of God and Luther's teaching, formed an integral part of Lutheran identity. In each age the church would have its foes, its Christ and Belial, and the church militant would never be without struggle, even in times of temporal peace, or the "peace of the belly," as he was wont to call it.

Hooper sought to advance Zwinglian theology and ecclesiology, as he understood it, in his teaching and ministry in England. His opposition to the consecratory vestments of a bishop and vestments in general was expressed in the terms and within the framework of the Reformed theology of Zurich. While Bullinger urged patience and counseled compromise for the sake of long-term reform in England, Hooper was not inconsistent in his Reformed arguments based upon what he had learned and seen modeled in Zurich. His approach to reform, like that of Zurich, worked from the top down and depended upon cooperation between the church and state. While England was the only Reformed reformation to take place under the auspices of a monarch and not along the lines of a godly republic, in his writings, Hooper attempted to synthesize and accommodate the Zwinglian pattern to the English Reformation.

As noted, Flacius and Hooper clearly differed in their approach to, definition of, and reasons for their opposition to practices in the church deemed adiaphora by their opponents—in Hooper's case, ministerial vestments in general, and, in Flacius' case, to the surplice, or chorrock. Flacius and the Magdeburgers were primarily concerned with the circumstances in which adiaphora were being employed—although they did clearly delineate that some things were in and of themselves not adiaphora. In contrast, Hooper and those who sided with him were chiefly worried about the inherently non-indifferent nature of longstanding church customs. Moreover, although the bishop's vestments were a cause for controversy in and of themselves for Hooper, had there been no imperial legislation regarding vestments in Germany, there is no indication that Flacius would have campaigned against the surplice. The surplice was in use in some Lutheran churches before the *Leipzig Interim*—Moritz' ancestral territories had experienced very conservative liturgical reform, so that the new measures introduced "little innovation" in liturgical practice—and nowhere in Flacius' writings do we find any trace of qualms with the established, continued use of vestments like the surplice in such Lutheran territories where they were the standard practice.[7]

Surely, although both men opposed certain vestments, Hooper, an English product of the Swiss Reformation, and Flacius, an Illyrian product of the German Lutheran Reformation, operated on very different theological grounds. They were confronted by dissimilar constitutional and governmental arrangements. They labored within distinct ecclesiastical structures. They were motivated by both common and contrasting fears regarding the relationship of the two kingdoms, the state and the Christian Church. Flacius was not outside the theological or institutional mainstream of German Lutheranism before the Adiaphoristic Controversy broke out, while Hooper had already departed from the mainstream of the English Church under Henry VIII well before the Vestment Controversy took place. Flacius, therefore, was forced into a fight by changes in practice introduced by the state. Hooper, on the other hand, emboldened by a promotion within the church granted him by the state, sought a fight in order to force the state to change the established practice of the church.

Special attention will be paid to how both men internalized the doctrine and reform efforts of their theological heroes, Luther and Zwingli. Particular attention will be paid to where and how each of them drew confessional lines. Recurring images and themes will be highlighted, as well as examples from the Scriptures and church history. This will serve to more fully demarcate, illuminate, and explicate the worldview, theological frameworks, and chief doctrinal concerns (what was at stake) of both men, and not merely in contradistinction to that of their opponents, as has usually

7. Arand, Nestingen, and Kolb, *The Lutheran Confessions: History and Theology of the Book of Concord*, 179.

been the case in the past. Consideration will also be given to the manner in which Flacius and Hooper approached the relationship between the church and the state, the duty of obedience and the possibility of resistance. Beyond the immediate scope of this exploration, greater appreciation for the nature, scale, and progression of these two controversies, one a precursor of Puritanism and the other a distinct and significant step toward confessionalization and state-building in Germany, will provide a better framework for contextualizing subsequent developments in the reformations in Germany and England, ecclesiastically, politically, and societally.

Matters will be addressed both chronologically and thematically. First, the reader will be provided with some helpful background and perspective regarding Luther's theology and Luther's teaching specifically on resistance. Special attention will be given to Luther's *Warning to His Dear German People*. A thorough study of Luther's doctrine of resistance would surely entail a good number of his other writings as well—for instance, his 1539 *Zirkulardisputation zu Matthäus*. Here the *Warning* will receive predominant and particular attention, because of its influence on Flacius and the Magdeburgers. Second, this study will trace the history of the Schmalkaldic League and explain the political and theological background of the Adiaphoristic Controversy. It will also sketch Flacius' life up to the time of the controversy. Third, the reader will be introduced to the primary sources utilized for this study and outline Flacius' general argumentation in the pamphlets under consideration, as well as the key Scriptures he used to ground his arguments theologically. Next, attention will be given to the noteworthy examples Flacius chose to use from Scripture, the Apocrypha, and ecclesiastical history in order to illustrate his points or motivate his readers. An examination of predominant or particularly interesting themes from his writings, which shed light upon Flacius' worldview and conception of the controversy at hand, will follow. These are: first, his apocalypticism; second, his remnant theology; third, his emphasis on confession and martyrdom as historical marks and identifiers of the faithful church militant; and finally his use of outsiders, like Spaniards and Turks, to reinforce his case. Finally, for comparative and contextual purposes, the last chapter will summarize the argumentation of the famous *Magdeburg Confession* as well as the final judgment of the *Formula of Concord* on the matter in its Article X.

In the second part, focus will shift to the writings and arguments of John Hooper in the Vestment Controversy. First, this second part will provide background on the Lutheran influence on the English Reformation in its first phase, the Henrician Reformation, and the general failure of Lutheran theology and ecclesiology to take hold in England. A brief sketch of John Hooper's life will then follow for the reader, as well as an outline of

Zurich's theological imprint upon him. Next, the reader will be familiarized with King Edward VI and his reform of the English Church as well as the general framework of the Vestment Controversy. The study will then engage Hooper's chief and sole surviving writings from the controversy, articulate his arguments, and identify key themes and recurring images and biblical precedents, examples, and illustrations. The conclusion will tie everything together, comparing and contrasting the thought and approaches of Hooper and Flacius vis-à-vis adiaphora as well as the circumstances in which they were developed and expressed.

Part One

Matthias Flacius and the
Adiaphoristic Controversy

Chapter 1 _____

The Path to the
Adiaphoristic Controversy

1.1. Luther's Theology of the Two Kingdoms

AT THE OUTSET, IT is important for the reader to understand an important distinction in Luther's and Lutheran theology, that is, the distinction between righteousness *coram mundo* and *coram Deo*, civic righteousness and the righteousness that avails before God. Article XVIII of the *Apology to the Augsburg Confession*, which the reformer considered a faithful explication of his teaching, helpfully elucidated this distinction. There the *Apology* conceded such a thing as civic righteousness, or righteousness *coram mundo*, in the sight of the world. The human will, it made clear, could "to some extent produce civil righteousness or the righteousness of works." The *Apology* explained further, "It can talk about God and offer God acts of worship with external works," for instance, and "it can obey rulers and parents." This meant that "by choosing an external work it can keep back the hand from murder, adultery, and theft." This was a whole different rightesousnes than justifying righteousness, however. The *Apology* stated, "Scripture calls this righteousness of the flesh, which carnal nature (that is, reason) produces by itself apart from the Holy Spirit."[1] Nevertheless, even this righteousness possible for human beings to achieve was rare because of the fallen state of humanity, as "the power of concupiscence is such that people more often obey their evil impulses than sound judgment" and "we see that not even the philosophers, who seemed to have aspired after this righteousness, attained it."[2]

---

1. KW, *Apology of the Augsburg Confession* XVIII.7, 233–34.
2. KW, *Apology of the Augsburg Confession* XVIII.5–6, 234.

According to the *Apology*, civic righteousness, *coram mundo*, was a blessing for the stability and benefit of society, but as much as it was to be praised, it also had to be distinguished from—and never esteemed higher than—the righteousness that avails before God, *coram Deo*. Righteousness *coram mundo* could do nothing to undo the damage sin had done with its eternal consequences. And so the *Apology* insisted, "Nevertheless we do not ascribe to free will those spiritual capacities, namely, true fear of God, true faith in God, the conviction and knowledge that God cares for us, hears us, and forgives us, etc. These are the real works of the first table, which the human heart cannot produce without the Holy Spirit, just as Paul says."[3]

Comprehension of this difference between the two righteousnesses is crucial to an understanding of Luther's writings concerning the temporal and spiritual realms. It is what drove him to include the famous *allein* in his translation of Rom 3:28: "*So halten wir nun dafür, daß der Mensch gerecht werde ohne des Gesetzes Werke, allein durch den Glauben.*" In Luther's view, people were saved through faith alone or they were not saved at all. People were righteous in Christ and with his righteousness or they were not righteous at all in God's sight (*coram Deo*), no matter how good a person or citizen they might have been (*coram mundo*). In fact, hell would be filled with such good people. As Article IV of the *Augsburg Confession* so succinctly made clear, "human beings cannot be justified before God by their own powers, merits, or works." Rather, it argued, "they are justified as a gift on account of Christ through faith when they believe that they are received into grace and that their sins are forgiven on account of Christ, who by his death made satisfaction for our sins. God reckons this faith as righteousness."[4] In short, as the *Apology* summarized Luther's teaching, "It is helpful to distinguish between civil righteousness, which is ascribed to the free will, and spiritual righteousness, which is ascribed to the operation of the Holy Spirit in the regenerate." This was important because "in this way outward discipline is preserved, because all people alike ought to know that God requires civil righteousness and that to some extent we are able to achieve it." The two, however, remained distinct, "philosophical teaching and the teaching of the Holy Spirit."[5]

In *Temporal Authority: To What Extent Should It Be Obeyed*, Luther emphasized the importance of Christ's conversation with Pilate, during which Jesus stated, "My kingdom is not of this world. If my kingdom were of this world, my servants would have been fighting, that I might not be

3. KW, *Apology of the Augsburg Confession* XVIII.7, 234.

4. KW, *Augsburg Confession* IV.1–3, 39–41.

5. KW, *Apology of the Augsburg Confession* XVIII.9–10, 234–35.

delivered over to the Jews. But my kingdom is not from the world."[6] He also pointed out that St. John the Baptist said to those soldiers—servants of the sword, the state—who came to him with crises of conscience, "Do not extort money from anyone by threats or by false accusation, and be content with your wages."[7] Christ did not overthrow the two kingdoms but placed them within their proper Christian context. St. John the Baptist did not toss out the role of the sword, but affirmed it, even while he at the same time informed the conscience of those who wielded it.

This, however, was not the first place Luther wrote in such a way or made use of these scriptural passages. As Luther was holed up in the Wartburg after Worms, Philip Melanchthon seems to have wrestled with the role and place of the state for Christians, particularly because of the agitation of the Zwickau prophets. Luther dismissed these men as *Schwärmern*, enthusiasts, who thought that they had swallowed the Holy Spirit "feathers and all," but they caused Melanchthon much consternation.[8] Among other things, the prophets urged the creation of a truly Christian society. In response, Luther wrote to his nervous friend and gifted colleague and reassured him of the divine institution of and will for temporal authority (the sword). Christ had not set forth guidelines and regulations for the use of the sword in the Gospels, but that was because it can "easily be regulated by human beings," and the accounts of the evangelists nevertheless make clear that Christ "commended it to us and affirmed it as instituted, or rather he clearly asserted that it is divinely ordained."[9]

According to Luther, the Christian was at the same time both a complete citizen of his nation and of heaven. As Christ is God and man in one person, so the Christian was a full member of both kingdoms in one person, and the two were hard to separate. An improper distinction between the two would, in Luther's mind, only serve to do harm to the Christian's person as a whole and confuse his work in both kingdoms. The Christian had to live with the tension and without neglecting either realm. Thus, while working in the kingdom of the left (the state) for the good of his neighbor, the Christian's conscience would rightly be informed by the teachings of Scripture. This would be so even as he argues on the basis of natural reason, the rightful guide for the kingdom of the left. While Luther famously described reason as the devil's whore (that is, fallen reason and reason misapplied in theology), he also frequently insisted that reason was God's gift to be used

6. John 18:36 ESV.
7. Luke 3:14 ESV; LW 45:88, 98.
8. LW 40:83.
9. LW 48:260–61.

wisely in the temporal realm. Paul Althaus sums up Luther's notion of the dual citizenship of the Christian well: "[The Christian] has two lords: one in the earthly kingdom and one in the spiritual kingdom. He is obligated to the emperor and to Christ at the same time; to the emperor for his outward life, to Christ inwardly with his conscience and in faith."[10]

For Luther, the world was fallen but not to be forsaken. Christians were not to scamper off to the wilderness to flee society. The world was full of sinners, but that was precisely why, in Luther's theology, it so desperately needed Christ's saints. God did not need the Christian's good works, but his or her neighbor did.[11] Luther proceeded in his thought from creation to redemption to vocation. God made you, God saved you, God placed you where he wanted you to walk in the works he had prepared in advance for you to walk in.[12] Luther wrote in his *Exposition of Psalm 127, for the Christians at Riga in Livonia*, "Indeed, one could very well say that the course of the world, and especially the doing of his saints, are God's mask, under which he conceals himself and so marvelously exercises dominion and introduces disorder in the world."[13] He preached in a festival sermon "the whole Gospel leads you to notice your neighbor and show mercy to him, to help him and advise him as God has helped you" and "concerning our works God tells us that they belong down here on earth for our neighbor, for the poor, miserable, desperate people whom we shall help, whom we shall comfort, teach and advise."[14] In his saints God worked not only for the good of his kingdom, that is, the kingdom of the gospel, but also for the kingdom of the state, the left hand, both to keep good order, and when necessary—through persecution and martyrdom, for instance—to bring change. The Christian Church not only had a place in this world but, with its works and prayers, salt and light, played an irreplaceable role in its survival and well-being.

Paul Althaus explains that Luther's ethics are inseparable from his teaching on the chief article, justification by faith, because "justification is both the presupposition and the source of the ethical life."[15] In other words, the Christian is set free from sin and free to serve, not for salvation—that inestimable burden has been lifted, since it was a yoke only Christ could

10. Althaus, *The Ethics of Martin Luther*, 61–62. It is worth noting that Luther's concept of outward and inward corresponds more with the concept of public and private in today's parlance than outward and inward.

11. Wingren, *Luther on Vocation*, 10.

12. Eph 2:8–10.

13. LW 45:331.

14. *Festival Sermons of Martin Luther: The Church Postils*, 60–61.

15. Althaus, *The Ethics of Martin Luther*, 3.

bear—but as one saved and supplied with the ability and impetus to serve. Thus, Flacius insisted that adiaphora ceased to be such when they came back under the law. The Christian serves, not under compulsion, but in love, with works that flow from faith, and that faith, through the same gracious love of a merciful God, finds great joy and satisfaction in such service, for how can the bride not delight to serve her doting Bridegroom? This service to God through earthly vocation, and even in governmental vocations, was fundamental to Flacius' later arguments concerning the duty of citizens, laypeople, pastors, and princes in resisting the *Interim* and to the *Magdeburg Confession*'s insistence that the lesser magistrate not only could resist a superior authority in certain instances, but had to do so as part of his or her vocation.

If the secular authorities in existence were ordained by God, and if the Christian was called to serve them, when might a Christian resist such authorities? Luther was forced to wrestle with this when an imperial invasion seemed imminent after the Diet of Augsburg of 1530. In addressing the question of when resistance was appropriate, this chapter will examine Luther's critical treatise of 1531, written in the heat of this tension, *Dr. Martin Luther's Warning to His Dear German People*. The prospect of imperial invasion seemed very real after the Diet of Augsburg of 1530, which failed to resolve the religious question. There the emperor had rejected the *Augsburg Confession* and accepted the *Confutation*, the response of select Roman Catholic theologians to the doctrine and practice confessed by the Lutherans. Moreover, in a rump session of the diet in November the emperor had declared his intention to use force if the Lutherans did not comply with his mandates. This was the temporal context of Luther's *Dr. Martin Luther's Warning to His Dear German People*.[16] There has been debate about Luther's intentions in writing the *Warning*—whether he really meant to say anything new by it or not, and whether it was, in fact, the call for resistance under appropriate circumstances that some later interpreted it to be—but here the later reception of the work by those who justified resistance to the emperor and his allies is most pertinent.[17] It is possible, but unlikely, that their reception of the work was quite contrary to the general spirit Luther exhibited within it. Worthy of note, though, is Robert von Friedeburg's reminder that Luther never endorsed any sort of natural law right of defense for individual citizens. Rather, throughout the *Warning* he restricted the right of defense to the princes, likely as a result of the constitutional and legal arguments

16. For Luther's *Warning*, see LW 47:6–55.

17. For the chief points of contention, see Friedeburg, "Confusion around the Magdeburg Confession and the Making of 'Revolutionary Early Modern Resistance Theory,'" 307–18; Whitford, "Rejoinder to Robert von Friedeburg," 301–3.

of the jurists which provided lawful grounds for such resistance.[18] The Magdeburgers, not Luther, extended the right of defense and resistance beyond princely magistrates to a "wide range of inferior magistrates" in their *Magdeburg Confession.*[19] A summary of the arrangement and argument of the *Warning* follows in order to familiarize the reader with it and make comparisons to the later works of Matthias Flacius and the Magdeburgers, especially the *Magdeburg Confession,* because these later Lutherans placed great emphasis on the *Warning,* quoted it, and even crafted some of their publications in similar style and arrangement to it.

In the *Warning,* Luther's answer regarding when resistance was permissible was rather simple: when obedience to God demanded it. He distinguished self-defense and rebellion and made clear that only the former was debatable for Christians. Luther blamed the stubbornness of the papal parties for the failure to reach religious peace so far.[20] For that reason, Luther concluded that God would swallow up these enemies in their hardness of heart, like Pharaoh in the Red Sea. Yes, "God sure loves this and takes delight in it," and "such defiance and contempt of his grace are most pleasing to him," teaching moments for the arrogant.[21] The possibility of violence, and even his own death, did not terrify Luther, for "whoever kills Doctor Luther in an uprising will not spare many of the priests either," so that "in the end we will undertake a little pilgrimage together—they, the papists, into the abyss of hell to their god of lies and murder, whom they served with lies and murder; I to my Lord Jesus Christ, whom I served in truth and peace."[22]

Luther would not countenance rebellion, though he held it understandable, given the great tyranny of pope and emperor. Rebellion was neither scriptural nor Lutheran, but God would surely use it, Luther made clear, should it arise. Such rebellion could serve as a means for God to humble his enemies, but if it did come, it would do so, not as the "fruit of Lutheran teaching," but rather as a result of the papists' desire for conflict.[23] Justified resistance in Luther's view was self-defense, although even in that instance he would not be the one to call for war, because "it is not fitting for me, a preacher, vested with the spiritual office, to wage war or to counsel war or incite it, but rather to dissuade from war and to direct to peace, as I have done

18. Friedeburg, "Confusion around the Magdeburg Confession," 312.

19. Ibid., 318.

20. LW 47:11.

21. LW 47:13.

22. LW 47:15.

23. LW 47:14.

until now with all diligence."[24] It was likely, however, that the enemies of God who sought war would, in good time, meet their Maccabees, a theme later developed by Mathias Flacius Illyricus and the confessors of Magdeburg.[25] Thomas Kaufmann calls the Maccabees the first and most important image and model of Christian defiance in the face of religious oppression.[26]

The *Warning*, therefore, offered pastoral counsel to those who may be faced with warfare, especially leaders who may have to choose between obedience to God or man, persecution of Christian subjects in their territories or protection of them. Conscience, as later for Flacius and the Magdeburg confessors, was central. Luther wrote, "I will not reprove those who defend themselves against the murderous and bloodthirsty papists, nor let anyone else rebuke them as being seditious, but I will direct them in this matter to the law and to the jurists." He noted that "when the murderers and bloodhounds wish to wage war and to murder, it is in truth no insurrection to rise against them to defend oneself."[27] He continued, "I do not want to leave the conscience of the people burdened by the concern and worry that their self-defense might be rebellious. For such a term would be too evil and too harsh in such a case. It should be given a different name, which I am sure the jurists can find for it."[28] The Lutherans desired peace, Luther argued, but were faced with enemies who had "no law, either divine or human, on their side," and so they needed to be ready, no doubt militarily, but especially spiritually.[29] No Protestant should want war, but they had to be spiritually prepared for the possibility, for their opponents' only recourse was to force, which, unlike God's Word, they did have on their side.[30] He explained:

> But since I am the 'prophet of the Germans'—for this haughty title I will henceforth have to assign to myself, to please and oblige my papists and asses—it is fitting that I, as a faithful teacher, warn my dear Germans against the harm and danger threatening them and impart Christian instruction to them regarding their conduct in the event that the emperor, at the instigation of his devils, the papists, issues a call to arms against the princes and cities on our side.[31]

24. LW 47:18.
25. LW 47:17.
26. Kaufmann, *Das Ende der Reformation*, 195.
27. LW 47:19.
28. Ibid.
29. LW 47:20.
30. LW 47:25.
31. LW 47:29.

Luther provided three reasons why the princes could disobey the emperor should the Roman Catholic parties press for war. First, "you, as well as the emperor, vowed in baptism to preserve the gospel of Christ and not to persecute it or oppose it."[32] In words echoed later by the Magdeburgers, Luther insisted that "he who fights and contends against the gospel necessarily fights simultaneously against God, against the precious blood of Christ, against the Holy Spirit."[33] Second, "even if our doctrine were false—although everyone knows it is not—you should still be deterred from fighting [along with the emperor, rather than in the defense of your subjects] solely by the knowledge that by such fighting you are taking upon yourself a part of the guilt before God of all the abominations which have been committed and will be committed by the whole papacy."[34] Third and finally, "if you did otherwise you would not only burden yourself with all these abominations and help strengthen them, but you would also lend a hand in overthrowing and exterminating all the good which the dear gospel has again restored and established," which he then described for them.[35] This was no trifling concern, for "if this doctrine vanishes, the church vanishes," and even if all should try to undo it, "it must remain and the world must continue to perish on account of it."[36] If the princes were to obey the emperor in this regard, they would "help to destroy Christ's kingdom and rebuild the devil's."[37] In short, the Christian "must obey God rather than men," as the *clausula Petri* of Acts 5:29 states.[38] He warned, "Christ will not be afraid of you and will also (God willing) stand his ground against you. But if he does, you will have quite a battle on your hands."[39] One can understand why those words would have resonated with Flacius and the Magdeburgers and why they would have found in them a justification for their resistance, as well as grounds to claim theological kinship with Luther in their course of action, even if, in the case of the pastors who ascribed to the *Magdeburg Confession*, their course included in the lesser magistrate argument an expansion of Luther's parameters regarding who is entitled to resist a superor magistrate.

32. LW 47:35.
33. LW 47:35.
34. LW 47:36.
35. LW 47:52.
36. LW 47:54.
37. Ibid.
38. Ibid.
39. Ibid.

1.2. The Schmalkaldic League and the Outbreak of the Controversy

To understand the development of the Schmalkaldic League, it is beneficial to consider how Luther saw himself vis-à-vis politicians and politics.
He no doubt recognized that his theological stances had set a Reformation under way which included clear political aspects and dynamics. He
also certainly realized that his continued personal survival, and not only
that of his theological reform, depended upon the princely protection, no
matter how piously and sincerely he commended himself to God's hands
alone. Luther's God used earthly means, both to bring forgiveness through
Word and sacrament and to bring protection and foster public welfare in the
temporal realm; his explanation of the Fourth Commandment in the *Large
Catechism* evidences that. With the death of Frederick the Wise—who did
not desire direct consultation with Luther and navigated his political course
largely without solicited advice from the theologians in Wittenberg—John
of Saxony, a committed Lutheran, came to power.[40] Luther was now regularly consulted, and his opinions carried noteworthy weight at the court.
And yet, for all of this, unlike Zwingli, Bucer, or Calvin, Luther was never in
the middle of civic dealings and lacked any comprehensive feel for the basic
mechanics of the civil realm.[41] He operated with a clear political naiveté and
without the cultivated savvy of the urban reformers. Luther was a university
professor and a preacher to the comparatively unrefined citizens of Wittenberg. He did not regularly interact with a powerful city council. He did not
daily grapple with the broader imperial politics that could swiftly and significantly impact the security and welfare of an imperial city as some other
reformers would have. Throughout his life and in every crisis, Luther continued to see himself tasked with the pastoral care of souls and consciences.
Eike Wolgast rightly explains, "Luther never saw himself as a politician, but
always and in every situation as a theologian and as one charged with the
cure of souls [*Seelsorger*]," so that that his politics were a derivative of his
theology, the testing of theological principles in political practice.[42]

The 1529 Diet of Speyer, not attended by Charles V, but overseen
by Ferdinand in his stead, marked an important shift in the course of
the Reformation in Germany. While the diet in the same city in 1526
had suspended execution of the Edict of Worms, which forbade anyone
to receive, defend, or support Luther and his ideas, the 1529 diet lifted

40. Wolgast, *Die Wittenberg Theologie und die Politik der evangelischen Stände*; Wolgast, *Die Religionsfrage als Problem des Widerstandsrechts im 16.*, 278, 291.

41. Wolgast, *Die Wittenberg Theologie*, 289.

42. Ibid., 13.

that suspension. This only fueled the suspicions of the Protestant parties that conflict was inevitable. This was especially true of Landgrave Philip of Hesse, who had already been pushing for an alliance of Protestant forces, particularly after getting his hands on a forged document detailing a Roman Catholic alliance supposedly formed after the earlier Diet of Speyer of 1526. Charles V had actually sent instructions for Ferdinand to act in a diplomatic and mollifying fashion with the Protestant parties, since he needed their assistance against the surging Turkish armies approaching Vienna. Nevertheless, Ferdinand brought the diet to a speedy conclusion before the emperor's counsel could be heeded, or perhaps he never had any intention of heeding it. Unlike at the earlier diet in Speyer, the Protestants were now in the clear minority, and there was little they could do to stop the new measures. Thus, the diet in the end forbade new reform measures and declared that the Edict of Worms was to be enforced in the territories of the empire. Effectively Roman Catholicism was to be the faith of the empire, regardless of the confessional convictions of its ruler. This was unacceptable to the Protestant princes and imperial cities, and so the road was paved to a defensive alliance like the Schmalkaldic League. In the end, unable to change or substantially influence the decisions of the committee of the diet—Landgrave Philip was not even consulted—all that was possible for the evangelicals was protest, the famous Protestation of Speyer of 25 April 1529, from which Protestants take their name.[43]

As the Turkish threat continued to materialize and grow, a solution to the German religious question became increasingly important for Charles V, and so, while the Diet of Augsburg of 1530 dealt with a variety of issues, religion dominated. The evangelicals presented a summary of their faith, the *Augsburg Confession*, written by Philipp Melanchthon and based upon a number of previous theological articles, which has since served as a shibboleth for Protestants, especially on the European continent. The Catholic theologians in turn presented their *Confutation*, with which Charles V was not impressed. In the end, however, the emperor rejected the *Augsburg Confession* and accepted the *Confutation*. The subsequent Protestant *Apology of the Augsburg Confession* had little bearing imperially, although it was widely disseminated in Germany, and the emperor's refusal to consider it bolstered the Protestant narrative that pope and emperor together were hardening themselves, or had hardened themselves, against the truth. It also became part of the 1580 *Book of Concord*, a collection of the confessional statements of the Evangelical Lutheran Church. Together with the lifting of the religious compromise of the 1526 Diet of Speyer at the 1529 Diet of Speyer,

43. Kohnle, *Reichstag und Reformation*, 368.

Charles V's actions at Augsburg served as the chief catalyst for the founding of the Schmalkaldic League, bringing, as Gabriele Haug-Moritz has noted, conflicts that had festered for a decade into open dissent.[44]

In addition to the actions of Ferdinand and Charles V, however, there were also important theological developments that cleared the way for a defensive alliance. In 1530 a disputation was held between Saxon jurists and theologians in Torgau, with the hope that consensus could be reached regarding the right of resistance of Lutheran princes, should they come under attack, and the formation a defensive alliance. This Torgau disputation was foundational both for the subsequent evolution of the Schmalkaldic League and the theories of resistance propagated by the city of Magdeburg during the interim crises. Torgau was a watershed moment for the possibility and permissibility of Lutheran resistance in the first half of the sixteenth century. And it was so not because Luther offered any ringing endorsement of such a path, but because he removed himself and the rest of the Wittenberg faculty from ongoing and meaningful debate of the issue with the court. The jurists were thus set free to formulate arguments and theories without the hindrance of the traditionally conservative and recalcitrant opinions of the faculty which had so frustrated them up until this point. In this, Bugenhagen had been the exception, the lone voice among the faculty articulating a position in line with the jurists, which made the case for resistance in certain circumstances.[45]

Luther's *Gutachten*, a product of the disputation of Torgau, therefore marked a victory for the jurists and their arguments, and they later used it to repel religiously motivated objections to resistance on a number of occasions.[46] Luther himself provided no clearly defined advocation, absolution, or framework for resistance in the document; in fact, resistance remained possible only by the jurists' definitions based upon natural and imperial law.[47] As one historian notes, "When the elector summoned both his lawyers and parson/professors to dispute the justifiability of resistance in the darkening political atmosphere after the failure of the diet at Augsburg to resolve the religious 'question,' it was the jurists who did elaborate the constitutional and legal arguments in favor of Saxon membership in the proposed league." The jurists argued that "the emperor had been elected upon specific conditions, they insisted, and thus had an obligation to rule in conjunction with the estates. If he violated the laws of the empire, as

44. Haug-Moritz, *Der Schmalkaldische Bund, 1530–1541/42*, 45.

45. For more on Bugenhagen, see Wolgast, *Die Wittenberg Theologie*, 136.

46. Ibid., 191.

47. Ibid., 178, 182

he had done by proceeding against the Protestants when their appeal to a council was still pending, all their obligations to him were erased."[48] Luther's *Gutachten* opened the door for the jurists, but they, not he, for the most part made the case for resistance. He merely demurred from arguing against their case, whether from conviction or by necessity.

Luther did not necessarily change his position at Torgau, therefore. Rather, he stepped back from the debate. He claimed incompetence in questions of imperial law. He declared himself unqualified to offer political counsel on such matters, so that the jurists, now unencumbered, could proceed with their argumentation from imperial law.[49] When this was coupled with the death of John of Saxony, who regularly sought Luther's counsel and, much to Landgrave Philip of Hesse's consternation, had adopted a more patient and moderate tone and approach because of it, a recipe for a precipitous turn emerged. Luther had long harbored suspicions regarding Philip of Hesse's ambitions, and these suspicions only grew with time. Luther feared the consequences of the youthful chest puffing and *Krieglust* of the young princes, especially the Landgrave, who were now at the head of the two most influential Protestant lands in Germany.[50] In Luther's eyes, they lacked the wisdom of Frederick the Wise and scruples of John of Saxony, with whose death Luther's influence with the Saxon court clearly waned.[51] John Frederick, young, ambitious, and much more amenable to Philip of Hesse's arguments and strategies, was much less interested in the faculty's opinions and was determined to act, even in theological matters, as he saw fit. This marked a crucial shift from Frederick the Wise's hands-off passivity and John of Saxony's devout desire to consult the theologians.

The Schmalkaldic League eventually would have a battle on its hands—one that it lost humiliatingly and disastrously to imperial forces. That does not mean, however, that it would not be quite a force for a number of years leading up to its demise. In fact, a good argument could be made that had it not been for its growing potency and, hence, its increasing ambitions, it might not have been undone. That is a thesis for another investigation, however. Here it is enough to briefly sketch the founding of the League, which took place in 1531 and included Landgrave Philip of Hesse and John of Saxony. The formation of a league was hardly innovative or shocking; leagues had a long history in imperial politics, and the emperor had depended upon

---

48. Shoenberger, "The Development of the Lutheran Theory of Resistance: 1523–1530," 71.

49. Wolgast, *Die Religionsfrage als Problem*, 20.

50. Wolgast, *Die Wittenberg Theologie*, 124–25.

51. Ibid., 296.

them in numerous instances in the past. The Swabian League, for example, had long been a powerful player in German political history. The novelty of the Schmalkaldic League rested in the fact that it was a defensive alliance formed for fear of attack by the emperor. Thus, it was an alliance *against* the emperor's feared invasion. The exclusion of the emperor was momentous, therefore. It raised important constitutional issues and challenged the basic nature of the Holy Roman Empire and the relationships of the rulers of its various territories and cities.

In 1535, membership in the Schmalkaldic League was opened to all who accepted the *Augsburg Confession*. This led to the entry of a number of important Protestant cities. Larger membership also increased the possibility of conflicts, however, as each member pledged defensive aid to any other that was attacked for the sake of its religion. More significantly, Francis I, King of France, also joined the League. Thus, the League lost any claim to a purely religious nature, as Francis and his realm did not accept the *Augsburg Confession*. By 1539, Denmark had been added to the alliance, making it a veritable force with which to be reckoned. This increased vitality and might emboldened the leading rulers of the League, the young princes Philip of Hesse and John Frederick. They increasingly flexed their muscle in the years to come, further generating skepticism about the genuine nature of their alliance, which may indeed have undermined the allegiance or sympathies of some princes and rulers who shared theological convictions but feared disturbances to the balance of power. Such noteworthy and controversial undertakings include the reinstatement of Ulrich in Württemberg, a deposed ruler, after which Lutheran reforms were introduced in his territory. Controversy as well was the League's occupation of Henry V's territory in Braunschweig-Wolfenbüttel, after the League had come to the aid of Goslar, which Henry V had occupied under his own religious pretexts. In retrospect, while the Schmalkaldic League was founded upon a religious premise and as a defensive alliance for confessors of the Augsburg Confession, it is improper to conclude that there were not significant, and even overriding, political dimensions. Haug-Moritz explains in her massive work on the League, *Der Schmalkaldische Bund, 1530-1541/1542*, which unfortunately only covers up to the year 1542, the pinnacle of the League's power in her view, that it is simply untenable, in the light of further research, to operate under the popular assumptions of the past which would consider the League only under the central concept of religion and defense, for the Schmalkaldic League was neither limited to religion nor aimed solely at defense.[52] Throughout the League's activities ran clear political

---

52. Haug-Moritz, *Der Schmalkaldische Bund*, 91.

concerns and consequences like property questions and other motivations of self-interest.[53] It's impact, therefore, extended beyond the scope of mere theological motivation and a hope for the preservation of religious doctrine and practice; it stretched deep into the realm of territorialization and confessionalization in the broad sense.[54]

It is important to note again the significant turn that occurred with the ascendancy to the throne of John Frederick of Saxony, who was much less reliant upon the counsel of Luther and the Wittenberg faculty and much more ambitious than his predecessor, John of Saxony. With John's death, the League now found itself with rulers several decades Luther's junior, largely untested, and full of vigor and aspiration. Gone was the cautiousness previously employed by the Saxon electors, and Philip of Hesse, whose aggressiveness had been tempered so far only by the opinions of Luther and Melanchthon, received a much more receptive hearing at the Saxon court for his arguments and strategies. In the end, perhaps as a direct consequence, the young prince, John Frederick, would eventually find himself captive, having lost his gamble, fallen from the apex of his power to loss of his electoral title, his lands, and the university in Wittenberg. For all that sorrow, however, he would become a hero for the Magdeburgers, second only to Luther in their hagiography, portrayed as a victim of the union of impious papistic and imperial forces, a figure around which to rally.

1546 and 1547 were cataclysmic years for German Protestants, each tinged with painful loss. Luther died in 1546 and Philipp Melanchthon, the reluctant heir-apparent, became the purported theological head of the Lutheran Reformation. He lacked Luther's charisma and prophetic voice, however, and theologians and historians ever since have debated whether he acted as he did in the years immediately following the reformer's death because he was a frightened academic or because he had long harbored latent differences in theological orientation with Luther. While the Holy Roman Emperor, Charles V, was unable to wage war against the Lutheran princes of the Schmalkaldic League during Luther's lifetime, there was now a lull in tensions with other European powers and the threat of the Turks, for which he was reliant upon the Lutherans for aid. The opportunity for decisive action arrived when the forces of several Lutheran imperial cities occupied Füssen. Thus the Schmalkaldic War began in 1546 and ended quickly thereafter with a decisive imperial victory at the Battle of Mühlberg 24 April 1547, largely made possible by the treachery of Moritz of Saxony, who was called by some the "Judas of Meissen" for having gone over

53. Ibid., 506–10.
54. Ibid., 518.

to the emperor's side. The significance of this factor deserves attention. A Lutheran prince's political and territorial ambitions, coupled with personal animosity toward his cousin, Elector John Frederick, led him to act against the Protestant Schmalkaldic League in cooperation with the Roman Catholic emperor and parties, not with any expressed intention to renounce the Reformation (indeed, an argument could be made that in the end his actions went a long way toward preserving the Reformation), but to enhance his status and increase his realm.

Buoyed by his victory, the emperor now tried to foist the *Augsburg Interim* upon the Lutheran churches of Germany. The *Augsburg Interim* sought to reintroduce a wide breadth of Roman Catholic ceremonies and doctrine. It restored the seven sacraments of Roman Catholicism, taught transubstantiation, reinforced the ecclesiastical authority and rule of bishops and the Roman pontiff, omitted *sola fide* from the formula of justification, and mandated a spate of long-abolished customs like fasts and festivals in evangelical territories. The evangelical churches in Germany protested and resisted steadfastly. Moritz of Saxony realized the impossibility of implementing it. He therefore commissioned his newly acquired Wittenberg theologians with the production of a mediating formula for Saxony. They primarily addressed ceremonies in the subsequent document, but also included some ambiguous doctrinal statements, even on the chief doctrine of justification. Thus, this very important chief article thus still remained weak and unclear. The Wittenbergers tried to moderate and avoid some of the more troublesome measures of the *Augsburg Interim*, like the eucharistic prayer, the formula for extreme unction, and the use of chrism in baptism, yet substantial sticking-points remained for many Lutheran pastors and theologians. Vestments like the surplice and festivals like Corpus Christi became symbolic of the controversial measures that remained in force in Moritz' compromise. The Gnesio-Lutherans, as they later became known, opposed the adoption of this compromise formula, which Flacius popularlized as the *Leipzig Interim*. The controversy that resulted, which shook German Protestantism to its core, generated or revealed a number of the fault lines along which Lutheranism would crack in the decades to come (e.g. Crypto-Calvinistic, Majoristic, Synergistic, etc.).[55] Gnesio-Lutherans and Philippists, as Melanchthon's supporters, many of them former students, were eventually termed, would subsequently battle over teachings on original sin, free will, good works, and a number of other matters— their disputes both academic and personal, theological and political. The

---

55. For more on Kaufmann's argument regarding the anachronism of speaking of Gnesio-Lutherans at this time, see *Das Ende der Reformation*, 74.

Formula of Concord of 1577 several decades later endeavored to resolve the bitter disputes that broke out over such teachings, often settling on a middle ground between the positions and emphases of the two groups. Several Gnesio-Lutherans, including Flacius, would have their positions explicitly disavowed by the *Formula*—in Flacius' case, his position on original sin. All of these positions, however, were stances taken after the conclusion of the Adiaphoristic Controversy in response to provocative theological statements made by opponents.

A brief explanation of the theological term adiaphora is necessary at this point, because it was a term central to the controversy that erupted. Some information on the background and content of the interims will also be helpful. Adiaphora is a term borrowed from the Greeks, and especially the Stoics. Bente defines them as follows: "ceremonies which God has neither commanded nor prohibited are adiaphora (*res mediae, Mitteldinge*) and *ceteris paribus* (other things being equal), may be observed or omitted, adopted or rejected."[56] Earlier Christian theologians, Thomas Aquinas, for instance, had addressed indifferent matters in their theological works, and the concept itself, though not the term, harkens back to the Pauline epistles and Paul's emphasis on Christian freedom exercised in Christian love, for example, in Romans 14 and 1 Corinthians 10. Luther used the term "adiaphora" in his lectures on Galatians. There he explained, "For to those who believe in Christ whatever things are either enjoined or forbidden in the way of external ceremonies and bodily righteousnesses are all pure, adiaphora, and are permissible, except insofar as the believers are willing to subject themselves to these things of their own accord or for the sake of love."[57] The *Formula of Concord* described adiaphora as "ceremonies or ecclesiastical practices that are neither commanded nor forbidden in God's Word but that were introduced in the churches for the sake of good order and decorum," which is a useful definition for the purposes of this investigation.[58]

It is important to understand what added extra sting to the *Leipzig Interim* for those Lutherans who opposed it. Indeed, while the *Augsburg Interim* united Lutherans in their opposition, the *Leipzig Interim*, so named in a publicity triumph by Matthias Flacius, fractured them irreconcilably in certain instances. Not only had Flacius' former Wittenberg colleagues betrayed Luther, but Flacius and the other anti-Adiaphorists insisted that they had also betrayed and forsaken their rightful temporal lord, the former

56. Bente, "Historical Introductions to the Symbolical Books of the Evangelical Lutheran Church," 109. This appears in Bente's description of the anti-Adiaphorists' position.

57. LW 27:161.

58. KW, *Epitome* X.1, 515.

elector, the captured John Frederick, when they decided to serve at the whim of the traitorous Moritz instead. This was theological and political infidelity. Interestingly, even John Calvin chastised Melanchthon, albeit diplomatically, for his complicity, or at least his failure to act as a more vocal opponent of the adiaphora.[59] In the minds of the Gnesio-Lutherans, the very Lutheran theologians and leaders who should have led the resistance had forsaken Luther's Reformation, their secular ruler, and the Word of God by their actions. This was betrayal from within instead of assault from without. Their opponents argued there was simply no reason for the Wittenberg theologians and their associates to have acted as they had, other than to appease the emperor and the Antichrist through liturgical concessions (the surplice, or chorrock, became a symbol of these concessions) and a compromise formula even of the doctrine of justification, the chief article. These were compromises, the Gnesio-Lutherans insisted, made and tolerated only for fear of persecution and for the sake of temporal peace—at the expense of true, lasting, spiritual peace. Certainly the conciliatory and deferential tone of the *Leipzig Interim*, so offensive to its vocal opponents, was apparent from its very beginning:

> Our concern is based upon our desire to be obedient to the Roman Imperial Majesty and to conduct ourselves in such a way that his Majesty realize that our interest revolves only around *tranquility, peace and unity*. This is our counsel, made in good faith; it is what we ourselves want to serve and promote wherever possible. For in contrast to what some say and write about us—without any basis—our concern and our intention are always directed not toward causing schism and complications, but rather toward *peace and unity*. We testify to that in the very presence of God, to whom all human hearts are known. Our actions will demonstrate that.[60]

1.3. Flacius' Life up to the Controversy

Matija Vlačić Ilirik, Matthias Flacius Illyricus, a Slav, was born into a relatively well-to-do family 3 March 1520, in Albona, which is now Labin, in the Istrian peninsula, which was then part of the Venetian Republic. His hometown is now a part of Croatia and rests comfortably only a few miles from the Adriatic Sea. This area had once been part of the Roman province

59. Kaufmann, *Das Ende der Reformation*, 115.

60. Kolb and Nestingen, *Sources and Contexts of the Book of Concord*, 184; italics added.

Illyria and Flacius, like others before him, used that designation as an iden-
tifier when he moved to Northern Europe.[61] At the end of his life he would
also add "Albonensis," another reference to his Croation origin.[62] Matthias
was the last of six children. His mother, Jacobea, appears to have died giving
birth to him. His father, Andrija, died when Matthias was twelve. His name
derived from the feast day closest to his birthday.

Flacius' great-uncle through marriage was Baldo Lupetino, a man who
would play an important role in Flacius' future, even though condemned to
death 27 October 1547 for his "Lutheran" faith after five years of imprisonment. The sentence was eventually carried out, after years of intercession
by some powerful supporters, in September 1556, when he was drowned
in a lagoon in Venice after ceremonial degradation as a heretic. Victims of
the Inquisition were not infrequently labeled Lutherans as a sort of general
designation of heresy, but Lupetino, unlike some others, legitimately seems
to have been influenced by the writings of Luther. He shared them with Flacius and conveyed to his young relative "how Luther has brought the Gospel
back into honor."[63] Significantly, the princes of the Schmalkaldic League had
requested Lupetino's release and Flacius himself bore a letter to Venice in
1542 signed by John Frederick, an impressive accomplishment, since he had
only been in Wittenberg about a year at that point. Sadly, this was to no avail
and Flacius' firsthand experience with the Inquisition left a lifelong impression. Lupetino's encouragement to him during his imprisonment would
strike home during later persecution: "non ricantare, anzi cantare," that is,
"Do not recant, but sing."[64] Flacius no doubt internalized the fact that his
dear great-uncle died for being a "Lutheran." Confession and martyrdom
were part of his family history.

When he was sixteen years old, his father dead, Flacius moved to Venice to pursue his education. He almost joined a Franciscan monastery at
seventeen, but his great-uncle introduced him to the Reformation. In 1539,
at the age of nineteen, a copy of Dante's *Divine Comedy* tucked in his bag,
and with the encouragement of Lupetino, Flacius ventured north to study
theology under the shining lights of the Lutheran Reformation in Germany.[65] He studied Hebrew at Basel before moving on to Tübingen and finally
Wittenberg. He made important contacts at each stop along the way and
was priviledged to study under men who were very respected in their fields

61. Ilić, *Theologian of Sin and Grace*, 31.

62. Ibid., 64.

63. Ibid., 39.

64. Olson, *Matthias Flacius and the Survival of Luther's Reform*, 51.

65. Ibid., 35.

(Simon Grynaeus in Basle and Matthias Garbitius Illyricus at Tübingen, for example). Thus, at this point of his life, much of his theological knowledge was self-taught, but, as can be seen, he had also received important educational opportunities along the way. Ilić notes regarding the phase of Flacius' life leading up to Wittenberg:

> First, he always saw himself as something of an outsider north of the Alps. Second, born outside the Holy Roman Empire and orphaned at an early age, he was initially oriented toward Venice and the Italian humanism that it represented. His humanist training there and his concomitant interest in history, on which many studies of his thought have focused, arose not so much from his later exposure to Martin Luther and Philipp Melanchthon but from his earlier education at the school of San Marco and in the shadow of the Aldine Press. His decision to leave the safe confines of Italian Catholicism and Venetian civic life had to have been a momentous one, inspired by his relative but also by the message emanating from Wittenberg and other centers of the Reformation.[66]

Drawn by Luther's theology, and driven by the counsel of Lupetino, Flacius made his way to Wittenberg, but when he arrived there, he had already received substantial training as a humanist and brought with him many of the skills and interests that would lead him to make substantial contributions to a variety of academic disciplines. Upon his arrival, he had a demonstrable familiarity with the classical and biblical languages, which he would hone in Wittenberg.

Flacius began his study in Wittenberg in 1541. As a student pursuing a Master of Arts degree, he studied under both Philipp Melanchthon and Martin Luther, who was now in the last phase of his life and ministry. He struggled throughout his life with the climate and diet in Germany, yet performed admirably as a student. He became particularly close with Philipp Melanchthon, who recognized his pupil's abilities. Even later in the scalding heat of the Adiaphoristic Controversy, Flacius openly admitted his indebtedness to Philipp, with whom he worked much more closely than Luther, as well as his other former Wittenberg instructors with whom he later engaged in polemics.[67] Melanchthon himself would still admit in 1556, long after the Adiaphoristic Controversy had broken out and concluded, as well

66. Ilić, *Theologian of Sin and Grace*, 40.

67. Matthias Flacius Illyricus, *Entschuldigung Matthiae Flacij Illyrici, geschrieben an die Universitet zu Wittemberg der Mittelding halben. Item sein brief an Philip. Melanthonem sampt etlichen andern schrifften dieselbige sach belangend. Verdeudscht*, Aiii r.

as other controversies begun, "I used to enjoy friendship and familiarity with Illyricus."[68] While studying at Wittenberg, Flacius also went through a bout of depression and spiritual angst, for which he sought Luther's pastoral counsel. Luther's spiritual insight and advice helped him find peace, and this relationship with the reformer became a defining feature of his life and later work, evident in his concern for the conscience of believers. Luther was also familiar with Flacius' work ethic as a scholar, referring to him as "*studiosissimus*" in a November 1544 letter.[69] The relationship between Luther and Flacius was close enough that Luther attended his wedding to Elisabeth in November of 1545.[70] The reformer would die just four months later.

Flacius received his Master of Philosophy on 24 February 1546, six days after Luther's funeral. He was first in a class of thirty-nine. His thesis, *That Holy Scripture was Written Completely from the Beginning Not Only with Consonants, but Also With Vowel-Points*, addressed the debate whether the Masoretic pointing of the Hebrew Old Testament was part of the original text. Flacius contended that it was, which scholars now know is untrue.[71] This was an important argument for debate with Roman Catholicism, however, because the papal parties argued that later Masoretic pointing lent support to the history and necessity of a magisterium within the church to authoritatively define and interpret Holy Scripture. Now married to a Lutheran pastor's daughter, and having taught Hebrew in Wittenberg since 1544, hired although he was acknowledged to be "as good as nameless," Flacius appeared to be settling down to a comfortable life in Wittenberg.[72] In but a few years, however, everything changed. The defeat of the Schmalkaldic League, the captivity of the former Elector of Saxony, John Frederick of Saxony, and the introduction of the *Augsburg Interim* seriously threatened the future of Luther's Reformation.

Throughout the Interim Crisis, Melanchthon and his colleagues in Wittenberg argued that their compromises involved only adiaphora and preserved the heart and core of the Lutheran faith, particularly the doctrine of justification, upon which Luther maintained the church stands or falls. Melanchthon and the so-called Adiaphorists, as Flacius called them, thus argued that Flacius and those of his party were introducing divisions into Lutheranism over indifferent practices lacking any meaningful doctrinal implications or detriment to Luther's foundational teachings. Flacius would

---

68. Ilić, *Theologian of Sin and Grace*, 67.

69. Ibid., 64.

70. Ibid.

71. Olson, *Matthias Flacius and the Survival of Luther's Reform*, 53.

72. Ibid., 52.

concede that such things normally could perhaps be adiaphora, but because the current compromises and ceremonies were drafted and initiated under compulsion, by the state and not the church, and in order to placate the enemies of the church, he refused to consider them adiaphora. In fact, he would later argue that in such a controversy nothing at all was an adiaphoron. He took this stand, not as someone unfamiliar with Wittenberg affairs, but as someone very much in the loop. Until Flacius' departure from the city, Melanchthon often discussed the various conferences he attended and the proposals under consideration with him. Philipp had even instructed Flacius to make a copy of the compromise formula on justification drafted at Pegau, at which time Flacius complained, "What treacle!"[73] Melanchthon confided his fears regarding the *Augsburg Interim* to the young Hebrew professor.[74] So highly had Melanchthon thought of him, in fact, that when he went to Braunschweig while the University of Wittenberg was closed because of the advance of Moritz' troops, Philipp recommended him to the schoolmaster there with a comparison to the fourth-century Bishop of Salamis in Cyprus, writing that Matthias "excels that pentaglot, the Salaminian, Epiphanius, not only in knowledge of languages, but in knowledge of affairs."[75] It was as a colleague who knew his opponents well, therefore, and still admired much about them and their accomplishments, that Flacius dismissed the Wittenbergers' claims that they dealt only with adiaphora and insisted that in their compromises crouched the real and present danger of "yawning atheism."[76] Crushed by his dear preceptor's timidity, he wrote that "Philomela had put the pipe in the sack and was afraid of the hawk."[77]

After writing a few pamphlets against the *Interim* under pseudonyms, Flacius decided to depart Wittenberg in 1549, initially leaving his "very pregnant wife" behind.[78] His first stop was Magdeburg, where Nicholas Amsdorf, Erasmus Alberus, and the city's other prominent theologians urged him to stay and help struggle against the *Interim*. He rejected their offer at first, though, because he feared that his health would not endure the siege he already foresaw on the horizon, since he "would have to eat smoked bacon and meat, and also salted and dried fish."[79] After further travels, however, he decided to accept the Magdeburgers' hospitality.

73. Ibid., 99.
74. Ibid., 121.
75. Ibid., 121, 68.
76. Ibid., 124.
77. Ibid., 118.
78. Kaufmann, "Matthias Flacius Illyricus," 183.
79. Ibid.

Nowhere was the opposition to the *Leipzig Interim*, forever known by the name he had given it, still utilized by scholars today, fiercer than in Magdeburg, a haven for theologians who, like Flacius, had fled other territories for reasons of conscience or to better oppose the new measures. Under the leadership of Nicholas Amsdorf, the longtime friend of Luther and head of the Reformation in Magdeburg, these theologians worked tirelessly, passionately, and uncompromisingly against all who had cooperated with the imperially mandated changes and thus, in their minds, against Luther's theological testament and legacy. In this fight, Flacius outstripped the rest in the vigor and magnitude of his efforts. As Kaufmann observes, "No other figure in the sixteenth century, not even Martin Luther, wrote and published so many pages in so short a time as did Flacius."[80]

It is important to remember that before the Adiaphoristic Controversy ever began, Flacius had personal experience with theologies in conflict and persecution. As mentioned earlier, his uncle, Baldo Lupetino, who had exerted a good deal of influence on him and his education and formation as a young man, was a victim of the Inquisition in Venice. He was imprisoned and sentenced to death, not merely for heresy, but for being a *Lutheran*. It is hard to imagine that this did not make a lasting impression on Flacius. He was a second generation confessor, so to speak, and he was carrying on the legacy of his uncle and all those who had risked worldly goods and fame for the sake of Christ and the truth of God's Word.

After Lupetino, no one had influenced Flacius' faith and Christian formation more than Martin Luther. Irene Dingel's article, "Flacius als Schüler Luthers und Melanchthons," sheds particular light on the relationship between Flacius and his teachers, Luther and Melanchthon, as well as Flacius' self-identification with Luther and his struggles.[81] Crucial is the fact that it was Luther who had brought the young Illyrian out of a spiritual crisis and depression with pastoral counsel and testimony from his own experience with the same. That Luther too had undergone a crisis of faith and great melancholy surely touched Flacius. They shared not only a confession of faith, then, but an experience of faith. Both had been touched by God through the gospel with healing, and this bore spiritual and emotional fruit. Flacius was a Lutheran, then, not only doctrinally, but existentially. Luther was part of his past and Flacius' personal faith bore the great reformer's fingerprints. This explains why references and appeals to Luther's person, work, and publications abound in Flacius' writings, as well as why he often mentioned Luther not only as "Martin Luther," but rather as "Dr. Martin

---

80. Kaufmann, "'Our Lord God's Chancery,'" 576.

81. Dingel, "Flacius als Schüler Luthers und Melanchthons," 77–93.

Luther of blessed memory,"[82] as "the honorable master and father Martin Luther,"[83] as "Reverend Father Martin Luther of pious memory,"[84] or similar titles. As a student of the great reformer, Flacius appealed not only to Luther's writings, but also to the reformer's lectures, which he had personally attended.[85] It was for true Lutheranism, Luther's Lutheranism, that Flacius had left behind fatherland, friends, and inheritance. He thus internalized the controversies of Luther's life, especially the contest with Agricola, in which Melanchthon had sought to serve as a mediator and thus failed, in Flacius' view, to remain sufficiently steadfast. Luther became, not only a spiritual father for him, but a *Leitbildcharakter*.[86]

As Luther had moderated Melanchthon's wavering during his life, so now it became Flacius' task to limit the damages that, in his view, Melanchthon's timidity was doing to Luther's theological legacy.[87] He hinted at this role in *Ein vermanung zur bestendigkeit*, where he compared the current situation to the circumstances at Augsburg. Once again, Melanchthon and some of the more timid Wittenbergers needed encouragement and emboldening. Flacius wrote there, "At Augsburg, at the Diet in 1530, some wanted to reconcile Christ and Belial in adiaphora, and if Dr. Martin had not at that time been on guard, which one sees in his letters, which are now in print, we now through our own wisdom would not even have a trace of the truth among us."[88] He strove to provide the same corrective to Melanchthon's proclivity to vacillate and moderate Luther's doctrine also in his *Vermanung Matth. Flacii Illyrici*.[89] A fine example is Flacius' and Melanchthon's relationships with Luther's *De Servio Arbitrio, On the Bondage of the Will*. This was one of Luther's works with which Melanchthon was most uncomfortable. For Flacius, however, it became foundational. In fact, Flacius' desire to defend Luther's teaching in that work drove his obstinacy in the later theological debate over original sin, on account of which the Flacian doctrine of original sin was condemned as excessive in the *Formula of Concord*.[90]

---

82. For instance, see Flacius, *Ein vermanung zur bestendigkeit*, Ai v.

83. Waremundus, "Eine gemeine Protestation," in *Reaktionen auf das Augsburger Interim: Der Interimistische Streit (1548–1549)*, 162.

84. Flacius, *Quod Hoc Tempore Nulla Penitus Mutatio in Religione sit in gratiam impiorum facienda*, A3 v.

85. Flacius, *Vermanung Matth. Flacii Illyrici*, Aii v.

86. Dingel, "Flacius als Schüler," 84, 89.

87. Ibid., 81.

88. Flacius, *Ein vermanung zur bestendigkeit*, Hiii r.

89. Flacius, *Vermanung Matth. Flacii Illyrici*, Cii r.

90. Dingel, "Flacius als Schüler," 90.

This does not mean, however, that Flacius learned nothing from Melanchthon or that he was ungrateful for Philip's instruction and hospitality in Wittenberg. He frequently admitted his indebtedness to his former teacher and mentor and his regret at having to contest his error. Moreover, he combined Luther's teaching with Melanchthon's methodology, especially in his *Clavis scripturae sacrae*. He commended Melanchthon's *Loci*, pairing it even with Luther's *Postille* as an expression and representation of sound Lutheran theology that should be upheld and preserved, and continued to hold it in high esteem.[91] Moreover, he frequently used Melanchthon's writing against Melanchthon, demonstrating his familiarity and appreciation for his former professor's earlier work.[92] Flacius, thus, bore the imprint of both of his mentors, Luther and Melanchthon, so that Dingel asserts, "In no other theologian of the second half of the sixteenth century does one find this synthesis of Melanchthon's method and Luther's theology so effectively."[93]

91. For instance, see Flacius, *Ein buch, von waren und falschen Mitteldingen*, Miv r.
92. For instance, see Flacius, *Ein buch, von waren und falschen Mitteldingen*, Piv r.
93. Dingel, "Flacius als Schüler," 83.

Chapter 2 ———————————————————————

Flacius' Case against the Interims

2.1. The Background and Nature of Flacius' Writings

IT IS HELPFUL AT this point to briefly sketch Flacius' main arguments in the Adiaphoristic Controversy against the *Augsburg Interim* and *Leipzig Interim*. Because their titles are quite lengthy in the fashion of his day, for the sake of brevity and clarity they will be noted here by the beginnings of their titles, *Ein vermanung zur bestendigkeit*; *Ein Christliche vermanung*; *Vermanung Matth. Flacii Illyrici*; and *Ein buch von waren und falschen Mitteldingen*. The *Admonitions* [*Vermanung*] for the most part made similar arguments and attacks against Flacius' opponents. The four additional works under consideration were comparable to the *Admonitions* [*Vermanung*] in approach, with the exception of *Breves Svmmae Religionis Iesus Christi, & Antichristi*, which presented first Luther's teachings on contested doctrines followed by those of the pope's church. *Ein buch von waren und falschen Mitteldingen* dealt in detail with the essence and proper handling of adiaphora in times of peace and particularly in a time of confession. The *Admonitions* [*Vermanung*] and *Ein buch von waren und falschen Mitteldingen* served for the most part a threefold purpose. First, they identified the issues involved in the controversy. Second, they identified the opponents—papists, ambitious magistrates, Adiaphorists—and then analyzed and dismantled these opponents' arguments. Third, they urged all true and faithful Christians to remain faithful to Christ and his Scriptures by opposing the interims and those who would impose them by force. The *Admonitions* [*Vermanung*], while similar in content, differed slightly in arrangement, and *Ein buch von waren und falschen Mitteldingen* was arranged much more methodically. Regarding its arrangement, Flacius stated at the beginning: "I will present this material in an orderly and methodical fashion."[1] He explained:

---

1. Flacius, *Ein buch von waren und falschen Mitteldingen*, Ji v.

> I will therefore now divide this book in three parts. In the first part, I will, with the help of Christ, speak about true adiaphora and the Christian ceremonies of the churches, about the reasons for them, and the ultimate benefit flowing from them. In the second part, I will speak about the current false adiaphora, compare the same with true adiaphora, and examine them. In addition, with the help of God, I will demonstrate that the same have neither the origin nor the benefit of true adiaphora, and that one should therefore by no means regard or accept them true adiaphora. In the last part, I will do away with certain meritless arguments of the Adiaphorists.[2]

Flacius began his *Ein vermanung zur bestendigkeit* by quoting Luther's prediction that "three things will destroy the true religion." These are: "First, ingratitude, that we forget the great benefits that we have received from the dear gospel. Second, the security that is now prevalent and reigns on all sides. Third, human wisdom that wants to bring all things into some sort of order and reform with godless counsel in the name of common peace."[3] The latter, Flacius argued, was precisely what was taking place with the composition and adoption of the *Leipzig Interim*. Under the threat of violence, the emperor and the victorious princes were now attempting to compel the evangelicals to adopt a number of Roman liturgical practices and watered-down theological formulas, all with the Adiaphorists' complicity for the sake of peace. The changes, the Adiaphorists reasoned, could be undone later when fortunes and the political balance had shifted. Flacius found this reasoning self-serving, harmful, and despicable. His writings endeavored to expose the disingenuous and detrimental nature of his opponents' sophistic argumentation.

Flacius provided the following "General Rule about Ceremonies" in *Ein buch von waren und falschen Mitteldingen*, echoed in his other writings:

> All ceremonies and church practices are in and of themselves free and they will always be. When, however, coercion, the false illusion that they were worship of God and must be observed, renunciation [of the faith], offense, [or] an opening for godless develops, and when, in whatever way it might happen, they do not build up but rather tear down the church of God and mock God, then they are no longer adiaphora.[4]

---

2. Ibid.

3. Flacius, *Ein vermanung zur bestendigkeit*, Ai v. Flacius quotes it again in the same work, Hii r—Hii v.

4. Flacius, *Ein buch von waren und falschen Mitteldingen*, Ai v.

He then concluded, "All these evil aspects are now in play, except that some things are not even adiaphora, but instead are patently godless."[5]

Flacius left no doubt in *Ein vermanung zur bestendigkeit* regarding who was to blame for the current crisis. Yes, the papists and the emperor bore much of the guilt, but most disturbing was the fact that those who should have written such an admonition, and could have done so much better than he, remained silent or even cooperated outright with the enemies. His former colleagues in Wittenberg had forsaken their holy offices and callings and instead were now attempting to reconcile Christ and Belial, so that one could serve two lords where they ought only have one.[6] Men willing to act in such a way were "epicurean sows" who would rather "persecute Christ with the godless" than "be persecuted by the godless for the sake of Christ."[7] According to Flacius, the Christian religion was not something to be molded to fit the spirit and perils of the time, but must be considered "firm and unchangeable, so that even if someone like Solomon upon his kingly throne should teach or assert something false, it does not cease to be false and incorrect on account of the person."[8] Furthermore, as if the personal apostasy of these prominent theologians and former friends of Luther were not enough, their example, excuses, and writings were drawing the common people into apostasy with them. Their statements were giving the masses the impression that the changes were not only harmless but salutary, which was an indefensible and damning transgression according to Flacius.[9] It was utterly appalling and shameful that they "dare even to brazenly lie from the pulpit that everything now stands better than before in both secular policy and ecclesiastical governance."[10]

In Flacius' opinion, there was no debating what was the only proper response for Christians. They had to remain firm and refuse to yield. They had to remain unswayed by the spineless sophistry of the Adiaphorists. They had to reject the interims out of hand and at all costs if Luther's Reformation were to survive. This was, in the end, the primary purpose of the *Admonitions*, to buck up and encourage those taking a stand to remain firm and exhort those who had, as of yet, not been steadfast to begin to become so. For those who had thus far waffled, Flacius recommended that "there is no better medicine and counsel than a persistent faith, and in this faith

5. Ibid.

6. Flacius, *Ein vermanung zur bestendigkeit*, Aii r–Aiii v.

7. Flacius, *Ein Christliche vermanung*, Bi r.

8. Ibid., Bii r–Bii v.

9. Ibid., Di v.

10. Flacius, *Ein vermanung zur bestendigkeit*, Hii v.

hefty, persistent, and unfailing prayer." This was the only remedy for fear and frailty, because "human counsel, help, and medicine is nothing but work, fidgeting, and anxiety of heart, as David says, which make the sickness worse the more they are employed."[11] He bid them, "Let us therefore be obedient to our dear God and Father in this cross and follow Christ, his dear Son and all saints in this," for "he can requite us very richly in this and yonder life."[12] This reminder, that it did little good to gain peace in this life at the expense of blessedness in the end, ran throughout Flacius' writings from the Adiaphoristic Controversy and was frequently echoed in the *Magdeburg Confession*. The future of Christ's Church was at stake and a failure of the German Lutherans to take a stand would have repercussions throughout Christendom. "The eyes of all men are upon us," he pled, "We must therefore concede nothing at all to the devil, nor give any glory to the impious, nor stir up disillusionment among the weak."[13]

It was all or nothing, and Flacius insisted that the Lutherans must accept absolutely nothing foisted upon the church by the magistrates. One simply could not confess Christ and accept the *Interim* and consider himself a Christian in Luther's mold, or perhaps of any kind. It was impermissible to make concessions to God's enemies—the Antichrist, the devil, and the impious. It would be much better to offend Caesar tenfold than to forsake Christ, and in the end there really would be no pleasing the emperor through these incremental changes. He would not be happy until the Lutherans were brought back into the papal fold.[14] Christians would suffer innocently for opposing this ploy of Satan and his ilk, but that did not mean they should suffer silently. "The Christian Church is responsible for adding to its innocence and defending its teaching openly in this time too," he counseled, "and it certainly should not and indeed cannot surrender in any way since the adversaries strive against God himself and against justice with the sword and with fire, and persecute our teaching, and try to force us to accept new false doctrine in the place of our teaching . . . even though it is no secret that our doctrine is clearly the divine truth."[15]

The defining Scriptures for Flacius' approach and argumentation were found in St. Paul's letters to the Romans, the Galatians, and his first letter to the Corinthians. Even in places where he did not quote them directly, the reader familiar with the New Testament will recognize their influence

11. Ibid., Fiii r.

12. Flacius, *Vermanung Matth. Flacii Illyrici*, Biii v–Biv r.

13. Flacius, *Quod Hoc Tempore*, B1 r.

14. Ibid., A4 r.

15. Waremundus, "Eine gemeine Protestation," 144.

upon Flacius. He turned to Romans to explain how one should approach differences of practice or sentiment within the church in so far as weaker brethren are concerned. Like Luther before him, Flacius turned especially to Galatians for a defense of Christian freedom, which he felt was being infringed upon by the new liturgical changes and formulae. 1 Corinthians provided the biblical basis for the teaching of adiaphora, for there Paul wrestled with the early church's conflict over how best to assimilate Jews and Gentiles with their different social cultures and religious backgrounds. 1 Corinthians and Romans both also emphasized for Flacius the importance of good order and a proper balance between Christian freedom and Christian love, so that neither detracted from nor existed in isolation from the other. Flacius himself located the foundations of the New Testament doctrine of adiaphora as follows:

> That such adiaphora are present in the church and her ceremonies can easily be proven from St. Paul, who writes about them in 1 Corinthians 8, 9, 10, and 14. Romans 14 also deals with such adiaphora as there are, for instance, to live married or unmarried (only that they are chaste matters), to eat food or not to eat it, to observe certain days or not to observe them, so long as they avoid superstition in so doing, to take a salary from the hearers or not to take one, and likewise to teach, to hear, and to sing in certain ways in the churches.[16]

Those hoping to comprehend and follow Flacius' line of thinking, therefore, do well to study these chapters of Scripture along with Paul's letter to the Galatians, especially the first two chapters.

Finally, Flacius provided three key characteristics of true adiaphora that can permissibly and with edification serve for the good of the church. First, they had to spring from the free will of the church. Second, they needed to be instituted by those who have authority to do so, namely, pastors and legitimate church authorities. Third, and most importantly, they had to flow from the general command of God regarding adiaphora.[17] This final requirement meant that Christians had to consider not only the things proposed as adiaphora in and of themselves, but also the circumstances surrounding them. In other words, did they carry theological or cultural baggage? With what were they associated? Who was imposing them? This was the chief reason why the adiaphora proposed, advocated for, or defended by various Adiaphorists during the controversy could not be accepted or deemed true and legitimate adiaphora in the biblical sense. He wrote,

16. Flacius, *Ein buch von waren und falschen Mitteldingen*, Jii r.
17. Ibid., Liv r.

"God does not want to have ceremonies that have for a long time served for godlessness and have been done away with set up again. He does not only become seriously angry about the godless essence [of ceremonies], but also about all the circumstances surrounding them." This was the heart and core of Flacius' resistance to the new liturgical changes being foisted upon the Lutheran churches in Germany by those with neither the proper authority nor spirit to introduce or require them.

2.2. Flacius' Use of Examples from Scripture and Ecclesiastical History

As a professor of Hebrew, Flacius had an intimate familiarity not only with the Scriptures as a whole, but specifically with the Old Testament. This is evident throughout his writings. While his arguments regarding the doctrine of adiaphora were grounded in the New Testament, especially Paul's letters to the Corinthians and Romans, the lion's share of the examples which illustrate these arguments were from the Old Testament and the Apocrypha. This study will now explore some of the examples Flacius employed in his writings, especially those from the Old Testament and Apocrypha. This will help the reader gain a sense for how Flacius used the accounts of the Scriptures and church history for reinforcement of his opinions and as a lens through which to understand contemporary events. For Flacius, contemporary challenges were to be understood not merely as new experience, but as part of a historical cycle, a new chapter in an ancient and ongoing story that would reach its climax in the last days and culminate in Christ's return.

By far the most predominant example Flacius employed throughout his pamphlets was the exodus of the Jews from Egypt. Indeed, the exodus was a pattern for the whole history of the Church in Flacius' view: "Now he leads them out of a safe and good position into great danger and need, and then soon he helps them out of their great need and brings them again into a peaceful state."[18] Just as the Jews during the trials of the wilderness longed for the perceived benefits of their earlier life in Egypt and imagined their slavery to have been much better than it really was, so also vacillating Lutherans were imagining better days in the past under the papacy and taking for granted the deliverance that God had worked for them through Luther from the traditions and legalism of men. Their ingratitude not only matched that of the Jews in the wilderness, but even excelled it, for the Lutherans had been delivered from a more burdensome and abominable slavery under

---

18. Flacius, *Ein vermanung zur bestendigkeit*, Fi v–Fii r.

the papacy, a spiritual servitude.[19] Just as the Jews had despised Moses and Aaron in difficult moments, so also many Lutherans now were despising faithful preachers of God's Word and the sainted reformer.

In a further elaboration of this picture, Flacius' writings cast the pope, emperor, and hostile magistrates as pharaohs for their stubborn refusal to permit the right preaching of the gospel and heed God's commands regarding their offices. Before pleading with the magistrates and religious leaders who were pushing the new changes to cease overstepping their jurisdictions and realms, he addressed them as follows: "Oh you antichrists, oh you pharaohs, oh you foxhounds, who are worse than the Pharaoh himself, you persecutors of the divine Word, you who are the devil's servants, and with him will be martyred in hellish agony and pain, listen, we now speak with you."[20] The Pharaoh of Egypt's demise ought to have been instructive for these opponents of God's Church. Flacius wrote, "There have been many a Cain, Pharaoh, Sennacherib, Manasseh, Antiochus, Nero, Mauritius, and Julian, and no matter how strong those who have set themselves up against the Lord and his anointed may be, they will in the end fall off into the abyss of hell."[21]

Continuing his development of this theme, Flacius suggested that in the *Leipzig Interim* the Adiaphorists had set up for themselves and their adherents a new golden calf, just as had happened in the wilderness when Aaron refused to lead boldly as a servant of God. They had "loosed and set the people free from the command, obedience, and fear of God, so that each one dared to do whatever he wanted."[22] They were like Korah and Dathan, who, ungrateful for God's deliverance, conspired to lead the Lord's people back into Egyptian servitude.[23]

Another prominent figure in Flacius' publications was the prophet Elijah. Irene Dingel points out that throughout the controversy Flacius saw his task, and to an extent the task of all theologians, like that of Elijah.[24] Moreover, like a number of other Lutherans of his day, he identified Luther as a third Elijah. Explaining the impropriety of the Adiaphorists' work, he noted, "They grieve the Holy Spirit with a special disgrace, since they reinstitute the ceremonies and practices of the Antichrist, the filth which the Holy Spirit through Dr. Martin Luther, the third Elijah, swept out of the house

19. Flacius, *Ein buch von waren und falschen Mitteldingen*, Giv r.
20. Waremundus, "Eine gemeine Protestation," 164.
21. Flacius, *Ein vermanung zur bestendigkeit*, Hiv r.
22. Ibid., Aiii v.
23. Ibid., Hii v.
24. Dingel, "Flacius als Schüler," 91.

of God through the inexpressible mercy of God."[25] Elijah's confrontation with the prophets of Baal became paradigmatic for the Interim Crisis and exposed the folly of the Wittenbergers' approach. He observed:

> Also, when the great prophet Elijah time and again fled from the godless tyranny of Ahab, he did not hand his church over to the wolves of Baal by doing so. Rather, he strengthened it in the truth through his steadfast confession and the pitiable misery he endured. If he had, however, accepted the ceremonies of Baal, painted up the same, and defended them in order to appease the priests of Baal, and only cursorily addressed the abuse in generalities (as the Leipzig theologians' letter to the preacher of the Margrave Albrecht does), had he wanted to make fine distinctions and serve the times, so that through such modera- tion (as they now call it) he might assuage the fury of the king . . . he would have completely betrayed and sold out the church, for the great majority would have thought, "See now, this admi- rable and great man, whom we regard so highly in our church, limps upon both sides for the sake of peace in order not to upset the king. I therefore may do the same even more compliantly, since I am in no way equal to him." In this way they would have been weakened, yielded and imitated him. Jezebel thus would not have had the blood of so many rude Stoics, pigheaded and unruly people in her kingdom to spill, as also this land does not now produce many martyrs.[26]

The Old Testament prophet-for-hire Balaam also made several appear- ances in Flacius' writings. The Book of Numbers in chapters 22-24 reports that when the Israelites were on their way to the Promised Land after escap- ing Egypt, Balak, the King of Moab, fearful of the advance of God's people, hired Balaam to curse them. The Lord, however, would not allow Balaam to do so, which resulted in the famous story of Balaam's ass, who refused to travel the path Balaam directed it upon, because it saw the angel of the Lord standing in the way. Only after cursing and beating the ass so that it finally spoke to him did Balaam realize that it had been protecting him. He thus reported to Balak that he could not curse the Israelites, because God would not permit him. Nevertheless, he did advise the king that perhaps the Isra- elites could be led into sin against the Lord, particularly with idolatry and sexual immorality, which did, in fact, happen. Similarly, the Adiaphorists were aiding the enemies of God by luring the Lord's people into idolatry and spiritual adultery through their compromises with the papacy. God would

25. Flacius, *Ein buch von waren und falschen Mitteldingen*, Ri r.
26. Ibid., Ti r.

help no one curse his teaching, the pure gospel as revealed by Luther, and yet through subtle seduction the compromise formulae and ceremonies of Augsburg and Leipzig were deceiving the faithful into open sin against the very God who had delivered them from papal oppression. Flacius complained, "For we sadly see, may God lament it, that some Jews and Balaams, so wily and unashamed, receive everything laid before them by the godless Ahithophels and dare to drag it into the church."[27] Elsewhere he wrote, "Many pious people complain that among them there are many consciences that have become erring, so that they now do not know whether or not they do well to listen to the intrusions of the adiaphoristic Balaam."[28] And likewise, he seethed that some Adiaphorists "through the help or instigation of Balaam and Ahithophel, forced out two truly God-fearing, steadfast preachers, who were not willing to go along with the new changes."[29]

Flacius also made use of the sins of Saul for his purposes. The enemies of the gospel in the Adiaphoristic Controversy were cast as Sauls. Flacius wrote that they were like Saul in 1 Samuel 15, when he offered unlawful sacrifice in the misguided notion that it would please God. He explained that, like Saul, "the godless suppose that it matters very little, yes, not at all, to have the correct teaching about God, a proper understanding of his will, and to follow the same. Rather, they place the greatest holiness in this, that we offer much to God and buy him off through our works and gifts."[30] Saul, together with several other men of the Old Testament, illustrated that, just as in his own day, "even the very best people in the church often become the most evil and shameful, such as Saul, Absalom, Solomon, and the like."[31] Saul's experience with David's godly music was also instructive. Flacius insisted that German hymns must be retained in the Evangelical churches because "in this way, young men and women can lead their hearts away from evil thoughts, awaken them to the fear of God, and drive the devil out from them, as we read in the history of Saul."[32]

Flacius also often termed the Adiaphorists "Ahithophels"; Ahithophel was King David's counselor who went over to Absalom during his rebellion.[33] The Wittenbergers and their allies were doing the same according to Flacius, serving the usurper, Moritz, as well as the emperor, who was

27. Flacius, *Ein Christliche vermanung*, Eii v.

28. Ibid., Hii r.

29. Flacius, *Ein buch von waren und falschen Mitteldingen*, Mii r.

30. Flacius, *Ein vermanung zur bestendigkeit*, Cii r.

31. Flacius, *Ein Christliche vermanung*, Eiii r.

32. Flacius, *Ein buch von waren und falschen Mitteldingen*, Oi v–Oi r.

33. 2 Sam 15:12.

overstepping his authority and trampling the Lutherans' religious freedom. Moreover, the current concessions were only stepping-stones to further power grabs. He warned Lutherans and Germans, "Such things demonstrate that the authorities nowhere will indicate how far the changes should stretch and do not want to establish an end goal, but rather day by day more and more is desired and demanded by the impudent Ahithophels."[34] He argued from Psalm 12, "The Holy Spirit prays further, and we should also pray, that the heavenly Father would yet once again root out the false teachers, tongue threshers, and Ahithophels, who fall to the Babylonian whore, her beast, and the great lords, who defiantly defend the unjust, both in spiritual and worldly things."[35] Nevertheless, just as Absalom's rebellion had ended in a defeat hastened by his pride and cunning, so also the current rebellion would end in failure. Man's wisdom could not ultimately triumph over God's will. The Antichrist could not defeat Christ. The Ahithophels would eventually push too far and be toppled by the mighty hand of God.

The examples above serve to give the reader a sense of Flacius' use of Old Testament examples and illustrations. Flacius also drew a number of illustrations from the Apocrypha. The first and most important, which originated with Luther's *Warning*, drew upon the history of the Maccabees, although Flacius focused especially on the case of Eleazar, the priest, while Luther broadly referenced Antiochus' tyranny. Flacius retold the account from 2 Maccabees, particularly chapter 6, for the reader: "When a Jewish priest by the name of Eleazar was counseled by a captain of Antiochus at the times of the Maccabees that he should in fact only eat from the Jewish sacrifice but allow the captain to say to his army associates that Eleazar had eaten from the heathen sacrifice, the pious priest was unwilling to approve of the plan and therefore was strangled."[36]

Eleazar, in short, was the perfect anti-Adiaphorist. The Adiaphorists approached their situation entirely differently than this faithful old priest. Flacius described their pragmatism: "Here an Interimist or Adiaphorist might say that it is only an indifferent thing to eat from the sacrificial flesh or not. Why should I not eat to perpetuate my life for the church and not for my own personal good?"[37] Eleazar, however, would have none of that. He realized that to go along with the captain's ploy would have had disastrous consequences, for himself and his fold. Flacius explained that by cooperating "he in that way would have denied his religion and acted against God's

---

34. Flacius, *Ein Christliche vermanung*, Dii v.

35. Flacius, *Vermanung Matth. Flacii Illyrici*, Eiii r.

36. Flacius, *Ein vermanung zur bestendigkeit*, Aiv v–Bi r.

37. Ibid., Bi r.

Word with great scandal."[38] The emperor himself was cast as Antiochus, in league with the Antichrist. Flacius protested, "For that reason, since the present ceremonies are being imposed upon the church against its will, not by the common people, but by the most manifest enemies of Christ, namely by the Antichrist and his beast, one can therefore in no way accept them, and they are no longer adiaphora, but the godless mandates of the Antichrist and the bloodthirsty Antiochus."[39] The only proper course for Christian pastors, therefore, was Eleazar's. They too must resist the captain's sly proposal. They too must avoid giving a false impression, misleading the people, and furthering the enemies' ungodly agenda. Flacius left no doubt about this. The reader need not draw his own conclusions.

> Just as in the history of Eleazar in 2 Maccabees 6, it would have been Christian for him to have eaten from his sacrificial meat, for such was commanded by God, but since scandal would result from it, and thereby a denial of the faith would have been inferred from it, it would in this way have been entirely and completely unchristian. Therefore, all the God-fearing should guard themselves with all diligence so that they do not make themselves participants in such scandal and [place themselves under] the wrath of God.[40]

Flacius also drew upon the example of Judith from the Apocrypha. Her story illustrated the foolishness of setting timetables for God. In Judith 8:11-17, Judith reprimanded some of the leaders of the Israelites, because, when the people complained about their prospects of surviving a siege and a looming military battle, they urged the people to allow five days for God to respond to their prayers and deliver them before seeking an alternate course. Their intention might well have been earnest, but in limiting God's time to act, even in an attempt to give him more time to act, they erred. God works in his own time, Flacius declared, and the Christian is called, not to set limits, but to wait and trust and pray. He wrote, "God does not want (as Judith says) one to prescribe the time and hour when or how He should help us, as our old Adam would like, and is accustomed to do."[41] This was part of the theology of the cross, "that we do not define for our Lord God the time and day of our pleasing, when and how he should help." Rather, "God has his particular plan and his particular way to rescue the oppressed Church, and for many reasons, according to his special plan and

---

38. Ibid.

39. Flacius, *Ein buch von waren und falschen Mitteldingen*, Liii v.

40. Ibid., Qi r.

41. Flacius, *Ein vermanung zur bestendigkeit*, Giii v–Giv r.

thoughts, he sometimes lets it fall into great burdens and remain stuck in them."[42] The Church was a waiting, expectant people with a promised future but not an appointed date.

Flacius did not limit himself to the Old Testament and the Apocrypha, however. He illustrated and undergirded his arguments with examples from the New Testament as well. He appealed occasionally to the life of Jesus, but more often to Christ's words. One chief example of Flacius' use of a New Testament account to illustrate his point provides an awareness of how Flacius utilized the New Testament. Even when he turned to it for illustrative examples, then he did so predominantly for proof passages and *sedes*. This is clearly evident in the case of Galatians. Flacius drew upon Paul's rebuke of Peter, which Paul recounts in Galatians 2. This account, however, cannot be separated from the various commands from Paul's Letter to the Galatians to avoid the traditions of men, new teaching, and most importantly, any new gospel. St. Paul's warning to the Galatians appears a number of times in Flacius' pamphlets, where the apostle commands his hearers, "But even if we or an angel from heaven should preach to you a gospel contrary to the one we preached to you, let him be accursed. As we have said before, so now I say again: If anyone is preaching to you a gospel contrary to the one you received, let him be accursed."[43] Flacius' use of this story to illustrate his point was hardly original, though. Paul himself used the incident with Peter as an illustration of the principles he laid down in the first chapter of Galatians. Flacius merely did the same. The same is likewise true of Flacius' use of Revelation. The illustrations from that book underscore the warnings and commands provided there. They are intimately tied together, not only in Flacius' writing, but in the apostle's own. There was less creativity, then, in Flacius' use of these New Testament accounts and images than in his use of the Old Testament, Apocrypha, and church history.

To return to the example from Galatians, why had Paul rebuked Peter? Paul explains:

> But when Cephas came to Antioch, I opposed him to his face, because he stood condemned. For before certain men came from James, he was eating with the Gentiles; but when they came he drew back and separated himself, fearing the circumcision party. And the rest of the Jews acted hypocritically along with him, so that even Barnabas was led astray by their hypocrisy. But when I saw that their conduct was not in step with the truth of the gospel, I said to Cephas before them all, "If you, though a

---

42. Flacius, *Vermanung Matth. Flacii Illyrici*, Ci v.

43. Gal 1:8,9 ESV.

Jew, live like a Gentile and not like a Jew, how can you force the Gentiles to live like Jews?"[44]

Peter had compromised the pure and clear message of the gospel. It is no coincidence that the next part of Galatians treats again the Pauline doctrine of justification by grace through faith. Paul insists in verse 21, " I do not nullify the grace of God, for if righteousness were through the law, then Christ died for no purpose.[45] So too in his day Flacius was convinced that the gospel was being nullified by the requirements and ambiguities contained in the *Leipzig Interim*. It diminished and clouded the work of Christ, the proof of God's love for the world. It muddied faith's proper focus upon the only Lamb of God who takes away the sin of the world, whose name was the only name under heaven given to men for salvation, the one bread from heaven, who was the vivifying righteousness of God for all sinners who hunger.[46] This was the great threat and tragedy of the interims, which threatened to lead the redeemed back once again into slavery to sin, like a dog returning to vomit or a sow to the mud.[47] The very core of the Christian faith was at stake. The chief article, the doctrine of justification, the article upon which the church stands or falls, was being challenged, watered down, and thus nullified, for it was all Christ or not enough Christ in Flacius' and Luther's teaching. This is similar to Paul's use of the account of the circumcision of Timothy and his subsequent refusal to have Titus circumcised. Once again the freedom of the gospel and the clarity of the doctrine of justification was at stake. In quoting this account, Flacius again used a biblical example from the New Testament that is first used by Paul, the author himself, in an illustrative manner and for which Paul himself supplies an attendant explication within the context of its original use in Galatians 2.[48]

Flacius provided additional examples from the life of St. Paul. Once again, though, these were often tied to applications that Paul himself made, with few exceptions. For instance, he noted that the Magdeburgers could not rightly be accused of causing an uproar or division, for they were as innocent as Paul was in the tumult that some raised in response to his preaching and teaching in Jerusalem and Ephesus.[49] Moreover, just as Paul continued to encourage the Ephesians, even after he had to flee, with prayer and his letter to them, so also Flacius held that faithful pastors should

---

44. Gal 2:8–14 ESV.

45. Gal 2:21 ESV.

46. Flacius, *Breves Svmmae Religionis Iesu Christi*, A2 v.

47. Ibid., A3 r.

48. Flacius, *Ein buch von waren und falschen Mitteldingen*, Tiii r.

49. Flacius, *Ein vermanung zur bestendigkeit*, Div v.

continue to look after their flocks, even if forced to leave. As it was better that Paul fled than stayed, if staying would have meant compromising the truth of God, so also, if a pastor's option were to stay and receive the new ceremonies or leave in protest, Flacius encouraged the latter as the faithful, biblical route.[50] These are two of a very few instances, though, where Flacius' use of an example from Paul's life was not tied to Paul's own application and interpretation of that event.

Moving beyond the time of the New Testament Scriptures, Flacius also utilized events from ecclesiastical history. He recounted the botched martyrdom of a number of Christians under the Emperor Valens, an Arian—he made use especially of persecution related to Arianism. When the Christians refused to back down in the face of an ambush commanded by the emperor, the captain charged with seeing that these believers were strangled refused to carry out his orders. His refusal sprang from his contact with a pregnant woman who was hurrying to the church. When the captain informed her that those at the church were going to be strangled, she replied to him, "I have indeed heard that and that is precisely why I am hurrying over there with my child, so that we might die together with the other Christians and become martyrs."[51] Flacius argued that if the Lutherans in his day would show the same courage and steadfastness they might meet similar results. Flacius recalled Athanasius' unwavering resolve in the face of numerous exiles on account of his rejection of the Arian heresy. Athanasius did not abandon his flock through his steadfastness. He would have abandoned them, rather, had he not held firm to the Word of God. Like Paul, when he was forced to flee Ephesus, Athanasius "through his prayer, writings, steadfast confession, pitiable misery, and his various crosses strengthened them and taught the Christian Church even up unto our own day."[52] Flacius contrasted the refusal of Christians in the early church to offer incense to the emperor with the Adiaphorists' willingness to cooperate in much more significant ways with the Antichrist himself.[53] He lamented, "In previous times it would have been a very intense slander of someone even if one had only alleged his falling away with two or three grains of incense. Now, however, even if one transforms the whole Christian Church into the abomination of the Antichrist, it still ought not be called a denial."[54] He pointed his readers to Book 7 of Eusebius' *Ecclesiastical History*, which covers the era

50. Flacius, *Ein buch von waren und falschen Mitteldingen*, Ti r–Ti v.

51. Flacius, *Ein Christliche vermanung*, Gii r.

52. Flacius, *Ein buch von waren und falschen Mitteldingen*, Ti v.

53. Flacius, *Ein Christliche vermanung*, Cii r.

54. Flacius, *Ein buch von waren und falschen Mitteldingen*, Qiii v.

of imperial persecution of the Christian Church, the famous era of martyrdom, which included the shameful folly of those who lapsed. Echoing the *Te Deum*, he urged, "We should in these things consider and imitate the example of the holy prophets, our dear Lord Jesus Christ, the apostles, and the holy martyrs, who in previous times and even gave up their lives for the Word of God."[55] In other words, Christians should follow the pattern of the one true Church that had existed from the Old Testament, through the New Testament, and into the present day.

Flacius made ample use of examples from the Scriptures, the Apocrypha, and church history. However, he made more use of the Old Testament, and indeed, perhaps even the Apocrypha, than the New Testament for creative illustrative purposes. This is partly because the examples he used from the New Testament were already tied by the original authors to their application. This is also likely because the Old Testament and Apocrypha provided more abundant examples of resistance to tyranny and the ungodly commands of those in power. Flacius also made use of church history. The examples chosen from church history served to illustrate the willingness of true Christians to suffer rather than to sin or compromise the Word of God. These examples did not provide the same instances of active resistance to governing authorities as could be found in the Old Testament, but they did demonstrate passive resistance, the willingness to suffer and die in order to obey God rather than men, as the *clausula Petri* demanded.

2.3. The Apocalypse and the End of Luther's Reformation in Germany

Matthias Flacius Illyricus, like many medieval and early modern Christians, was convinced he lived in the end times. In Christian theology, all time since Christ's ascension has been the end times. All that remains is Christ's return. Like Luther, Flacius did not think his Savior's return could be far off, given the great commotion in the world and the open persecution of the gospel which he decried. He was not ignorant, however, of earlier ages in which the end had appeared near. Rather, his church history erased the boundaries between the various ages of the church. Past, present, and future ran into each other in Flacius' view of the end times in which the church has found itself since apostolic times. Haberkern notes, "In this view, history was both a record of former times and a forecast of imminent events, offering solace and understanding for contemporaries by collapsing the temporal distinctions between the revealed past, a tumultuous present, and a potentially

---

55. Flacius, *Ein vermanung zur bestendigkeit*, Di r.

glorious future."[56] Thus, Flacius did not rule out that the interims might be a testing of Christ's Church like that which it had endured so often throughout its past, which would be followed by a continued history for this world. Flacius' understanding of the cyclical nature of ecclesiastical history—times of particular testing followed by times of more relative ease—can be seen in a number of places, most prominently in *Ein Vermanung zur bestendigkeit*, which began with a review of such cycles in the Old Testament and Apocrypha. "So also, it appears that the dear gospel of Christ has a different status at one time than at another," he observed.[57] The exodus, Flacius argued in the same work, "has always been a figure and pattern of the entire Church and all Christians, for God the Lord always leads His own in a wonderful manner."[58] He elaborated on his view of church history even further in the pages that followed. What more reason could there be to examine oneself, to state one's convictions, to reveal one's allegiances and worldview than the prospect of standing before one's Maker? He began *Ein Christliche vermanung*, therefore, with an emphatic insistence that he had a good conscience in this venture.[59] He contended that his opponents had a bad conscience, as he demonstrated with Caspar Cruciger's deathbed soul-searching.[60]

Flacius made regular allusion to imagery from the Revelation of St. John. Whether referring to the papacy as the Antichrist or speaking about the whore of Babylon, the enemies of Luther's doctrine (or those whom Flacius perceived as such) were clearly painted in apocalyptic hues. They were not merely enemies who pose contemporary dangers. They were manifestations of the constant enmity and danger faced by Christ's Church, whose opposition and hostility it would only escape through Christ's return. Paul described the man of lawlessness who was to arise within the church in 2 Thessalonians. He wrote, "Let no one deceive you in any way. For that day will not come, unless the rebellion comes first, and the man of lawlessness is revealed, the son of destruction, who opposes and exalts himself against every so-called god or object of worship, so that he takes his seat in the temple of God, proclaiming himself to be God."[61] Like Luther, Flacius insisted that this man of lawlessness was at work within Christianity through the office of the papacy. The devil, who could not overcome the Church through his

56. Haberkern, "Flacius' Human Face of Doctrine: Sacred History Between Prosopography and Dogmatics," 150.

57. Flacius, *Ein vermanung zur bestendigkeit*, Giv v.

58. Ibid., Fi v–Fii r.

59. Flacius, *Ein Christliche vermanung*, Aiv v.

60. Ibid., Bii v–Biii r.

61. 1 Thess 2:3, 4 ESV.

fury, was now busying himself infiltrating it as an angel of light, introducing corrupting changes under the pretext of piety.[62] Flacius expounded, "The old serpent could adorn himself in a stately fashion not only at the time of Eve but also in these times, as he appears under the facade of holiness above measure, bringing forth smooth and sweet words. In the back, though, is his black, poisonous, dragon's tail, together with eternal condemnation."[63] Flacius suggested to his readers that the fact that the same old enemies were at it again should be both comforting and alarming for the Christian. It was comforting because church history in Flacius' view was the tale of God's deliverance of his Christians from such enemies and yet alarming in that these were formidable foes with much experience in their ungodly labor.

Illyricus identified the chief enemy as the devil. And the devil was no dolt. He was sly, patient, and shrewd. He did not limit himself to the devilish, but worked sometimes most effectively, as at Flacius' time, through churches and liturgies themselves. His greatest successes not infrequently took place through what is presented as piety. This explains Flacius' special venom for the Adiaphorists, those evangelicals who were cooperating with the changes mandated by the *Interim*. Their cooperation lent the alterations, or adulterations, as Flacius preferred to call them, the guise of propriety and theological warrant and sanction. Why would they do this? They had underestimated the wiles of the devil and themselves been beguiled by the old evil foe through the papists and the emperor. Unlike Flacius, they had not discerned the devil's ploy to work through the church against the Church. Flacius explained, "The devil strives all the time to commence his wickedness in a little and insignificant thing, but plans to move forward gradually as far as he can, so that we slowly surrender our ability to back out, having dealt with the devil and his works in a friendly manner."[64] This, he noted, was precisely how the devil had operated with Eve, and it was how he now was duping the Adiaphorists, who should have learned from Eve's example. Elsewhere he compared the devil's tactics to a wedge, "which in the front is thin and sharp in the leading edge, so that one does not suppose, were it pounded into wood, that it would be able to break it apart very much." That was the deception and "yet, although it is very thin at the point, it does not on that account make any less of an entrance for the thickness that follows, and so proceeds in such a way that, after the first part is in, the other will follow closely after it until at last the wood is

62. Flacius, *Quod Hoc Tempore*, A2 r.
63. Henetus, "Ein kurzer Bericht vom Interim," 99.
64. Flacius, *Ein vermanung zur bestendigkeit*, Dii v.

entirely split."[65] The splitting of the wood would mean nothing else than the end of Luther's Reformation, at least in Germany.

While the devil was the Church's greatest and most perplexing foe in Flacius' literature, perhaps no enemy appeared more often than the Roman papacy, identified by Flacius, as by Luther, as the Antichrist. While Lutheran theology has historically made a distinction between the papacy and the pope himself as the Antichrist, no such distinction was evident in Flacius' writings. The pope was the clear enemy of Christ's Church and biblical doctrine and had to be resisted at all costs. Even the smallest concessions would compromise the whole of scriptural teaching. Even seemingly harmless liturgical practices would become an enormous threat when readopted in deference to Rome. The Adiaphorists, Flacius declared, "take a clear step toward reestablishing the papacy, for the ceremonies are the foremost foundation of the papacy and the greatest worship of God among the papists are just plain ceremonies."[66] The devil, together with the whole papacy, was in the liturgical details. Moreover, allowances toward the papacy would mislead and confound the common people, Flacius held, so that they would think, "O, the devil is not as dark as one paints him. The pope is not as bad as Doctor Luther made him out to be, for otherwise why would such great men permit uniformity with the Antichrist? Since Doctor Luther was quarrelsome and overdid it, why should we want to follow him? Why should we not compromise a little for the sake of peace and the common good?"[67] This was a real threat, he insisted, because "our teachers have hardly been able to root out all the abuses [from the past so far], although they have rooted out the foundation."[68] "When the papists now have these advantages," Flacius asked, "who can doubt that after that, when Sidonius and other ravenous papistic wolves and bears fall upon us, they will easily smother us, and thus drag the whole papacy into the church?"[69] For this reason Flacius maintained that "the adiaphoristic devils"—those granting the papists increasing advantages through their yielding—"are nothing other than the forerunner of the great devil, who is the originator and lord of the entire papacy."[70] They were pawns of the pope, the Antichrist, and his lord, the devil. One cannot reason with such enemies, Flacius said. Instead, he claimed that one had to oppose them from the outset and in every way. This ought not surprise

---

65. Flacius, *Ein Christliche vermanung*, Di v.

66. Flacius, *Ein buch von waren und falschen Mitteldingen*, Oii v–Oiii r.

67. Ibid., Pi r.

68. Ibid., Oiii r.

69. Flacius, *Ein Christliche vermanung*, Di r.

70. Ibid.

anyone, according to Flacius. God's Word had already revealed as much. "Daniel and Revelation say that the Antichrist, after he has been revealed and weakened," which was Luther's work, "will try to set up again his former honor and power with the help and assistance of the powerful."[71]

The title of Thomas Kaufmann's magisterial monograph, *Das Ende der Reformation*, summarizes well the threat Flacius deemed posed by the Adiaphoristic formula of Leipzig.[72] In 1524 Luther wrote in *To the Councilmen of All Cities in Germany that They Establish and Maintain Christian Schools*:

> O my beloved Germans, buy while the market is at your door; gather in the harvest while there is sunshine and fair weather; make use of God's grace and word while it is there! For you should know that God's word and grace is like a passing shower of rain which does not return where it has once been. It has been with the Jews, but when it's gone it's gone, and now they have nothing. Paul brought it to the Greeks; but again when it's gone it's gone, and now they have the Turk. Rome and the Latins also had it; but when it's gone it's gone, and now they have the pope. And you Germans need not think that you will have it forever, for ingratitude and contempt will not make it stay. Therefore, seize it and hold it fast, whoever can; for lazy hands are bound to have a lean year.[73]

Flacius had taken this warning to heart. He firmly believed that the gospel would move on if taken for granted. What stunned him was such ingratitude so soon after Luther's death, but as noted earlier, that was the pattern in the history of the Christian Church. The gospel assumed was the gospel lost. In Flacius' opinion, it was just a matter of time. Flacius explained, "Help, dear God! How can the people be so epicurean, yes, become so entirely brutish that they throw God and eternal life to the winds and despise it? They have continually clamored that they want to change something for the sake of peace and unity. Yes, they want to have peace and unity with the Babylonian whore and its gruesome beast."[74] He lamented that God would ask, "Why has the faithful city so shamefully become a whore?"[75] The threat loomed perilously and immenently, he warned: "For the devil certainly prowls around through his servants the papists, Interimists, and Adiaphorists, so

---

71. Flacius, *Vermanung Matth. Flacii Illyrici*, Civ r.

72. Kaufmann, *Das Ende der Reformation*.

73. LW 45:352–353.

74. Flacius, *Vermanung Matth. Flacii Illyrici*, Bi v.

75. Flacius, *Ein Christliche vermanung*, Hi r.

that through your wavering he might draw all churches back again to the papacy."[76] He complained:

> What horrible ingratitude it is, which our Lord God will yet earnestly and heavily punish, that we forget and are ungrateful for such revealed grace and kindness, that we are unwilling, in order to maintain the pure teaching, not only to lose our life, but also our goods, and that we do not want to do without or lack even the tiniest bit from our income and profit, but rather to continue to buy and sell, as it stands in Revelation 13. We take the sign of the beast on our foreheads and pray to his image, that is, so that we may ply our wares, we accept the Interim and submit to all godless things.[77]

Flacius clarified that the war against the Christians was not merely that. It was a war against Christ himself—a final great battle between God and the devil, the Savior and the beast. Repeatedly Flacius stated that Christ himself was persecuted, taken captive, and crucified in the person of his people. He appealed to the Duke of Saxony, Augustus, the brother of Moritz, who himself would become the Elector of Saxony in 1553, "to see to it that you tame the Epicurean, the destroyer of the religion of Christ, and hold yourself to the Christian religion." He warned the duke to take care especially "so that it may not be truthfully said in foreign places, such as in Denmark and other kingdoms, that through domestic war nothing else has been accomplished except that Christ himself, together with the pious prince, was captured and exiled from the land."[78] John Frederick, whose electoral title Augustus' brother had received from the emperor for joining forces against his cousin, was the pious prince who would be captive and exiled together with the Lord Jesus Christ himself should the duke not be careful. Elsewhere Flacius cried out, "Oh how hard the swift threats of our Lord Christ strike us now—'Woe to you, Chorazin! Woe to you, Bethsaida!'—we who are pushing away the Christ who is so clearly depicted before our eyes or want to crucify him again."[79] He explained the Adiaphorists' cooperation with the emperor's demands thus, "They are anxious that the Romans perhaps might come and take their land and people and therefore they are willing to crucify Christ, that is, they fear men more than God."[80] Moreover, the devil's wrath, expressed through the Antichrist and his minions, was

76. Ibid., Hi r.

77. Flacius, *Ein vermanung zur bestendigkeit*, Civ r.

78. Flacius, *Ein Christliche vermanung*, Bi r–Bi v.

79. Flacius, *Ein vermanung zur bestendigkeit*, Hiii r–Hiii v.

80. Flacius, *Ein buch von waren und falschen Mitteldingen*, Riv r.

not limited to Christians. No, he said, "from their deeds and profanity one can well establish that this is such a war in which the hellish devil himself persecutes the poor Christians with especial hatred, yes, rants and rages against the Lord Christ himself."[81]

This was not mere purposeful hyperbole on Flacius' part either. It was his sincere conviction. He honestly held that Christ was being persecuted, crucified again, by the open enemies of the Lutheran churches and those members of it who worked with the enemies. Christ was inseparable from his Church. The two were bound intimately together. And so his insistence that Christ himself was wronged when his church was victimized served a dual purpose. It illustrated the heinous and devilish nature of the Adiaphorists' conciliation of the Antichrist and his accomplices and emboldened those Christians who were under siege. Christ was with them. They bore Christ's cross and Christ would not abandon them under their crosses. Flacius counseled, "Inasmuch as we have been so born and called to faith in Christ, we should expect much adversity and carry the cross of Christ. It is a small thing that we patiently suffer such misfortune, and we ought not trouble ourselves too much and thus through foolish and godless fear and worry make the misfortune greater."[82] A later section will cover the suffering of the church militant and Flacius' theology of the cross, but it is worth noting this connection here because it reinforces the nature of the battle Flacius was watching play out in his time: a cosmic battle between good and evil, Christ and Satan—the battle foretold in Revelation, the culmination of the end times. What was happening was "taking place through those persons about whom the Holy Spirit has previously prophesied would storm the kingdom of Christ and earnestly prohibit us from obeying him, namely the whore of Babylon and the beast upon whom the whore rides."[83] Christ was fighting the beast. The Savior who suffered with his Christians also struggled together with them and in the end they, with him, would emerge victorious. Therefore, Flacius explained, "I also condemn and separate myself not only from the Babylonian harlot and its beast, but also from the image and signs of the beast, about which it is written in Revelation."[84] This was precisely the great tragedy of what the Adiaphorists were doing. Exactly when they ought to have been leading the charge and sounding the battle cry, they were making peace with Christ's ultimate enemies. Flacius grumbled, "I shrink back with my whole heart from the present horrid and

81. Flacius, *Vermanung Matth. Flacii Illyrici*, Di v–Dii r.

82. Ibid., Aiv r.

83. Flacius, *Ein buch von waren und falschen Mitteldingen*, Tiv r.

84. Ibid., Uiii v.

entirely diabolic harlotry taking place with the Babylonian harlot." His former colleagues, instead of fighting the good of fight, were rather toiling "in
order to reconcile themselves to the Antichrist, together with his beast, so
that the cross might not be laid on them . . . for the sake of Christ."[85]

In keeping with his apocalyptic viewpoint, Flacius also made use of recent signs and visions to reinforce his case (126). He devoted several pages to a
number of these phenomena in *Vermanung Matth. Flacii Illyrici*.[86] He alluded
to a prophecy from Nuremberg. He cited earlier prophecies of Melchtilde, an
eleventh century female mystic, and Hildegard, a twelfth century female mystic. He pointed out that three suns were seen on the twenty-first of March and
three moons that same evening. Moreover, there had been particularly omi-
nous and arrogant boasts from the enemies, which would surely come back
to bite them. Thunder was reported to have been battering and lingered in the
areas the enemy had occupied. Finally, a medical student who had stayed as a
boarder with the sister-in-law of one of the authors of the *Augsburg Interim*,
Johann Agricola, had died after expressing his strong support for the emperor.
While dying, however, he recanted and prophesied "extremely terrible things
and threatened by name those who had led the foreigners into Germany or
had helped in any way to allow innocent blood to be shed in Germany."[87] This
was not the only time Flacius made use of such a deathbed conversion and
vision either. In *Ein Christliche vermanung*, he devoted several pages to the
deathbed recantation of Cruciger, who had cooperated in the formulation of
the *Leipzig Interim* and in death declared, "I have spoken incorrectly. God be
my witness, I have spoken incorrectly."[88]

Flacius' writings contain clear apocalyptic elements. These elements
do not essentially define his works, but they do undergird and lend them
a sense of urgency. The devil and the Antichrist, who had been revealed by
Martin Luther, were making their final assault—at least it seemed—upon
the Christian Church. They were frantically battling against the newly restored and rejuvenated preaching of the gospel ushered in by the Reformation. This might well have been but another chapter in a long church history
of struggles and persecutions, but Flacius liberally employed the imagery of
St. John's Apocalypse, the Book of Revelation, to describe and interpret it.
The fate and legacy of Luther's Reformation in Germany was at stake. Judgment Day was drawing near. It was impossible for Flacius to imagine anything more being at stake. There was no time to spare. The clock was ticking

85. Ibid., Uiv r.

86. Flacius, *Vermanung Matth. Flacii Illyrici*, Civ v–Dii v.

87. Ibid., Dii r.

88. Flacius, *Ein Christliche vermanung*, Biii r.

down. Christians therefore needed to do what Christians have always been called to do: stand firm and confess Christ and the Christian faith.

2.4. The Church as Remnant

Flacius wrote of the church of his day that "this remnant of believers, otherwise in all respects entirely trifling and weak, is persecuted in a hostile manner by many thousands of devils, by the papists, interims, and the traitor Judas."[89] The Judas was likely Moritz, the so-called Judas of Meissen, so named because he sided with the emperor against his cousin and fellow Lutherans of the Schmalkaldic League. The object of interest here, though, is that "remnant of believers." Flacius was convinced that God's Church would almost always be a remnant. Even when churches swelled and were adorned with various glorious ornamentations, the true Church was often but a fragment, a small invisible *ecclesiola* within a perhaps more impressive visible *ecclesia*, though not in any puritanical sense. Philip Haberkern writes:

> At the heart of Flacius' historical enterprise, and lying at the very foundation of Lutheran perceptions of the past, was a belief in the continuity of God's true church on earth. This 'invisible' church, which constituted a small body within the institutional church and was often persecuted by the hypocritical majority, was marked by its fidelity to the Word of God and its propagation of the essential doctrines contained within it.[90]

The Church in Flacius' thought was "the little flock of the Lord."[91] Noting that the Adiaphorists and other opponents had failed to listen, Flacius stated, "I, however, since one admonishes them to no avail, will only admonish the little sheep of Christ who are still remaining in Meissen and elsewhere to guard themselves most carefully from the papistic, interimistic, and adiaphoristic, and flee and in no way receive all the adulterations of the recognized and true doctrine of Christ, be they as they may."[92] We see here and throughout his works Flacius' conception of the true Church as a percentage of those claiming to be Christians, often a tiny minority of those who call themselves Christians. According to Flacius, there was a reason that Jesus called the road to hell wide. The masses would walk it, even race down it. The road to heaven was narrow, its pilgrims few.

---

89. Flacius, *Ein buch von waren und falschen Mitteldingen*, Oiii v.
90. Haberkern, "Flacius' Human Face of Doctrine," 147.
91. Flacius, *Ein buch von waren und falschen Mitteldingen*, Riv v.
92. Flacius, *Ein Christliche vermanung*, Biv r–Biv v.

Not only were true Christians frequently few in number, according to Flacius' theology, but they were often unimpressive, unlettered, and unsophisticated. In fact, Flacius sometimes presented this lack of sophistication as a virtue. Again and again in his pamphlets, Flacius praised the laity in contrast to the clergy. His praise focused upon the laity's adherence to the plain meaning of the Word of God and their suspicion regarding the recent, poisonous changes. In *Ein buch von waren und falschen Mitteldingen* Flacius twice noted that the laity were rightly skeptical of the reintroduction of old practices. He blamed their possible apostasy upon the learned who abuse their reputations to mislead and confuse the simple. First, he cautioned, "For the laity, who hate the papacy like the devil himself, want to have no part of the abused, corrupted ceremonies that they must see in the church, and they thus regard all ceremonies and church usages, and even the entire religion, as trifling, and altogether despise it."[93] Second, he warned, "Therefore, the poor laity, especially in temptation and crosses, do not necessarily buy into such subtle arguments, but because they look more upon the person than upon the words, they put their trust in the person more for the sake of his reputation than his words."[94] In both instances, it was the simple faithful at risk because of the learned and sophisticated unfaithful. Flacius maintained that if the Church were to persevere, the laity needed to be admonished, encouraged, emboldened, and reassured, as he strove to do with his *Admonitions* [*Vermanung*].

There is a tension between wisdom and folly in Flacius' works. His enemies, he argued, operated upon the former, using worldly wisdom to avoid the cross and preserve temporal peace at the expense of the truth. The remnant, he insisted, was to cling to the latter, the foolishness of the cross. St. Paul's teaching from 1 Corinthians 1 runs throughout. Flacius wrote, "What [Paul] said certainly is to be marked well, for our Lord God has a special way and manner for ruling and preserving the entire world, and especially his Church, that is entirely contrary to human wisdom."[95] Man's thoughts had to bow where God's thoughts stood revealed. Moreover, when God was hidden, the Christian was not to dare to divine the the Lord's purposes beyond or outside of what Scripture had made known. Flacius wrote, "Our Lord God wants the human race to esteem his ways and counsel highly, follow it, judge itself according to it, and not ask how or why such happens, and what result will be accomplished by it. In particular he wants us to entrust every affair and all our life and care to him." All the

93. Flacius, *Ein buch von waren und falschen Mitteldingen*, Oii r.

94. Ibid., Pii v–Piii r.

95. Flacius, *Ein vermanung zur bestendigkeit*, Biv r.

Christian needed to know was God's promise that the Lord would work all things for good in the end.[96] True wisdom was God's wisdom. Man's wisdom, on the contrary, was prone to overstepping its bounds, twisting the truth for its convenience, and forsaking the love of one's neighbor. Reason had its place, but it had to remain faith's handmaiden and not its master. Flacius liked to point out that Dr. Martin himself had warned against navigating by reason.[97] It was an unreliable guide, for wisdom divorced from Christ, God's Wisdom, was folly and this "foolishness of men, their blindness and perverse nature, is so great that, while they cannot grasp the things that belong to God, they pay attention much more attentively to earthly and transitory things (which can help us little, as experience itself teaches us) rather than to that which is from God, to the divine teaching, and to those things which God has promised in it."[98]

Not only was Flacius' remnant often small in number and insignificant in stature, but it was heavenly-oriented. It was focused not only upon this life and its goods and goals, but upon the eternity promised by Christ. In fact, Flacius exposed one of the chief dangers facing Christians in his day as a willingness to compromise heavenly doctrine for earthly peace, spiritual truth for temporal well-being. He wrote, "This present world therefore errs when it assumes that a Christian will have all good days here, for Christ himself has said, 'You will have angst in this world, but peace in me.'"[99] The Adiaphorists, however, had either forgotten this or disregarded it outright. He asked rhetorically, "Should then the Church, which Christ has redeemed with his blood for the praise of his Father in heaven, shame and blaspheme God for the sake alone of bodily rest and good days?"[100] He warned of the temptation being presented to simple Christians under the pretense that they "will bring good order, proper discipline, reconciliation, and peace of the belly and the world, and clearly do not know what serves the divine good."[101] He observed, "The most important reason why almost everyone is stuck in error now is the god which one calls the belly and the life that one calls good and peaceful . . . . Such a god grows at a furious pace, even among those who perhaps have been somewhat God-fearing in the past."[102] Such was the peril facing the little flock of Christ. The simple were being duped

---

96. Ibid., Biv r.

97. Flacius, *Quod Hoc Tempore*, A3 r.

98. Flacius, *Ein vermanung zur bestendigkeit*, Cii v.

99. Ibid., Ei v.

100. Flacius, *Ein buch von waren und falschen Mitteldingen*, Ri r– Ri v.

101. Flacius, *Ein Christliche vermanung*, Diii r.

102. Flacius, *Ein buch von waren und falschen Mitteldingen*, Aii r.

by the learned, who were choosing good days here over the heaven won for them by Christ. The insignificant were being oppressed by the powerful and through threats and hollow promises wooed away from the true Christian faith and confessional faithfulness.

The concern for the belly mentioned above Flacius elsewhere described as epicureanism. In fact, he utilized few identifying adjectives more frequently than "epicurean." Nowhere is his assault on epicureanism more pronounced than in the preface to *Ein Christliche vermanung*, addressed to Augustus, Duke of Saxony. He began by retelling Jesus' lament of Jerusalem before his passion, when the Savior said, "If you knew what would serve for your peace."[103] The situation in Flacius' age equated closely, he contended. Just as the Jewish leaders had argued that it was best for Jesus, one man, to die, in order to keep peace with the Romans, so also now the little flock of Christ was being sacrificed in order to keep peace with the Holy Roman Emperor. Flacius held that the root of the problem was impatience and a lack of faith. When God failed to send help immediately and in the way desired, many despaired. Flacius explained, "Some, however, go so far as to surmise that there must be no God, or no more divine counsel available, and therefore have become entirely godless, associating themselves with those for whom things go best and grandest in this present life, thus assuming an epicurean way of life more and more each day."[104]

Flacius often joined the adjective "epicurean" with the noun "sow." In his preface dedicated to Duke Augustus of Saxony, the brother of Moritz, Flacius put the following words, clearly intended as a warning for the court at Meissen, into the mouth of Christ as he looked down upon Jerusalem before his passion: "O, you fools, have your wise and your teachers of the law become such entirely epicurean sows that they dare to think that someone can achieve peace between the wrathful God and sinning men! O, you godless, dunderheaded city, this very thing will be the chief cause of your ruin!"[105] This language was not original with Flacius. In *Against the Roman Papacy as an Institution of the Devil*, for example, Luther had written, "Do you hear, Pope Paul, first of all you have no faith, and you and your sons, the cardinals and the curia's riffraff, do not honor God, for you are Epicurean sows, just like all the popes, your predecessors."[106] Luther regularly termed contempt for the Word of God epicureanism. Lauterbach's *Table Talk* has Luther commenting, "How great is the presumption and security of the world! Whoever

---

103. Flacius, *Ein Christliche vermanung*, Aii r; Luke 19:42.
104. Flacius, *Ein vermanung zur bestendigkeit*, Ci v.
105. Flacius, *Ein Christliche vermanung*, Aii v.
106. LW 41:287.

thinks he's something dares to scoff at Christ and lift his foot against him. It'll get even worse; epicureanism will make great headway. For contempt of the Word, which is characteristic of this world and believes neither in God nor in a life to come, is nothing else than a preparation for epicureanism before the last day."[107] Viet Dietrich recorded a similar statement.[108] Flacius, thinking that last day at hand, surely found affirmation in such statements of the reformer, perhaps even personally having heard some in Wittenberg. In *The Bondage of the Will*, Luther attacked Erasmus with words that could have been spoken by Flacius against the Interimists: "By such tactics you only succeed in showing that you foster in your heart a Lucian, or some other pig from Epicurus' sty who, having no belief in God himself, secretly ridicules all who have a belief and confess it."[109] Flacius would similarly write later, "Now let the epicurean sows, the Interimists and Adiaphorists, scorn the wrath and threatening of God as they will, regard all this blasphemous depravity as little, simple, pure adiaphora, until they at last finally fall under the punishment of God." [110] Finally, in a letter to Wenceslas Link, Luther wrote of the end times, "Now is the time which was predicted to come after the fall of Antichrist, when people will be Epicureans and atheists, so that the word of Christ might be fulfilled: 'As it was in the days of Noah and Lot, so will it be on the day of the arrival of the Son of Man.'"[111] Once again, the impending last day necessitated clear, blunt language for Luther, and the same was true for Flacius, who certainly saw in the circumstances of his day a fulfillment of the prophecies of Luther, the third Elijah. Here, then, when Flacius unflatteringly classified a lack of trust in God in tribulation, attempts to circumvent the cross and suffering through human wisdom, and an overriding desire for temporal peace and well-being, he merely adopted the language of his spiritual father, Martin Luther. Even more, for the most part, he employed such language against his enemies less vehemently than Luther did, although not without fervor and sting.

Flacius demanded that Christians in this life focus not merely on their earthly welfare, but above all upon their eternal salvation. Again and again Flacius called upon his fellow Christians to refocus their perspective and rearrange their priorities. What good would it be, after all, to lose heaven for a little peace on earth? And yet the temporal was not unimportant in Flacius' view. It was not wrong to pray for one's daily bread, as the Lord's

107. LW 54:255–56.

108. LW 54:69.

109. LW 33:24.

110. Flacius, *Ein Christliche vermanung*, Biv r.

111. LW 50:243–44.

Prayer and Luther's *Catechism* encourage. Rather, the Christian had to be sure to do so in the right frame of mind. He explained, "The temporal, however, such as body and life, good health, peace, money and goods, etc., we should always pray for with the distinction and condition that they might serve to God's glory and for our own and other's salvation and well-being." In doing so, he continued, we must "place ourselves under the will of God, who may will that we should take up the cross, but with the hope that he will save us, just as Christ himself places himself under the will of his Father, when he says, 'Father, if it is possible, may this cup pass by me, but not what I will, but what you will.'"[112]

The appeal to Christ's petition in Gethsemane was important. Luther's flock, like Christ, faced a dilemma. Surely Christians, like their Christ, desired to avoid suffering if it were possible according to God's will, but never, Flacius insisted, if contrary to it or God's honor. This was Lutheranism's Gethsemane. God's remnant's cross awaited, and it would be sin and apostasy to refuse it. It was one thing for God to remove it. It was another thing entirely to flee it. This was no time to plot "whereby one might wiggle himself out of danger and need and increase his own goods and honor."[113] Flacius' theology of the cross and convictions concerning the church militant will be explained further in the next chapter, but it is helpful here to see how each of these themes together. They were indeed inseparable in Flacius' view. Not only was God's true Church a remnant, but it was a remnant in the end times called to carry its cross, as the Church had done in every age.

Flacius argued that the devil strived for victory by turning the hearts of Christ's little flock. Jesus said, after all, in Matthew 6:21, "For where your treasure is, there your heart will be also."[114] Flacius therefore warned, "It is better for the goods, body, and assembly of the God-fearing to be disturbed than for consciences. The spiritual wolf, the devil and false teachers, does not devour the sheep of Christ until he has made it adherent to him with its heart."[115] In a section on the steps the faithful should take to preserve the peace in a godly fashion, Flacius pointed out that there were human means through which the little flock of Christ could yet work. Not all human strategy was wrong, therefore. This strategy, though, was once again framed by the eternal. Flacius contended that the faithful should vocally express a willingness to trade earthly goods for religious freedom. He wrote, "We should also employ human plans and means, and not discard them,

112. Flacius, *Ein vermanung zur bestendigkeit*, Gii r.

113. Flacius, *Ein Christliche vermanung*, Aii v–Aiii r.

114. Matt 6:21 ESV.

115. Flacius, *Ein buch von waren und falschen Mitteldingen*, Ti v.

and in that way test our Lord God." He explained some of these human means in what follows: "You poor and entirely downtrodden churches"—in other words, the remnant—"petition your worldly lords diplomatically . . . begging them to remain satisfied with temporal rule and governance and leave the spiritual to Christ."[116]

Flacius did not expect the rulers to be satisfied with mere pleas and begging, however. After an attempt to shame the temporal lords by a comparison to the liberality of the Turks in their treatment of Christians, and before a warning that it is not fitting for a Christian lord to treat the Jews better than fellow Christians, Flacius continued his counsel to the faithful few: "Promise them even more than you owe them by right, if only they will permit you the gospel free and unadulterated. Give the tyrants your goods (if it is what they want to have), so long as you retain the treasure of eternal life, so that in all of these great difficulties and burdens you might maintain your grasp on the grace of God, his comfort, and the hope of eternal life."[117] In this way, he suggested, "you poor churches of Christ can diligently and sincerely beseech your earthly authorities for the sake of Christ, whose name is common to them and us."[118]

Already poor, pitiable, downtrodden, and tiny, the faithful few could plead only Christ with an appeal to Christian charity and a promise to become even poorer, trading all their goods, if necessary, in order to retain heavenly doctrine and the promise of the life to come. There was no other God-pleasing recourse left them, certainly not human scheming. If there were to be resistance, that was the office and responsibility of their rulers, to whom Flacius would certainly appeal for the same throughout the Adiaphoristic Controversy. The Church, however, was to be content with its pitiable existence so long as it could maintain its hold on Christ and His Word.

2.5. Confession, Martyrdom, and the Theology of the Cross

According to Flacius, it was time for Christ's Church, reinvigorated through Luther's doctrine, to buck up and bear the cross. He challenged his fellow Lutherans: "It is your duty, if you are a Christian at all, yes, if you are a man. You are no different than others."[119] While simple and of lowly stature in the eyes of the world, the Christian had to be no less manly than those of earthly might. Speaking about the removal of faithful pastors, Flacius fumed,

116. Flacius, *Ein Christliche vermanung*, Fii r.
117. Ibid., Fii v.
118. Ibid., Fiii r.
119. Ibid., Giii v.

"When weak-kneed, godless, and unlearned ninnies are set in the place of pious, faithful, learned, and steadfast preachers, as happened in Torgau, then already the entire papacy has been accepted."[120] Powerful enemies necessitated courageous resolve: "We should see to it that we manfully withstand the devil when he attacks us in his gruesome manner and endeavors to lead us to abandon God."[121] Flacius exorted Christians to struggle with their eyes on the prize: "We must stay alert and struggle manfully against the devil and we will be blessed."[122] While their foes might have impressive weaponry and power, the Christian had potent arms as well: "We should arm ourselves with God's Word not only so that we can guard ourselves with it, but also so that we can strengthen our brothers and struggle manfully against those who counsel unfaithfulness, and those who do not walk correctly according to the teaching of the gospel in full sight, and those (as Paul says) whose mouths must be stopped."[123]

For Flacius the cross was not merely part of the Christian life, a temporary inconvenience; the cross defined the Christian life—Christ's cross and the individual Christian's. In a certain sense Flacius' *Ein vermanung zur bestendigkeit* was nothing other than an extended commentary upon and development of Luther's theology of the cross. Flacius reminded his fellow Lutherans that "we must be obedient to God, since he subjects the Church to the cross, and through much sorrow and distress wants to conform it to his Son, so that afterward he may give it a place with him in glory."[124] The cross, then, was not only a burden to be borne; it was salutary. It had a remedial purpose. It reminded the Christian that his whole life is a cycle of repentance— contrition and trust in Christ for forgiveness, from which flows a desire to sin no more.[125] The Christian should thus be thankful for the cross. It prepares him for glory—lasting glory. Flacius expounded, "God wants the Church to be conformed to the likeness of his Son and suffer with him, so that he may be praised and the heavenly Father honored both in the confession of his teaching and the expectation of his help, as many passages in the Holy Scriptures attest."[126] The choice was easy when faced with theological compromise or suffering: "We should be willing, glad, and prepared to take up the cross upon our shoulders so we may follow the Lord

---

120. Ibid., Civ v–Di r.

121. Flacius, *Ein vermanung zur bestendigkeit*, Di r.

122. Ibid., Hiv v.

123. Flacius, *Ein buch von waren und falschen Mitteldingen*, Ui r.

124. Flacius, *Vermanung Matth. Flacii Illyrici*, Bi 4.

125. Flacius, *Breves Svmmae Religionis Iesu Christi*, A3 v.

126. Flacius, *Ein vermanung zur bestendigkeit*, Eiv r.

and enter through the narrow door to eternal life."[127] This was the path of all true Christians, Flacius held, for "all those who are blessed by God in Christ Jesus must be formed as one through the cross and thus enter into eternal life, as all of Holy Scripture abundantly indicates."[128] Moreover, the cross was instructive: "This miserable deplorable time has indeed written a fitting and somewhat large commentary about the Bible. For the daily experience of the cross makes everything in the Bible clearer and more meaningful."[129] He summarized this teaching about the place and role of the cross:

> In sum, the Holy Spirit regards and speaks about the cross much differently than our old Adam. Christ says in Matthew 5, "Blessed are those (yes, not poor and miserable) when people insult, abuse, and speak all manner of evil against you for my sake," so long as they are not lying. Be happy and comforted (and not sorrowful and despairing), you will be rewarded well in heaven. St. Paul also esteems the cross highly when he writes to the Philippians, "You are not only called to believe in Christ, but also to suffer for his sake." St. Paul tells us that it is a great gift from God to suffer for the sake of Christ. And the damned world doesn't begrudge us such gifts, although the old Adam does not desire them at all. Yet we will see in the last day whether the old Adam has been wiser and more truthful or the Holy Spirit.[130]

Christ's stirring words to his disciples are echoed again and again throughout Flacius' writings as a stern reminder for those tempted to buckle under the cross: "Whoever confesses me before men I will confess before my Father," and likewise, "Whoever denies me before men I will deny before my heavenly Father."[131] Similarly, Flacius urged his readers to fear much more than men "the one who can cast body and soul into hellish fire however and whenever he wills."[132] The only escaping the cross at the present time was apostasy, and the reward of apostasy was, as it always had been, hell. There was thus no greater danger in Flacius' mind than that Christians "forsake the true gifts of God and his Word, deny him in that way, and lose all faith in our Savior when he says, 'What does it profit a man to gain the whole world and yet lose his own soul?'"[133] It was a simple equation for the

127. Flacius, *Ein Christliche vermanung*, Fiv v.

128. Henetus, "Ein kurzer Bericht vom Interim," 110.

129. Flacius, *Vermanung Matth. Flacii Illyrici*, Eii v.

130. Flacius, *Ein vermanung zur bestendigkeit*, Eiv v–Fi r.

131. Flacius, *Ein buch von waren und falschen Mitteldingen*, Tiv v; Matt 10:32–33.

132. Flacius, *Vermanung Matth. Flacii Illyrici*, Bi v; Matt 10:28.

133. Flacius, *Ein vermanung zur bestendigkeit*, Cii v.

frightened Christian: "For it is undoubtedly true that whoever wants to save his life will here lose it in this life also through the just judgment of God. Whoever loses something for the sake of God, however, will be rewarded a hundredfold in this life also by our Lord God."[134] Everything was filtered through the cross, then. All were lost without Christ's cross and believers were lost if they shirked their own, for they were laid upon them by a loving God to conform them to Christ's image. "If, however, our Lord God ordains that they should martyr and strangle us, then we would flee such misfortune in vain, and in so doing would deny him," Flacius argued.[135] What thankless children the Lutherans would be, Flacius was convinced, if after God in his mercy brought Luther's bright light of the pure gospel to shine among them, they should refuse to withstand or risk anything in exchange. Flacius reminded them that they of all men, for this very reason, had a responsibility to stand firm and fight for the truth. He maintained:

> It is truly a great and inexpressible kindness of God that the almighty God in these last times, in such darkness, has rekindled the light of his dear holy gospel and invited all men in such a friendly fashion into eternal life. It is therefore an entirely unspeakable sin, yes, plainly a sin against the Holy Spirit, that we are so lax that we let the Word of God, and likewise the eternal life that the Son of God, Jesus Christ, has won for us with his own precious blood, be taken away from us with our full knowledge and will.[136]

Flacius considered the present a time for martyrs, perhaps especially so. He wrote, "Up until now we have briefly said that one should persevere in the truth and the pure, godly doctrine and confess the same also with his mouth before men. Now, however, since the cross continually follows the confession, and the same is the reason that many go astray from Christ, we want to say a little about crosses."[137] The cross was thus tied to a right and pure confession of the truth, which the devil and the world could not countenance. "The cross is always and especially now near the confession of the Word of God," he observed.[138] Such was the nature of the Christian life, and so while the danger might have increased in Flacius' time, the nature of the struggle never changed. It was part and parcel of the Christian faith. Flacius held firmly that faith had consequences, often unpleasant, in this life: "The

134. Ibid., Eiii v.

135. Ibid., Hi v.

136. Flacius, *Ein Christliche vermanung*, Giv r–Giv v.

137. Flacius, *Ein vermanung zur bestendigkeit*, Div v.

138. Ibid., Giv r.

God-fearing will have peace, not in this life, but in the next life."[139] Flacius
lamented, however, how few were prepared to meet such a fate, should God
require it. He wrote, "Now, however, in this time of martyrdom one sees
almost no Christian anywhere who is willing to follow after Christ with the
cross."[140] Sadly, "Maybe only one or two or a very small group might yet
follow, but from afar."[141] There were martyrs on both sides, however. Even
those who sought to escape the cross faced a martyrdom of sorts. Flacius
wrote, "This is a confusion of the entire religion, a terrible martyrdom of
the conscience, dishonor of the name of Christ, and results in innumerable
souls entering into eternal damnation."[142] If one was going to die, Flacius
thought, it was better to die to this world than to God and one's own conscience. At least in Christian martyrdom, death for Christ, Christians had
a reliable and glorious pattern established for them: "We should in these
things consider and imitate the example of the holy prophets, our dear Lord
Jesus Christ, the apostles, and the holy martyrs, who in previous times even
gave up their lives for the Word of God."[143]

In Flacius' teaching, the church this side of Christ's return was and
remained *ecclesia militans*, the church militant. Like Christ, it would have
its holy week, or weeks. Like Jesus, Flacius sought to demonstrate that the
church of his day was undergoing a holy week at the hands of those who
claimed to be religious scholars and priests.[144] Flacius spelled this out clearly
for his readers: "Just as at the time of Christ no one opposed the true teaching more than the high priests and scribes, and after them the other Jews,
so in our time the Turks do not condemn and persecute the teaching of
God's Word like the pope and priests . . . and the accomplices of the pope
who still yet praise the name of Christ."[145] Jesus had promised his followers as much: "If they persecuted me, they will also persecute you."[146] And
so, Illyricus wrote, "It goes for the poor Christian in this martyr week as
it went for Christ before his death."[147] The fact that the true Church is a
church militant reassured the Christian in the present crisis that he was not
alone. What he was experiencing was not unique, and things had in fact

139. Ibid., Div v–Ei r.

140. Flacius, *Vermanung Matth. Flacii Illyrici*, Eiii r.

141. Ibid.

142. Flacius, *Ein buch von waren und falschen Mitteldingen*, Hiv r.

143. Flacius, *Ein vermanung zur bestendigkeit*, Di r.

144. Waremundus, "Eine gemeine Protestation," 143.

145. Henetus, "Ein kurzer Bericht vom Interim," 112.

146. John 15:20 ESV.

147. Flacius, *Ein vermanung zur bestendigkeit*, Hi r.

sometimes even been worse, and yet God had not forsaken his people: "The situation has at times been worse for the Church than it is now, and our dear Lord Jesus Christ has surely enlightened the Church with the brilliance of his grace and given it joy."[148] It was a privilege to suffer for the sake of the truth, endure the loving discipline of the heavenly Father, and become part of such a noble fellowship of prophets, apostles, and martyrs, as Christians sing in the *Te Deum*. These were those, after all, who had chosen to lose their head in order to gain their crown, who rightly esteemed what Christ had done and won for them, what he had bestowed upon them through pure love and grace alone. Flacius reminded Lutherans that they possessed no less the same sweet promises of Christ that inspired and motivated such steadfast obedience in earlier times of church history. The question, Flacius maintained, was whether they still believed those promises now that their faith was put to the test. He challenged, "If we Christians now still believe the words of Christ, then let us accordingly hold fast to the opinion that it is better that we endure war and every misfortune, yes, even be plunged into the Elbe by the Spanish."[149]

In *Vermanung Matth. Flacii Illyrici* Flacius devoted several pages to reasons why the Christian should bear up under the cross and stand firm for Christ even unto death.[150] He gave ten chief reasons. First, God had protected Martin Luther and other great teachers of the church most wonderfully even though all the world ranted against them. Second, the Holy Spirit promised that, while God's rod may fall upon his people, in the end it is his enemies who would pay the ultimate price. Third, while Daniel and Revelation prophesied that the Antichrist would lash out against the Church, Christ's coming would bring his warfare to a futile end. Fourth, God promised to hear prayer through his Son, Jesus. Fifth, the obstinacy of the enemies testified to their final doom that awaits them, for "pride goes before destruction."[151] Sixth, in all history, no one who had persecuted the gospel had escaped unscathed. The seventh and eighth dealt with recent prophecies and signs reported in Germany. Ninth, God had already preserved his faithful in the war up to this point, so that, although many foes had risen against them, Magdeburg had stood firm and tall, unvanquished. Tenth and finally, Luther's heirs had so far survived three years of persecution already, the *Augsburg Interim*, the Council of Trent, the adiaphora of the

---

148. Ibid., Hiv r.
149. Flacius, *Ein Christliche vermanung*, Hi v.
150. Flacius, *Vermanung Matth. Flacii Illyrici*, Ciii v–Dii v.
151. Prov 16:18 ESV.

the Adiaphorists, and all terrors, so that the enemies had been confounded and exposed through their own cruelty and plotting.

Flacius pointed out that Christians were not unique in that they suffer. Even unbelievers faced adversity and endured sorrow. Suffering eluded no one in life, no matter how hard someone might try to escape it. It was simply part of life in a fallen world. Flacius wrote, "Although the Christians are especially and more than others called to the cross in this life, yet the godless, that is, those who have not been called to the Word of God, suffer as well, and no less than the Christians."[152] Flacius then went on to provide a number of examples of contemporaries who were suffering with no connection to the Christian faith. He explained, "I do not say this to rejoice at their misfortune. Rather, I would like to make clear to us gentle, yielding people that others also who have not been persecuted for God's Word nevertheless suffer just as much as we do."[153] Suffering was a given, in other words. The Christian was simply fortunate enough to know that God used such suffering to provide, not merely hardship, but a cross, which served a remedial, salutary, instructive purpose. To forsake the cross was not to escape suffering. It would likely simply come in some other form. Rather, Flacius said, to forsake the cross was to lose the benefits of suffering, to suffer, in essence, to no end and for no good purpose. With this in mind, He counseled, "Since we accomplish nothing through our sad, doubting, godless concern, but rather only make the suffering worse, and add a new special suffering onto the suffering of the day, let us, therefore, be patient and humble ourselves under the powerful hand of God, who has laid this cross of persecution upon us."[154] Escaping God's rod was unwise, if not impossible, Flacius advised. There was nothing preventing God, should the Christian despise the rod, from bringing the hammer to "smash us entirely to pieces."[155]

Flacius was convinced that the cross was a simple fact of the Christian life, and a blessed one at that. God loved his children, and because he loved them, he sometimes allowed them to suffer, to bear the cross, in order to train them in righteousness, refocus them upon Christ, and prepare them for the glory of heaven. So also, some Christians were called to martyrdom, to confess their Lord and Savior Jesus Christ even unto death. This was a special privilege. This was something that all Christians could be called to face. And martyrdom too served a salutary purpose. It testified to the truth of God's Word, honored God, and gave witness to

---

152. Flacius, *Vermanung Matth. Flacii Illyrici*, Aiii v.

153. Ibid., Aiv r.

154. Ibid., Aiv v.

155. Flacius, *Ein vermanung zur bestendigkeit*, Hiv r.

others. Christ's words were clear. Christians were called to confession no matter the cost. Any attempt to flee the cross or avoid suffering for the sake of Christ was a denial of Christ, who had suffered for the Christian. In tribulation, Flacius was convinced, Christians confessed or apostatized, became martyrs or hypocrites. There was too much at stake to let fallen human wisdom and reason take the lead. God's Word alone had to be the guide, because the old Adam, the sinful nature, would never willingly suffer even a minor inconvenience for the faith, because it was opposed to faith and in enmity toward God. Trust in God and prayer were the Christian's weapons and refuge. This was Flacius' theology of the cross, which framed and guided his response to the Interim Crisis.

2.6. An Outsider on Outsiders

Flacius' use of outsiders in his arguments, especially in order to shame his opponents, also deserves attention. It is especially interesting because Flacius himself was an outsider, a non-German, as was not infrequently pointed out by his opponents. His German was clearly non-native, together with his mannerisms and palate. As mentioned earlier, one of the reasons the Illyrian was at first hesitant to move to Magdeburg after leaving Wittenberg was that he "would have to eat smoked bacon and meat, and also salted and dried fish."[156] His foreignness was conspicuous and exploited by his adversaries in the Adiaphoristic Controversy, and yet that did not stop the Illyrian himself, like his opponents, from employing the outsider status of others to his own advantage in the heat of theological contest. For instance, he was quite capable and adept at using the Spanish in order to trump up German disdain toward foreign influence in their lands. We will now examine some ways in which Flacius employed outsiders to bolster his case, beginning with Turks and Muslims, or Mohammedans, as he called them.

In a number of instances, Flacius argued that the Lutherans would be treated more fairly under the Turks than they were being treated under their fellow Christians. For instance, he noted that the gospel "is also taught in Turkey and Greece and the Turks consent to it being preached in their territory and yet our tyrants are so insane, ranting and raving, that they do not permit it or want it."[157] In another place, when urging his fellow believers to plead with their rulers for freedom to practice their religion, he advised, "Indicate to them also that even the Turks are content with tribute and allow Christians to preach Christ. How much more rightly, then, should those

156. Kaufmann, "Matthias Flacius Illyricus," 183.
157. Henetus, "Ein kurzer Bericht vom Interim," 112.

who want to be called Christians, and indeed praise themselves for being such, permit the same and imitate the Turks, open and avowed enemies of God?"[158] Similarly, he added that the rulers should be ashamed for it to become known that "they would persecute their own Christian brothers and the true gospel of Jesus Christ, the Son of God, and want to cause them more trouble than the Turks, the Tartars, and other Mohammedans."[159] Elsewhere, when reassuring the persecuted that their oppressors would not escape unpunished, he promised that this would especially be true for the current persecutors because, after the gospel had been enkindled again among them in these last days for more than thirty years, they had nonetheless attacked this good news of Jesus Christ "more than the Turks and heathen."[160] He scolded the magistrates and papists, on the one hand, for failing to fulfill their offices, and on the other hand, for overstepping them. He promised not to yield no matter how much they threatened, challenging, "Rage and bluster against us according to your pleasure and satiate yourself with the blood of the Christians, for which you have until now so fervidly thirsted and endeavored to pour out a hundred times more than the Turks!"[161] He cautioned, "Consider again, you blinded, hardened hearts—for even unbelievers' tiny infants will be cast into eternal death for their original sin when they die, unless planted through baptism into the Christian Church—how will it fare with you, all you open sinners, who outdo the bandits, all tyrants, and even the Turks in blasphemy and bloodthirsty gruesomeness?"[162] The rulers also made the gospel and Christ a laughingstock among outsiders like the Turks. Flacius argued that through the Lutherans' inappropriate accommodations to the emperor and the pope "Jews, Turks, papists, and all the godless laugh at and scorn us, our gospel, and Christ, and God's name is blasphemed on account of our shameful inconstancy."[163] In addition, the changes proposed by the emperor and the Adiaphorists presented no less danger than if the Turks were attempting to foist Mohammedan adiaphora upon them and merited equal opposition.[164]

In addition to his use of the Turks, Flacius also made use of the Koran. By comparing the *Augsburg Interim*, the *Leipzig Interim*, and papal teaching to the Koran, he derided it as new revelation, about which Jesus warned

---

158. Flacius, *Ein Christliche vermanung*, Fii r.

159. Ibid., Fiii r.

160. Flacius, *Vermanung Matth. Flacii Illyrici*, Civ v–Di r.

161. Waremundus, "Eine gemeine Protestation," 164.

162. Ibid., 165–66.

163. Flacius, *Ein Christliche vermanung*, Cii v.

164. Flacius, *Quod Hoc Tempore*, A6 r.

his Christians to be on guard. Complaining about the brazen willingness to compromise the truth among the religious and political rulers of his day, Flacius sneered, "Almost any knight can now write a new interim or Koran and set up his own golden calves for worship with the appearance that the honor of the gospel of Christ will be maintained in that way, just as Aaron said that in the morning they would hold a festival of the Lord, yes, and not of the calf."[165] Taking a jab at what had happened in Torgau, where Georg Mohr replaced Gabriel Zwilling as pastor after Zwilling preached against the new liturgical changes and prayed for the deposed Elector John Frederick, Flacius quipped, "For Mohr and other Adiaphorists, and the additional dunderheads of Meissen, when one presents them with the prospect of some great benefit or promises them some great good, will in the end accept the entire papacy, indeed the Koran itself."[166] Similarly, returning to the earlier epicurean theme, Flacius denounced the spirit of the times with these words: "We would rather sit quietly by, look on, and let someone each day prescribe and devise a new Interim and Koran for us. Oh, what real and true epicurean sows we are and not attentive listeners to the Lord!"[167] Here the allusions to the Koran obviously served to shame his opponents by comparing their twisting of the revealed truth to the revelations of Mohammed, seen by his contemporaries as the great enemy of the Christian faith, a malevolent and enterprising inventor of a new and diabolical faith.

Continuing the theme, Flacius also labeled his enemies Mamluks. Mamluk warriors were Christians, frequently prisoners of war or slaves, who converted to Islam and then were enlisted in military service by the Ottomans, thus gaining their conquerors' respect and a higher position within that society. They were renowned for their ability in battle, especially in the Crusades, as well as in more recent Turkish incursions, which were still fresh in the memory of Flacius and his contemporaries. Calling someone a Mamluk, therefore, was a timely way of besmirching him as a turncoat, especially in the minds of Christians once again threatened by Turkish military incursions. Not only had Mamluks converted to another faith, but they subsequently waged warfare against Christianity, and in Flacius' thinking, this was precisely what the Adiaphorists were doing. Urging his readers not to follow the example of the Wittenbergers, Flacius counseled, "Let the Mamluks go their way, fear men more than God, and pay more attention to transitory than eternal things. Let us all the more instruct and strengthen ourselves and others who are fleeing eternal damnation and want to inherit

---

165. Flacius, *Ein vermanung zur bestendigkeit*, Aiii v.

166. Flacius, *Ein Christliche vermanung*, Civ v–Di r.

167. Ibid., Fiv r–Fiv v.

the eternal life (Ephesians 6)."[168] Elsewhere he wrote, "Above all, however, we should (would we otherwise be Christians?) condemn godless wisdom, or rather the foolishness of our defecting Mamluks." He continued, urging true Lutherans to let the pretenders go their way and "ape the Antichrist and his band, first in religious things, and thereafter also in the persecution of Christians, in which they show themselves to be the Antichrist's obedient children to the full."[169]

Flacius saw Adiaphorists as persecutors, not in the sense that they themselves taken up arms, but because they empower others to do so. It was only because they had gone along with Moritz' desire for compromise in liturgical matters that it was possible for the traitorous elector to attempt to enforce those changes with force. If he and other rulers did not have the reputation and consent of the Wittenberg faculty and other similar esteemed theologians behind them, they might well never have dared to act in such a way. The Adiaphorists were, therefore, enablers. Flacius wrote:

> First, our persecutors, the Mamluks, cry out that they also have the true religion and we can certainly have peace and the true Christian religion at the same time, if we ourselves only wished to have it. This devil's lie is easy to lay aside . . . . Additionally, many of them have not only approved the Interim, but also our persecution. They are therefore for the sake of peace not only Mamluks but also persecutors of Christ.[170]

The only explanation Flacius could fathom was that they had lost their senses and their previous convictions for fear. They, and not he and the Magdeburgers, had changed their attitude and stance. Flacius noted, "I certainly do not doubt that, if they returned to their senses and thought back, should someone earlier have laid before them such adiaphora—even Luther himself—they would have screamed, 'O pope, this Mamluk will impose the entire papacy on us, wrapped up under some deceptive words.'"[171]

Muslims were not the only useful fodder for the Flacius' argumentation; he also utilized the Jews in order to shame the rulers and expose the feebleness of the Adiaphorists' Christianity. Just as he warned that Lutherans should not make the faith and Christ a laughingstock among the Turks, so also he warned that they should not make it the same among the papists and Jews. He advised, "We should persevere in matters of the faith, as in other things, so that when the Jews and papists must mock us, they are in

---

168. Flacius, *Ein vermanung zur bestendigkeit*, Civ v.
169. Flacius, *Vermanung Matth. Flacii Illyrici*, Bi v.
170. Ibid., Bii r–Biii r.
171. Flacius, *Ein buch von waren und falschen Mitteldingen*, Aii v.

truth rejecting, blaspheming, and casting aspersions upon our gospel and our Christ himself."[172] Nor should Christians in their sophistry and duplicity become like "Jews and Balaams," Flacius urged, "for we sadly see, may God lament it, that some Jews and Balaams, so wily and unashamed, receive everything laid before them by the godless Ahithophels and dare to drag it into the church."[173] In addition, Christians should avoid Jewish ceremonies, by which Flacius meant ceremonies established as a new law—the traditions of men Jesus warned about in the gospels. He wrote, "Many nowadays are becoming bored with the simplicity of the gospel, marvel over the pomp and ostentatious appearance of the Jewish, heathenish ceremonies of the pope, and praise the external discipline and order of our opponents just as foolishly as one would praise excrement."[174]

Flacius also argued that the Jews within the empire were treated better than the faithful Lutherans. He urged his fellow Lutherans, "Show [your magistrates] that it would indeed be very bad and unjust for those who want to be called Christians to be patient with the Jews—openly godless people and slanderers of God—and permit them to have sufficient treasure, while they at the same time do not permit us to retain the plain truth of Jesus Christ."[175] If those who rejected Christ were left in peace in the empire, so much more ought those who confessed and preached him rightly be protected and afforded the freedom to practice their religion in peace.

The Jews were not always objects of derogatory statements or negative examples, though. In several instances Flacius contended that Christians should learn from the Jews. While their religion was backwards and impious, at least they were committed to it, he reasoned. He wrote, "The Jews . . . busy themselves with this the most, that they may keep their religion whole and pure, even though it is false, godless, and entirely damning, and they are willing to suffer and trade all for it, even their greatest treasures, before they would let it be changed."[176] He placed the steadfastness of the Jews in their convictions is placed in sharp contrast to the yielding attitude and approach rampant among the evangelicals. He continued, "We, however, most unfortunately, want to hand over the holy, saving gospel and the known truth even though we are not in much danger at all."[177] Elsewhere he recounted a

---

172. Flacius, *Ein Christliche vermanung*, Cii v.

173. Ibid., Eii v.

174. Flacius, *Ein buch von waren und falschen Mitteldingen*, Hi r.

175. Flacius, *Ein Christliche vermanung*, Fii v.

176. Ibid., Hi v; Fiv r.

177. Ibid., Fiii r.

story to illustrate just how foolish the vacillating evangelicals compliant and elastic spirit appeared to outsiders. He recalled:

> A year ago, in the Christmas season, when an assembly [*Land-tag*] was held in the marketplace about the new Interim at Leipzig, certain Jews (as one says) asked certain Christian merchants why they held so many assemblies about their religion, whether they perhaps had doubts about it. They were Jews, a godless people according to the Christian opinion, yet they rather would have died a thousand deaths than have the religion that they followed changed. We thus carry ourselves so subtly with our adiaphora, new Interim, and so many days that Jews, Turks, papists, and all the godless laugh at and scorn us, our gospel, and Christ, and God's name is blasphemed on account of our shameful inconstancy.[178]

Once again, as with the Turks and the Mamluks, Flacius employed a group of perceived outsiders or foreigners in order to demonstrate the shamefulness of rulers' harsh treatment of the faithful and the shamelessness of the Adiaphorists' lack of resolve.

Finally, Flacius also exploited German patriotism and hostility toward foreign occupiers by connecting the Spanish with the *Augsburg Interim*. He did not hesitate to call the *Augsburg Interim* a "Spanish Interim," for instance. He wrote, "But the present peculiar and Spanish interims, which secretly are patched together by a few in a little hut, are full of dubious and long-winded speech" and "are forcefully foisted upon the church."[179] This was Spanish infringement upon the German Reformation's will and rights, and the Adiaphorists, because they were willing to collaborate with the Spanish, were *de facto* bad Germans. They were willing to serve an outside power for security and advancement. This was in Flacius' eyes a backhanded jab at the emperor as well, who preferred to reside in Spain instead of within Germany. Flacius asked:

> Our Adiaphorists, on account of a little danger, dare us to make room for "mere" adiaphora in such weighty matters, which they earlier objected to with great cries. What do you suppose they would do if the Spanish set hangmen, chains, and fire before them on one side and great prelates and gracious lords on the other, who promised them bishoprics, positions as provosts,

---

178. Ibid., Cii v.

179. Flacius, *Ein buch von waren und falschen Mitteldingen*, Miv r.

canonries, good benefices, etc., where they could craft yet more
adiaphora?[180]

No Spanish threats or fear of Spaniards should have moved the heirs of
Luther's German Reformation. They should have been willing to suffer
all before they would give into the Spanish brutality serving at the behest
of emperor and pope. As mentioned above, Flacius contended that the
evangelicals should have been willing to choose death, even drowning in
the Elbe by Spanish hands, over causing "so many Christians to stumble,
yes, even so many churches, change our religion and teaching into that of
the papacy."[181]

   In all of the examples provided above, we see that Flacius found it useful to make use of outsiders and foreigners in order to bolster his arguments.
He did so even though he himself was an outsider and a foreigner, who
openly admitted his lack of proficiency in German, and whose enemies had
used his foreign origins against him. In spite of all this, he chose to expose
the faults of his opponents through comparisons to foreigners and members of other religions, and with remarkable success. In addition, in order
to shame his opponents, he compared the treatment of Christians in foreign
lands of other faiths with the treatment those Lutherans who were unwilling to accept the *Augsburg Interim* or *Leipzig Interim* were receiving in the
supposedly Christian lands in which they lived. It would have been better,
he surmised, for the Lutherans to live under non-Christian rulers than their
current political and religious leaders who he was convinced were opposing
the gospel and Christian freedom. This served not only to undermine the
tact of the authorities he opposed but also provided an important rationale
for resistance to them.

2.7. The *Magdeburg Confession* and the *Formula of Concord*

Flacius did not write the *Magdeburg Confession*, which has been called the
"birth certificate of the Gnesio-Lutheran movement," but the author or
authors (most likely Nicholas Gallus and/or Nicholas Amsdorf, Luther's
longtime friend) certainly knew his work and shared his convictions in
this regard.[182] Flacius' influence has not been appreciated in the past, but
as the *Confession* receives more attention, it is important that it be noted.
Kaufmann very correctly states that Flacius was almost certainly involved

180. Flacius, *Ein Christliche vermanung*, Giv v.
181. Ibid., Hi v.
182. Kaufmann, *Das Ende der Reformation*, 176.

in its formation, whether indirectly or directly, and has called him the heart
and motor of Magdeburg, the Lord God's Chancery.[183] In support of this
judgment is the astounding fact that Flacius' writings accounted for roughly
forty percent of the publications in the city during the years of the Adiaphoristic Controversy.[184] Flacius did not sign the *Confession* because he was
not a pastor (Flacius probably never preached in German in his entire life).
Regardless, the *Confession* uses the same imagery as Flacius, the same Scriptures, largely the same argumentation, and labels its opponents similarly
(Adiaphorists, Interimists, Ahithophels, etc.). Readers find in the *Confession*, then, if not the direct product of Flacius' hand, an indirect reflection
and discernible echo of his thought and argumentation during the controversy thus far. It provided an orderly, clear, and forceful articulation of the
Flacian propaganda, theology, and apologetic for the cause of Magdeburg
both with respect to the objectional nature of the interims and the proper
relationship between church and state in such matters.

Before addressing the content of the *Magdeburg Confession*, it is imperative to understand the political background in the city, where there
had been enduring power struggles since the very first intrusions of the
Reformation. The *Confession*, it must be remembered, was as much a political document as a theological one. Written at the behest and with the
permission of the city council, its chief task was the legitimatization both of
the council's actions thus far and any future possible resistance. While clear
apocalyptic themes run throughout the writings of the Magdeburg theologians, as Thomas Kaufmann has duly noted, the city council clearly had
very temporal ambitions involved in the resistance they offered the emperor
and later Moritz. There had been a long struggle for increased spiritual and
temporal autonomy from the archbishop, evident in vocal bitterness toward
the Roman Catholic clergy still active there, especially the cathedral canons.
After the adoption of the Reformation in 1524, only the cathedral chapter
in the city, the collegiate church, a few other churches and monasteries had
remained Roman Catholic, with frequent confrontations, beginning with
the abolition of the Roman Catholic Mass, also in 1524. Both political and
religious tensions became evident, for instance, in the seizure by the city
of many of the choice properties of the cathedral chapter and the Roman
Church; the confiscation of the Augustinian monastery, which in time became a municipal library; the threatened arrest of the cathedral chapter's

183. Ibid., 177, 74.
184. Ibid., 73.

clergy, which led most of the canons to flee; and the occupation of the lands of the archbishopric, for which defensive excuses were offered.[185]

In the survey that follows, emphasis will be placed upon the Latin version of the *Confession* with noteworthy text in the German bracketed. The *Confession* begins with three Bible passages on its cover page, and they are significant: Psalm 119:46 (incorrectly cited as Psalm 18 in the Latin, but correctly in the German), which is Nathan's call for David to repent; Romans 13:3; and Acts 9:4,5.[186] The most significant is Romans 13:3 because the confessors do not follow Luther's translation, but employed their own with a crucial departure from Luther's. Luther translated Romans 13:3 as follows: "*Denn die Gewaltigen sind nicht den guten Werken, sondern den bösen zu fürchten. Willst du dich aber nicht fürchten vor der Obrigkeit, so tue Gutes, so wirst du Lob von derselbigen haben.*"[187] The German edition of the *Magdeburg Confession* translated it thus: "*Die Gewaltigen sind von Gott nicht den guten wercken, sondern den bösen zufürchten verordnet.*" The authors added three words, *verorden* and *von Gott*, which help explain their use of the passage to support their argument. They wrote, "First, they are the good, and second, by terrorizing them, the ruler has forsaken his God-given mandate to rule."[188] This was a fundamental point of their argument and foundational for the lesser-magistrate doctrine they would establish in the *Confession*, that when the superior magistrate had forsaken his proper mandate from God to rule, the lesser magistrate could and should intervene in just defense of his realm and subjects. The final passage, Acts 9:4,5, set forth Jesus' question to Paul before the saint's conversion, asking Saul why he was persecuting not merely the church, but Christ himself. The Magdeburg confessors, like Flacius, and also like Luther in his *Warning*, returned to this thought numerous times, that the emperor and the pope persecuted not only Christians, but indeed the Christ whom they claimed to follow. For instance, they later wrote that their enemies desire by their actions "with Satanic fury to persecute Christ in his members and pollute their hands

185. Kaufmann, *Das Ende der Reformation*, 26–38. See also Rein, *The Chancery of God*, 58–60, 130ff.

186. *Bekenntnis Unterricht und vermanung der Pfarrhern und Prediger der Christlichen Kirchen zu Magdeburgk*; *Confessio et Apologia Pastorum & reliquorum ministrorum Ecclesiae Magdeburgensis*. The *Confession*'s translation of Ps 119:46 reads: "I will speak about your testimonies before kings and not be put to shame." Rom 13:3 is rendered, "Rulers are not for terror for good conduct, but for bad." Acts 9:4,5 is translated, "Saul, Saul, why do you persecute me? It is hard to kick against the goads."

187. Luther Bibel, 1545.

188. Whitford, *Tyranny and Resistance*, 68.

with the blood of Christ and trample him underfoot."[189] They pled, "We appeal to you, Emperor Charles, most merciful lord, that you would in no way allow the papal cohort to exercise your majesty and power in order to drive away Christ and in the end crucify him again," and warned that Christ was not faring well under the emperor's rule, which, in the end, could not fare well for Charles.[190] For that reason, they urged him to change course, "so that he may repay your faithfulness in these gifts with his greater gifts in eternal life."[191] They added that even if the emperor did not regard them as fellow Christians, he nevertheless afforded Jews and Turks religious liberty within his realm. Why would he, then, not afford the Lutherans the same, whose confession shared so much in common with his own? Thus, they wrote, "You allow certain Jews and heathens to remain in their religion and do not compel them to accept yours with arms."[192]

The *Confession*, like Flacius' *Ein buch von waren und falschen Mitteldingen*, is divided into three main parts.[193] It progresses in similar fashion to Luther's *Warning*—"a survey of the present situation and the theological issues at stake, an apology for just resistance, and a warning."[194] In the opening of the work, the authors stated the crux of the crisis:

> When the higher magistrate persecutes his subjects' rights by force, whether natural or divine rights, or the true religion and worship of God, then the inferior magistrate ought to resist according to the command of God.
>
> The current persecution we now suffer from our superior authorities in particular pertains to the oppression of the truth of our religion, the true worship of God, etc. [and the reestablishment of the lies of the pope and his abominable idolatry].
>
> Therefore, our magistrate [and every Christian authority] ought to resist this oppression according to the command of God.[195]

The first section of the *Confession* was, for the most part, a restatement of the *Augsburg Confession*, intended to demonstrate that the Magdeburgers were not doctrinal innovators. This part of the work is not as important for the purposes of this study as the next two. The second part of the *Confession* is

189. *Confessio*, H4 r.

190. Ibid., E4 v.

191. Ibid.

192. *Confessio*, F1 r; *Bekenntnis*, Ji r.

193. Flacius, *Ein buch, von waren und falschen Mitteldingen*.

194. Whitford, *Tyranny and Resistance*, 78.

195. *Confessio*, A1 v; *Bekenntnis*, Ai v.

the most pertinent. It sets forth the rationale for resistance. This was also the section most crucial to the city council's quest for legitimization. While theological arguments and citations run throughout, it often reads like a juristic work. Robert von Friedeburg details the legal arguments set forth in the *Confession* and their significance for later thought, as well as the ways in which the *Confession* marked a break from or evolution of earlier Lutheran argumentation.[196] Among a number of other things, he notes three key developments in the *Magdeburg Confession* worth mentioning here. First, it established the right, and indeed the obligation, of the Magdeburg Council as a ruling authority to act in defense of its subjects, locating this authority in Romans 13. This was an important expansion of divine authority, as Lutherans had previously argued that the emperor, and sometimes the princes, were the authorities established by God with others in leadership positions, individually or as a body, holding their authority through them, but not from God himself. Second, the *Confession* recognized the defense of the fatherland and its freedom from tyranny as a responsibility of all citizens within their vocations. Third, it portrayed the struggle of the people of Israel as instructive for all the faithful in their struggle against the Antichrist.[197]

As to the basis of the conflict, the Magdeburg confessors left little doubt: it "pertains to [the gospel,] the glory of God and the eternal salvation of all men." They insisted that the city's citizens long to be faithful, obedient, peace-loving subjects.[198] They acted only for the defense of God's true Word and religion.[199] They might have been pathetic and despised by their superior foes—the remnant of Christ—but they had to act according to their conscience and within their rights, for their own good, and the good of the church everywhere, "especially foreign ones."[200] In short, the authors framed the city's resistance as a defense of religious liberty and true Christianity within a nominally Christian empire. The lesser magistrate doctrine was founded, therefore, not simply upon natural, German, and imperial law, but most especially upon the Christian obligations of those magistrates toward Christ and for the sake of their subjects, as seen in this blunt admonition to the Emperor Charles V himself:

> These dual obediences [to God and to the emperor] serve and
> animate each other [in a Christian manner] without harm or dis-
> turbance to conscience on either side when both are constituted

196. Schorn-Schütte, ed., *Das Interim*, 389–437.

197. Friedeburg, "Magdeburger Argumentationen zum Recht," 429.

198. *Confessio*, E3 v; *Bekenntnis*, Hiii r–Hiii v.

199. Ibid.

200. *Confessio*, A3.

between the limits prescribed by God and the laws of offices [so that each is given what belongs to it]. When, however, one is deficient, horrible sins and grievous tumult [and outrage] necessarily result, just as you now, Emperor Charles, have exceeded the limits of your rule [and office] and extended it into the realm [and office] of Christ. You are the cause of this turmoil [with us and some others before us], as Elijah told Ahab [and we must just as freely inform you], and not those who do not want to give you the honor that belongs to God nor are able to do so for fear of the wrath of God and eternal punishments.[201]

Magdeburg's resistance might be justified with arguments from natural and civil law, but its cause, they argued, was the emperor's intrusion into the realm and rule of God's law.

The third part was a warning to fellow evangelicals hesitant to rally to Magdeburg's cause or tempted to provide aid of any sort to the emperor and his allies. To do so, as Flacius repeated in his writings, would be nothing but abandonment of the faith and persecutions of Christ. An extended quotation from this portion of the *Confession* should suffice to demonstrate the general tone and argument:

And as their willful ignorance does not excuse them in the least, they thus are [and remain] persecutors of Christ, and [therefore those who know better and to a certain extent confess, even though they pretend that they do not do what they do gladly, but have to do it, all the same do it and become knowing persecutors of Christ]. For that reason, they are not excused any more because they have been compelled by others contrary to their will. Indeed, for that reason they are more worthily counted persecutors of the gospel than the ignorant [and will receive greater recompense]. You may now certainly produce many who have up until now professed with us the gospel of Christ [and God's Word], who, if anyone today were to threaten them with punishments or death, with the loss of honors or riches, would, if they were able to bring Christ bodily back [from heaven] indeed would be prepared to destroy him again, some for the sake of the pleasures of this life, [favor], advantages, and honors, others having been overtaken by the circumstances, [out of fear for loss of their life and goods]; if only they should see his lowly state and him forsaken by God in his weakness, they would altogether [willingly and knowingly] crucify Christ again in his own person according to the will of the tyrant. How is that now any

201. *Confessio*, F1 v–F2 r; *Bekenntnis*, Jii v–Jiii r.

different from what is now happening among us? Christ himself testifies concerning this, "Whatever you have done to one of the least of these you have done to me" (Matthew 25). And to Saul he says, "Saul, Saul, why do you persecute me" (Acts 9).[202]

Nothing less than Jesus' gospel and eternal salvation hung in the balance. The authors of the *Confession* intended to set forth everything in such a way as to leave all without excuse. There was no wiggle room, in other words, especially not such an expanse of it as the Interimists claimed. This was a time of confession, and in a time of confession nothing at all was adiaphora, let alone everything in every way.

The siege ultimately ended with a treaty. Moritz continued his seemingly duplicitous ways and, when it became clear that a stalemate was inevitable, switched sides "to solidify his rule."[203] Both the city and Moritz declared victory. The Peace of Augsburg was established four years later, in 1555, which "recognized the central claim of the Magdeburg pastors and the *Torgau Articles*—religious diversity does not equal imperial disloyalty."[204] Whether or not Moritz or Magdeburg were the real victor, Magdeburg ultimately solidified its iconic place in the story of the defense of Lutheranism and the preservation of Luther's doctrine.

The Flacian principle, *nihil est adiaphoron in statu confessionis et scandali*, that is, nothing is an adiaphoron in a state of confession and offense, was the position adopted by the *Formula of Concord* in 1577. The *Formula*, signed by roughly two-thirds of the Lutheran pastors in Germany, concluded that it had been wrong to compromise in a time of confession. Without saying as much, the Formula *de facto* conceded that the Magdeburgers had been right in their actions and convictions. It resolved, "We reject and condemn as false the opinion of those who hold that in a time of persecution people may comply and compromise with the enemies of the holy gospel in indifferent things, since this imperils the truth."[205] Moreover, "Likewise, we regard it as a sin worthy of punishment when, in a time of persecution, actions contrary and opposed to the confession of the Christian faith are undertaken because of the enemies of the gospel, either in indifferent things or in public teaching or in anything else which pertains to religion."[206] The general arguments of Flacius' *Book on True and False Adiaphora* here were approvingly restated. Flacius and the Magdeburgers were vindicated regard-

202. *Confessio*, H3v; *Bekenntnis*, Nii v–Niii r.

203. Whitford, *Tyranny and Resistance*, 89.

204. Ibid., 90.

205. KW, *Solid Declaration* X.28, 640.

206. Ibid.

ing adiaphora and confession. Their approach was accepted by the *Formula* as the Lutheran approach, the one consistent with the teaching of Martin Luther. In addition, one of the chief authors of the *Formula of Concord*, Martin Chemnitz, outlined an approach to ceremonies in his *Examination of the Council of Trent* that was not unlike Flacius' own. [207]

In approaching the *Formula*'s answer to the challenges and questions raised by this tumultuous time in Lutheran history, it would perhaps be best to first look at the Scripture on which Article X stands. This will afford a helpful comparison with the arguments of Flacius and the Scriptures he employed in the controversy that preceded and necessitated this article of the *Formula of Concord*. Following are some of the passages quoted by the *Formula* with brief comments when beneficial.

The *Formula* operated on the theological assumption that the Roman Catholic Church had not changed its stripes from the days preceding Luther's death. It was still a church wrapped in a semi-Pelagian system prone to the inducement of either self-righteousness or despair in those subject to it. The *Formula* asserted that Jesus' words regarding the religious leaders of the Jews were equally true of the pope's followers: "They worship me in vain; their teachings are but rules taught by men."[208] In permitting Rome to invade Wittenberg under the guise of indifferent rites and rubrics, therefore, the Adiaphorists betrayed the cause of the very man buried beneath the pulpit from which some of them preached on the Lord's Day.[209] The lay person's eyes, which Luther had labored so tirelessly by the grace of God to pry from an unbroken fixation upon works, relics, novenas, processions, and penances, were now, whether by the intention of the Adiaphorists or not, once again directed to the ceremonies and superstitions that had once before filled and transfixed them. For that reason, Christ's warning once again needed to be sounded during the controversy, which was what Flacius did. Ceremonies, even when instituted for good order and with fine intentions, were nevertheless, "in and of themselves no divine worship, nor even a part of it."[210]

Like Flacius, the *Formula* drew upon St. Paul's first letter to the Corinthians and his letters to the Romans and Galatians. The focus upon 1 Corinthians was understandable and unoriginal. As noted earlier, was any congregation in the New Testament any more embroiled in an adiaphoristic

---

207. Chemnitz, *Examination of the Counil of Trent*, 2:109.

208. Matt 15:19 ESV; KW, *Epitome* X.3, 515.

209. Krauss, *Lebensbilder aus der Geschichte der christlichen Kirche fuer Lutherische Leser Nordamerikas ausgewaehlt und bearbeitet*, 479.

210. KW, *Epitome* X.3, 515.

controversy of its own than the one at Corinth? Paul therefore provided a felicitous principle for the congregation there which is echoed and stated more succinctly in Romans 14:13: "Therefore let us not pass judgment on one another any longer, but rather decide never to put a stumbling block or hindrance in the way of a brother."[211] The Epitome, the shorter summary of the arguments of the *Formula of Concord* (the Solid Declaration, included along with it, comprised the longer statement), grounded part of its response to the Adiaphoristic Controversy directly in Paul's call for care in regard to the weak in faith: "Of course, all frivolity and offense must be avoided, and special consideration must be given particularly to those who are weak in faith."[212] Galatians 5:1 also clearly applied. There Paul wrote, "For freedom Christ has set us free; stand firm therefore, and do not submit again to a yoke of slavery."[213] Precisely when rites and practices, excepting of course the Sacraments, which are by nature mandates, were commanded as though they were necessary to please our God or merit salvation, those rites and practices, according to the *Formula*, became an affront to the gospel, robbing the Christian of the freedom that Christ has won for him at such an inestimable price.[214] Continuing with Galatians, like Flacius, the *Formula* cited Paul's rebuke of Peter.[215] Echoing Flacius' insistence that the Christian could not reconcile Christ with Belial, the *Formula* alluded to St. Paul's words in 2 Corinthians 6:14, "Do not be unequally yoked with unbelievers. For what partnership has righteousness with lawlessness? Or what fellowship has light with darkness?"[216] Indeed, where there was no commonality in teaching (*lex credendi*), there should be no impression of commonality in teaching presented through the worship practice of a congregation or church body (*lex orandi*). The *Formula* taught that church rites had to be rejected under the following circumstances:

> We should not regard as free and indifferent, but rather as things
> forbidden by God that are to be avoided, the kind of things pre-
> sented under the name and appearance of external, indifferent
> things that are nevertheless fundamentally opposed to God's
> Word (even if they are painted another color). Moreover, we
> must not include among the truly free adiaphora or indifferent

211. Rom 14:13 ESV.

212. KW, *Epitome* X.5, 515.

213. Gal 5:1 ESV.

214. KW, *Solid Declaration* X.10–12, 637.

215. KW, *Solid Declaration* X.13–14, 637–638.

216. 2 Cor 6:14 ESV; KW, *Solid Declaration* X.6, 636; KW, *Solid Declaration* X.23, 639.

matters ceremonies that give the appearance or (in order to avoid persecution) are designed to give the impression that our religion does not differ greatly from the papist religion or that their religion were not completely contrary to ours. Nor are such ceremonies matters of indifference when they are intended to create the illusion (or are demanded or accepted with that intention), as if such action brought the two contradictory religions into agreement and made them one body or as if a return to the papacy and a deviation from the pure teaching of the gospel and from the true religion had taken place or could gradually result from these actions.[217]

Why?

Thus, submission and compromise in external things where Christian agreement in doctrine has not already been achieved strengthens idolaters in their idolatry. On the other hand, this grieves and offends faithful believers and weakens their faith. Christians are bound to avoid both for the welfare and salvation of their souls, as it is written, "Woe to the world because of stumbling blocks" [Matt. 18:7], and, "If any of you put a stumbling block before one of these little ones who believe in me, it would be better for you if a great millstone were fastened around your neck and you were drowned in the depth of the sea" [Matt. 18:6].[218]

If this were not a clear enough echo of Flacius' own arguments and use of Scripture, the *Formula* then quoted one of the passages Flacius utilized most frequently in his propaganda against the *Leipzig Interim*: "Special attention should be given to Christ's words, 'Everyone therefore who confesses me before others, I also will confess before my Father in heaven . . . ' (Matt. 10:[32])."[219] David Scaer aptly summarizes Article X's answer to the challenges and questions raised at this tumultuous time in Lutheran history as follows:

The answer given by Article X was the one adopted by Flacius, who refused to tolerate the reintroduction of Roman Catholic customs. Christians have freedom to practice or to avoid customs and rituals which are neither forbidden nor commanded in God's Word, but they are duty bound to resist where compliance in customs would give the impression that they were

217. KW, *Solid Declaration* X.5, 636.
218. KW, *Solid Declaration* X.16, 638.
219. KW, *Solid Declaration* X.17, 638.

complying with false doctrine. Should a human ordinance be given the stature of a divine command or be viewed as necessary for salvation, it must be resisted.[220]

The *Formula of Concord* did not merely side with Flacius' teaching regarding adiaphora. By adopting Flacius' approach, the *Formula* in essence declared it Lutheran, the position consistent with Luther's teaching. The authors of the *Formula* consciously grounded its conclusions in earlier confessional documents, such as the *Treatise on the Power and Primacy of the Pope* and the *Smalcald Articles*.[221] They also cited several of Luther's letters. The fact that Flacius had first published these letters during the Adiaphoristic Controversy only reinforces this impression that the *Formula* accepted Flacius' stance as Luther's own.[222] It is not surprising, then, that the *Formula's* doctrine of adiaphora largely read like Luther's own regarding the place and criteria for the acceptance and rejection of ceremonies—it was Luther's teaching, after all, that Flacius endeavored to preserve and uphold throughout his theological contest with the Adiaphorists. Luther's words, echoed by Flacius, found further reiteration in the *Formula*, and through them Flacius' own assertions with respect to the controversy, which he had fortified and undergirded with such statements of the reformer:

> Other matters will adjust themselves as the need arises. And this is the sum of the matter: Let everything be done so that the Word may have free course instead of the prattling and rattling that has been the rule up to now. We can spare everything except the Word. Again, we profit by nothing as much as by the Word. For the whole Scripture shows that the Word should have free course among Christians. And in Luke 10[:42], Christ himself says, "One thing is needful," i.e., that Mary sit at the feet of Christ and hear his word daily. This is the best part to choose and it shall not be taken away forever. It is an eternal Word. Everything else must pass away, no matter how much care and trouble it may give Martha. God help us achieve this. Amen.[223]

220. Scaer, *Getting into the Story of Concord*, 91.

221. Marquart, "Article X. Confession and Ceremonies," 265.

222. KW, *Solid Declaration* X.24, 640. See ibid., n316.

223. LW 53:14.

Chapter 3

Concluding Thoughts on Part One

MATTHIAS FLACIUS ILLYRICUS WAS one of the most vocal and important figures of post-Luther Lutheranism. His refusal to accept the interims and his campaign against them became definitive for Lutheran identity for generations and even centuries to come. His stance was vindicated in the *Formula of Concord* and its tenth article. No one published more than Flacius during the tumultuous years of the Adiaphoristic Controversy. These writings, prolific and powerful, were produced during one of German Lutheranism's earliest most significant internal crises and thus deserve much more attention than they have thus far received in historical scholarship, together with the broader life and thought of the man who wrote them. Dozens upon dozens of Flacius' writings await analysis as well as those of his colleagues in the fight against the imperially imposed "adiaphora." Furthermore, the social and cultural aspects of the crisis deserve further study.

This study has focused particularly the intellectual aspects of the debate—how one of the main protagonists and propagandists framed the struggle, argued his case, and identified his cause with Luther, the earlier Melancthon, and confessors of the past. In addition, the first part of this work explored what was adiaphora in Flacius' view, when it became such, and what the response should be when adiaphora ceased to be indifferent, or when purportedly indifferent matters had never been indifferent at all. In order to do this, at the outset Luther's theology of the two kingdoms has been examined, as well his teaching regarding resistance to secular authorities in religious matters, which so influenced Flacius' thought. Moreover, special consideration has been paid to the religious and political background which made this controversy possible. Attention has also been paid to Flacius' formative years in what is now Croatia, in Venice, and in Germany, where he was a student of Luther and Melanchthon. This background enables the reader to better understand the Adiaphoristic Controversy as well as those who contended on both sides during it, how Flacius' identity and worldview was shaped, and what that identity and worldview entailed. Attention was then paid to Flacius' doctrine and proposed practice with respect to adiaphora, especially in a state of confession, as expressed in key publications during the crisis.

Flacius saw himself as a Lutheran through and through. His uncle, Baldo Lupetino, was martyred as a Lutheran by the Venetian Inquisition. He himself left behind family, friends, and his future in the south to venture north to Wittenberg and study the theology of the German Reformation. Sacrifice for the faith of the Scriptures marked his life and defined his understanding of the Christian Church. While in Wittenberg, in the throes of depression and spiritual angst, Luther himself counseled the young Illyrian and shared with him his own experiences with *Anfechtung*. Luther thus became more than an instructor; Luther became a spiritual father. Flacius' Christianity was, therefore, Lutheran not only in theological confession but also in existential orientation. Even more, he saw the theological and liturgical battles in which he competed through the lens of the religious controversies of Luther's life. It was the same devil attacking the same Scriptures, the same Antichrist undermining the saving work of the same Christ, who, as Luther insisted, alone mediates between God and man, not through manmade ceremonies or rites, but through the Word and the sacraments alone. What was at stake, in Flacius' view, was nothing less than the entirety of the Reformation, because for Flacius, as for Luther, doctrine consisted not of disparate parts, but formed a *corpus doctrinae*, "a whole that functions as God's instrument of accomplishing his will."[1] The wavering of the Adiaphorists endangered nothing less than the central doctrine of Christianity, its very heart through which life came to the whole body, justification by grace through faith alone—pope, priest, superstition and human tradition parading as true worship of God necessarily therefore excluded.

The works researched for study were chosen because they present, not only contrasts, but positive statements of Flacius' convictions. They stated why resistance was necessary and what was at stake. They argued why Christians had to support faithful pastors and reject those who compromised. They drew confessional lines and delineated between true adiaphora and false. They established the ultimate authority in the church: the Bible and Luther's teaching, especially as encapsulated in the *Augsburg Confession* and, because of its applicability to the current crisis, his *Warning to His Dear German People*. These pamphlets also warned against a respect for persons that would detract from this authority and denounced the overstepping of

1. Kolb, *Bound Choice*, 18.

authority exercised by secular rulers, bishops, and the papacy. These writings defined what Flacius held Lutheranism to be, how it should act, and what it should look like after the death of the great reformer.

Flacius' teaching concerning adiaphora was grounded in the epistles of St. Paul, especially Romans, 1 Corinthians, and Galatians, but he preferred examples from the Old Testament to illustrate his points. He did make use of accounts from the New Testament, but they were frequently tied to applications already set forth by the biblical authors themselves and therefore less creative in nature. The Old Testament also provided more fitting and numerous examples of resistance toward those holding political powers, particularly when they infringed upon religious devotion and faithfulness. For this reason, Flacius also made use of the Apocrypha, whose accounts of the times of the Maccabees, for instance, proved remarkably valuable. An exception might seem to be his regular employment of scenes from St. John's Apocalypse, the Book of Revelation, but this is not so. In Revelation, Flacius found imagery and prophecy, not historical precedent. For precedent he turned primarily to the Old Testament, the Apocrypha, and also to ecclesiastical history. Throughout Flacius demonstrated his deep familiarity with the Scriptures and the impressive facility in the Old Testament he possessed as a Hebrew professor. He also made plain his knowledge of church history, which would be displayed in grander detail in his organization of the *Magdeburg Centuries* and his *Catalogue of Witnesses of the Truth*, a collection of historical testimonies against the Roman papacy and its theological and ecclesiastical claims.

Flacius saw not merely his church, but the Church, Christ's Church, under siege, as often before, but perhaps as never before. Church leaders and magistrates were conspiring together to undo what God himself had graciously wrought in recent decades. The light of the Word, no longer obscured under the bushel of papal pestilence, shone brighter than it had since apostolic times. The Babylonian captivity was ended, but now threatened to return and bring Luther's work to naught. The danger was serious and had to be confronted. The Church had been given only two tools through which God promised to deliver to his people the benefits of Christ's cross. There were only two means through which God promised his Spirit would create and preserve faith, the beggarly hand which received the salvation Christ won for them. The Church had the Word and the sacraments, preaching and the administration of the visible, efficacious signs and seals of God's promises. The liturgical changes the magistrates were seeking to enforce threatened both. They censored preaching and shrouded the sacraments in superstition and false teaching. The Church was thus handcuffed and the Spirit's means of grace impeded.

In order to help the reader understand Flacius' arguments and appeals to Scripture, key themes and imagery in his writings have been identified and explored, especially those from the Bible. His apocalypticism is evident throughout. He feared that the Adiaphoristic Controversy could spell the end of the Reformation, and even more, of the world. Christ's return appeared imminent, the prophecies of Revelation fulfilled in the papal Antichrist's war against Christianity, recently revitalized and renewed through the preaching and teaching of Martin Luther, the third Elijah. No enemy harbored greater enmity and contempt toward God than the Antichrist of Rome, not even the Egyptians and the heathen.[2] He was the man of lawlessness from 2 Thessalonians. In fact, Flacius ended his *Breves Svmmae Religionis Iesus Christi, & Antichristi* with 2 Thessalonians 2, together with Daniel 11.[3] This was not a new battle in church history but a culmination of the ancient and original battle between God and Lucifer, Christ and the serpent.

According to Flacius, the Church was battered and bruised. Confessionally Lutheran churches and individuals were dwindling in numbers. Like Christ in Holy Week, Lutheranism was having its martyr week, its time of suffering and trial. But this was to be expected; the Holy Christian Church had been a remnant throughout most of its history, if not all. It was small, unlearned, and foolish in the eyes of the world, whose epicurean and temporally obsessed mindset could conceive of it in no other way. Moreover, as often had been the case in its history, a serious threat came, not only from outside the ranks of professing Christians, but within. As Judas had betrayed Christ and his little flock of twelve, so also now the Adiaphorists were betraying their brothers and sisters in the Lutheran Church and Jesus himself in the person of his Christians.

Flacius reminded his coreligionists that suffering in the Christian life was not a sign of God's displeasure, but of his love. God had often tested his Church. God had often let it bear crosses, and these crosses were never in vain. They were salutary and instructive. Bitter trial and strife here would only make the glory and peace of heaven sweeter and all the more appreciated. In fact, crosses, Christ's and the Christian's own, were such a predominant part of the Christian life and Christian teaching that they were definitive of true Christianity. A lack of crosses often indicated a lack of faithfulness to the truth. Right confession had historically garnered stiff opposition, and so it must be in Flacius' day. It was a fear of such crosses that had driven his former colleagues in Wittenberg into consortium with

2. Flacius, *Breves Svmmae Religionis Iesu Christi*, A6 r.
3. Ibid., A6 v–A8 r.

the Antichrist. It was the prospect of such crosses that led some princes to waver in their opposition. This was in stark contrast to the courageous stand taken by Magdeburg, Flacius' adopted home during the Adiaphoristic Controversy. Magdeburg benefitted greatly from welcoming the Illyrian publicist, too. His swift and steady stream of publications offered continuous and articulate defense of the confessional and political stance taken by the city's pastors and council.

Finally, even as an outsider himself, Flacius was able to exploit outsiders in order to stiffen the spine and stoke German and Lutheran pride among his audience. He charged that the Christian rulers of the empire and various German lands were more cruel toward orthodox Lutherans than the Turks were toward Christians in their lands. He contended that the Adiaphorists had written a new Koran with the *Leipzig Interim*, while the papacy had for centuries been writing new Korans. Lutherans who compromised with Moritz, Charles V, and the Roman pontiff were depicted as Mamluks. As the Mamluks had forsaken Christianity and adopted Islam for political and economic gain, so the Adiaphorists had done the same. And as the Mamluks had persecuted Christianity by warring against it with Muslim armies, so also the Adiaphorists and those who failed to oppose them not only apostatized but actively strove against the Christianity of the Bible and Luther, its faithful expositor. The *Augsburg Interim* may have been foisted upon them by a German emperor and the *Leipzig Interim* by a Lutheran prince, but Flacius connected their enforcement to Spanish power. Spanish troops were foreign occupiers undermining the integrity of German sovereignty, papal foot soldiers conjuring in Protestant minds thoughts of the cruelty of the Spanish Inquisition. And there would be no end to the papists' and magistrates' confusing of the two kingdoms and their power grabs unless faithful Christians—German Christians—collectively put their foot down and stood firm. Flacius insisted that only a fool could not see that. The trend was clear: "First they claimed that they only wanted to punish a few disobedient princes and in no way sought to contest with our freedom and fatherland . . . but now, after they have with a great cry and sense of urgency extended their reach to the end of German land, one must reconsider what they have attempted here.[4]

In the end, Flacius' pamphlets were in his consideration nothing more than a call to faithfulness to the truth as he knew and understood it through Luther's instruction and writings. He processed the crisis through the lens of his own self-identity and worldview, shaped by past experience with persecution, theological consolation in the midst of uncertainty, and instruction

---

4. Henetus, "Ein kurzer Bericht vom Interim," 99.

at the feet of the two great Wittenberg pillars of the Reformation, Martin Luther and Philip Melanchthon. It was a sad and unplanned twist that led Illyricus into conflict with the latter, which no doubt shook him to his core, challenging friendships, past experience, and the trajectory of his academic career. It is hard to conceive how Flacius possibly gained more than he lost through his bold stance against the *Leipzig Interim*. He gained fame, but not without even greater notoriety. He later landed a position at the University of Jena, but this was a step down from the more illustrious University of Wittenberg, where he taught before his flight to Magdeburg, and no such professorial prospect seemed likely, let alone imminent, when he took his bold stand in the heat of the Adiaphoristic Controversy. He published widely, but with little or no personal profit. He lost friends, made enemies who would yearn and work for his downfall long after the Adiaphoristic Controversy, was isolated from family, and began a lifetime of wandering. He had argued that Israel's exodus was the pattern of the Church's history and present, and it certainly became the pattern of his own life. As his writings warned, though, the faithful Christian could hardly protest such a lot. Christ had warned his little flock of a life of crosses and persecution. In each age the Christ's Church would have its foes, its Christ and Belial, and the church militant would never be without struggle, even in times of temporal peace, or the "peace of the belly," as Flacius was wont to call it. The task of this life for the believer was not the attainment of comfort and ease but the preservation of God's Word and Luther's teaching. Nothing testified and abounded more to God's glory, after all, than unwavering steadfastness and commitment to the unadulterated confession of Christ's work and person, through which alone the Christian finds justification and an eternal life more precious than anything this world and its powers could offer or provide. Sadly, Flacius died an isolated, wandering man in Frankfurt am Main in 1575. Even more sadly, as a result of his confession and his controversial nature, he was denied a Christian burial.[5] The cross, suffering for the sake of his confession, marked, if not his burial plot, certainly his death, as he likely long expected it would.

5. Olson, "Matthias Flacius (1520–1575)," 88.

Part Two

John Hooper and the Vestment Controversy

Chapter 4

The Path to the Vestment Controversy

4.1. Wittenberg and Henry VIII: Doors Open

LUTHERANISM HAD SOME OPPORTUNITIES in England. Its top-down, prince-driven pattern of development in Germany would seemingly have served well what was taking place in England. There were a number of sympathizers with Luther's doctrine. Some prominent Englishmen even studied at Wittenberg. German merchants smuggled Luther's writings into England. Some of what the German theologian taught had long been held there by the Lollards. Luther's Ninety-Five Theses and his refusal to recant at the Diet of Worms sent waves throughout Christendom, and England could hardly ignore them as they reached its shore. In order to understand the shift that took place with Cromwell's death and then later with Edward VI's rise to power, it is important to appreciate the extent to which Lutheranism had the opportunity to shape English Protestantism, to which it did so in any meaningful way, and the movement made away from Wittenberg and to Zurich that took place in the 1540s. It was this shift that made both Hooper's appointment to a bishopric and the Vestment Controversy that resulted possible and shaped its course.

England's Catholicism before the Henrician Reformation was vibrant in comparison with the continent. There was a degree of corruption and moral laxity among the clergy, as elsewhere in Europe, but not a commensurate amount.[1] A number of Englishmen had expressed irritation at papal intrusions upon national sovereignty and the disproportionate role certain

---

1. Tjernagel, *Henry VIII and the Lutherans: A Study in Anglo-Lutheran Relations from 1521–1547*, 34. See also Duffy, *The Stripping of the Altars: Traditional Religion in England c. 1400–c.1580*.

prelates, like Cardinal Wolsey, played in national politics, often at the expense of pastoral ministry. Nevertheless, many such prelates did indeed serve with genuine and evident interest in the well-being of their fellow citizens. There is little doubt that a significant portion of the English population would have welcomed reforms, but few could have imagined the English Reformation. The Henrician Reformation would be both unexpected and unique, the result of a peculiar state of affairs and distinct influences, quite "its own thing," as Alec Ryrie has called it.[2] In the end, the Henrician Reformation seized upon, more than it was seized by, continental evangelical thought, and the continental reformations often served more to provide theological justification for politically motivated actions than to incite and guide religious and ecclesiastical measures taken for their own sake.[3] James Pragman expresses it well when he concludes, "The English Reformation never was a transplanted growth from the European continent."[4] This half will explore why this was so, especially in connection with continental Lutheranism. There were three main issues that presented intriguing prospects for Lutheranism in England: questions of authority, Henry's famous marriage question, and a concern for alliances. When Wittenberg's support ceased to be necessary or useful in these three areas, Lutheranism lost its prospective role as a viable guide or mold for the English Reformation. Erwin Doernberg has argued that "Henry VIII remained favourably disposed to causes or persons only as long as they could be expected to be useful for his own schemes."[5] This study is not concerned with the veracity of that statement in every aspect, but it will demonstrate the truth of that statement with respect to Henry's relationship with Lutherans and Lutheranism.

The initial exchange between Henry VIII and Martin Luther played no small role in shaping future dialogue. This interaction began with Henry VIII's *Assertio Septem Sacramentorum*, or, *Defence of the Seven Sacraments*. Debates about Henry's authorship of this book—whether he wrote any or all of it—will not be resolved any time soon. Diarmaid MacCulloch matter-of-factly asserts that "previous teams had ghost-written his *Assertion* against Luther."[6] Richard Rex concludes that Henry most likely did not write the *Assertio* on his own, but that he surely played a vital role in

2. Ryrie, "The Strange Death of Lutheran England," 66.

3. Bernard, *The King's Reformation: Henry VIII and the Remaking of the English Church*, 277.

4. Pragman, "The Augsburg Confession in the English Reformation: Richard Taverner's Contribution," 85.

5. Doernberg, *Henry VIII and Luther: An Account of their Personal Relations*, 3.

6. MacCulloch, *The Reformation*, 199.

its production, most likely having begun it on his own.[7] Sir Thomas More certainly played some role, even if he was "only a sorter out and placer of the principal matters," as he later claimed.[8] Yet the authorship of the *Assertio* matters little for the present study, because the fact remains that it was published in the king's name. It was Henry VIII's official response to Luther's teachings, especially those expressed in the reformer's famous treatise, *On the Babylonian Captivity of the Christian Church*, which assailed Rome's sacramental system. As will be seen later, one of Henry's consistent concerns throughout his reign was the maintenance of proper authority in general and his own personal authority specifically. One of the things that the king found especially bothersome in Luther's writings, therefore, was the doctrine of the priesthood of all believers and what he considered its implications.[9] In this way, Henry endeavored to defend the very papal ecclesiastical and political claims and structure that he would subsequently undermine, shirk, and overthrow in his land.

Henry was not driven to write his *Defence of the Seven Sacraments* only by a Christian zeal for the truth. He also wanted to increase his prestige on the continent. Henry had eyed a papal title for some time, especially *Defensor Ecclesiae* or *Defensor Fidei*.[10] Such a title, as Peter Gwyn notes, would enable Henry "to keep company on equal terms with the Most Christian king of France and the Catholic king of Spain."[11] Luther's new heresy provided a fortuitous opportunity to obtain such a title. Wolsey and the king made sure that the book was not published for general consumption until the papal bull bestowing Henry's new title, *Defensor Fidei*, could be included with it.[12]

Few in Henry's court probably doubted that the precocious Wittenberg theologian would reply in some manner to Henry's literary assault on his doctrine. What few likely could have expected, however, was the tone and the forcefulness of the reformer's reply. For his own part, Henry had not been a model of courtesy in what and how he had written at various places in his *Assertio* (Luther was said to spew the poison of vipers in anger and hatred at the instigation of Satan), but he was far from Luther's equal in the employment of vituperation.[13] Even though his own friends confronted him

7. Rex, "The English Campaign against Luther in the 1520s," 88.

8. Gwyn, *The King's Cardinal: The Rise and Fall of Thomas Wolsey*, 484.

9. Tjernagel, *Henry VIII and the Lutherans*, 23.

10 Doernberg, *Henry VIII and Luther*, 5.

11. Gwyn, *The King's Cardinal*, 484.

12. Tjernagel, *Henry VIII and the Lutherans*, 10; Henry VIII, *Defence of the Seven Sacraments*, 166–73.

13. Henry VIII, *Assertio Septem Sacramentorum; or, Defence of the Seven Sacraments*, 186–87.

over the tone of his reply to the king, the reformer was unrepentant.[14] Henry was scandalized. He had been called "an ass, a pig, a drunkard, a dreamer, a mad and most ignorant monster," and other names of that sort.[15]

Luther later wrote an apology when the King of Denmark intimated that Henry had become more amenable to the Reformation, but Henry exploited the letter and circulated it as evidence of a recantation on Luther's part, which only exacerbated the reformer's skepticism concerning Henry's general sincerity and religious convictions.[16] In 1527, Luther summed up his thoughts concerning his apology to Henry in a letter to Wenceslas Link:

> Persuaded by the King of Denmark, I wrote a suppliant and humble letter to the King of England; I certainly had high hope and [wrote] with a guileless and candid heart. He has answered me with such hostility that he sounds just like Duke George, and as if he rejoiced in the opportunity to have his revenge. These tyrants have such weak, unmanly, and totally sordid characters that they are worthy of serving the rabble. But thanks be to Christ, I am sufficiently avenged, for I disdain them and their god, who is Satan, and this is my joy.[17]

And so it was, with harsh words and bitter polemics, that the dialogue between Henry VIII and Luther began. While the relationship was not fatally poisoned, there was much to be overcome.

Alec Ryrie writes, "The king's suspicion of Lutheranism in general, his loathing for Luther in particular and his heartfelt attachment to his own authority guaranteed that the English Church would remain beyond Wittenberg's sphere of influence."[18] Yet the thesis of Ryrie's article, "The Strange Death of Lutheran England," is that the "Reformed dominance was late in coming" in England and that "until shortly before the king's death the dominant strain of English evangelicalism was broadly Lutheran in its doctrine and non-confrontational in its politics."[19] Lutheranism was not destined to

---

14. Doernberg, *Henry VIII and Luther*, 33.

15. Gwyn, *The King's Cardinal*, 485.

16. This skepticism, tampered by an openness to God's hand in developments that offered hope of an opening for the gospel in Henry's lands, continued through Luther's life. When news of Robert Barnes' death reached him, the reformer commented, "That king wants to be God. He establishes articles of faith and forbids marriage on pain of death, which not even the pope did. I have something of the prophet in me. What I prophesy will usually come true. Therefore I keep it back and don't say much" (LW 54:384).

17. LW 49:157.

18. Ryrie, "The Strange Death of Lutheran England," 66.

19. Ibid., 68.

fail in England. It had its opportunities. In fact, it had its moments of supremacy, at least among the reformers of the English church. One important reason for this was the question of authority. Richard Rex argues that "in this one word, obedience, we have the essence of the Henrician religion. It would not be going too far to say that Henry's Reformation turned, or began to turn, English religion into a distinctive and coherent version of Christianity, one in which obedience was the paramount virtue or value—as important as faith in Lutheranism or the real presence in catholicism."[20] As it became clearer that Henry VIII's marriage to Catherine of Aragon would not be annulled, some of his counselors and theologians began to argue that the English monarch was by divine right the head of the church in his land, employing whatever ancient precedents they could find. It was not lost upon these men that Luther's appeal to the German nobility to undertake the reformation of the Christian churches in their lands, stated clearly in his treatise of 1520, entitled *To the Christian Nobility of the German Nation*, was beneficial as a bulwark in their arguments for royal supremacy in the church.[21] Whether Henry was in his own conscience ever fully convinced this was true was not nearly as important as the fact that he was convinced it was useful, for Henry VIII was a pragmatic ruler. As Richard Rex has shown, evangelicals in England "sought to exploit the obedience theme in order to make further progress towards other aspects of Lutheran theology, including the all-important doctrine of justification by faith alone."[22]

In his explanation of the Fourth Commandment, Luther extended the realm of authority involved with obedience to that commandment from the home to the church and the state. Speaking of the need for children to honor and respect parents, he wrote, "The same may be said of obedience to the civil authority, which, as we have said, belongs in the category of 'fatherhood' as a walk of life, and is the most comprehensive of all."[23] In his lectures on Romans 13, he reiterated the fundamental authority of civil government and the obedience the Christian owed it.[24] In this way, as

20. Rex, "The Crisis of Obedience: God's Word and Henry's Reformation," 894.

21. The fact that Henry later adopted so much of Luther's view in this regard is made even more striking when one considers passages like the following from *To the Christian Nobility of the German Nation*, which would surely have upset the English king immensely at the time he wrote his *Assertio*: "It follows from this argument that there is no true, basic difference between laymen and priests, princes and bishops, between religious and secular, except for the sake of office and work, but not for the sake of status. They are all of the spiritual estate, all are truly priests, bishops, and popes. But they do not all have the same work to do" (LW 44:128).

22. Rex, "The Crisis of Obedience: God's Word and Henry's Reformation," 865.

23. K-W, *Large Catechism* I.150, 407.

24. LW 25:468–84.

Rex explains, "In a significant alteration of the traditional order, he then extended the commandment from families to households, to civil government, and finally to preaching pastors, emphasising the paternal status of all human authority."[25] The interest of Henry's court and the English reformers in the question of authority and Luther's teachings over against the papacy regarding it is evidenced by the fact that, as Carrie Euler has shown in a recent study, almost all of the Henrician translations of Luther's works "fall into one of two categories: anti-Catholic polemic or spiritual devotion."[26] Luther's writings bolstered the case for Henry's authority in church affairs both by attacking the foundations of papal power and by fostering a high esteem for civil government. As Luther's useful doctrine of obedience then gained prevalence in the Henrician Reformation, a door was opened for the further penetration of other distinctively Lutheran doctrines.[27] Whether theologians of Lutheran inclinations would succeed in that endeavor was yet to be determined.

A second opening for Lutheranism in England was Henry's campaign for support for the annulment of his marriage to Catherine, or his divorce from her, from the universities and theologians of the continent. Here Tjernagel makes a worthwhile observation: "The term divorce is a misnomer, of course. What Henry contemplated was the annulment of a marriage which he believed had been improperly contracted. He was led to this by the firm conviction that God had cursed his marriage by not giving him a male heir to the throne."[28] It was becoming clearer by the day that the pope would not side with the English monarch, as he was deeply entangled at the moment in Italian political maneuvering and caught between the ambitions of Charles V and Francis I. Charles V in effect had the pope captive at the moment. It would have been very inconvenient, therefore, for Clement VII "to admit a papal error in an important dispensation, at a time when the judiciary function of the Holy See was more strongly debated in the world than ever before and totally rejected by the Lutherans."[29] Lutheranism failed to take advantage of the window of opportunity afforded it, though, on theological grounds. Luther abhorred divorce, to the point, even, of his infamous advice to Philip of Hesse to take a second wife rather than divorce his first. His opinion was similar in Henry's regard. He agreed that the original

25. Rex, "The Crisis of Obedience: God's Word and Henry's Reformation," 867.

26. Euler, "Does Faith Translate? Tudor Translations of Martin Luther and the Doctrine of Justification by Faith," 85.

27. Rex, "The Crisis of Obedience: God's Word and Henry's Reformation," 884.

28. Tjernagel, *Henry VIII and the Lutherans*, 73.

29. Doernberg, *Henry VIII and Luther*, 65–67.

papal dispensation granted to allow Henry VIII to marry the wife of his late brother, Arthur, was suspect, yet, because marriage had been contracted, he was unwilling to sever the bond established between Henry and Catherine. He wrote to Robert Barnes in September of 1531, "Even if the King might have sinned by marrying the wife of his deceased brother, and even if the dispensation granted by the Roman pope might not have been valid (I do not debate this now), nevertheless it would be a heavier and more dreadful sin [for the King] to divorce the woman he had married."[30] His colleagues were of the same mind, to differing extents. Luther's inclination toward bigamy rather than divorce was not unique to him, however. Pope Clement VII himself had expressed the possibility of the English monarch instead marrying a second wife. Doernberg writes, "There is a curious tendency among some English historians, by no means confined to the Roman Catholics, not only to preserve a conspiratorial silence about the Pope's genuine conviction but to follow up their silence about the Pope with a disgusted exposure of so 'typically Lutheran' an immorality."[31] He continues, "Monogamy was the normal thing among Christians and nobody in Henry VIII's time, with the exception of the Anabaptists of Münster (1534), denied its normality. Neither the Pope nor Luther regarded bigamy as *desideratum*; but both of them, and not they alone, regarded it as the lesser evil compared with divorce."[32] Even Erasmus, not one to speak controversial notions openly or outside of satire, offered bigamy as an option as well.[33] Zwingli, however, took a more favorable view of the divorce and maintained his opinion even after learning of the stance of the Wittenberg theologians.[34] Henry had reached out to the Lutherans, then, for support in his marriage dilemma, but Luther and his colleagues failed to ingratiate themselves to him for the sake of conscience. In the end, however, this did not prove to be an insurmountable obstacle. Whether the Lutherans had helped him or not, Henry VIII got his divorce, and the fact that Luther and the German princes who supported him stood, like Henry, in opposition to imperial policy and papal power endeared them to the English king.[35]

As time passed and both the Lutheran princes of Germany and the newly declared head of the English church, the king, became keenly aware

30. LW 50:32.

31. Doernberg, *Henry VIII and Luther*, 73–74.

32. Ibid., 74.

33. Ibid.

34. Euler, *Couriers of the Gospel*, 55; Olsen, *The New Testament Logia on Divorce*, 68–69.

35. Tjernagel, *Henry VIII and the Lutherans*, 91.

of their awkward and precarious standing in diplomatic affairs, the possibility of reconciliation arose. Both Henry and Luther demonstrated a willingness to swallow their pride. Henry expressed regret for his book against Luther. Luther's apology, written when the King of Denmark advised him that Henry VIII was more inclined to the gospel than before, marked a shift in tenor. Both men demonstrated a willingness to humble themselves, at least in some measure, Henry for political and diplomatic capital and Luther for the spread of the gospel in England.

Henry VIII expressed interest in joining the Schmalkaldic League, but was from the beginning an odd fit. Secular policy concerns trumped ecclesiastical affairs in Henry's mind, whereas the League insisted upon theological agreement for diplomatic cooperation.[36] Henry's divorce and his unwillingness to subscribe officially and outright to the *Augsburg Confession* proved to be roadblocks to his relationship with the League. Henry hinted that he might declare theological agreement with the Lutheran doctrine of the League, should they accept him first, but was unwilling to do so beforehand, or to promise to do so at all. The Wittenberg Articles of 1536 attempted to clear the way to theological agreement and did influence the Ten Articles in some obvious ways.[37] In spite of such incremental progress, however, significant and thorough doctrinal consensus was never reached.[38] In the end, the crushing defeat of the Schmalkaldic League at the Battle of Mühlberg destroyed any political utility in an alliance with the now routed German princes of that alliance.

4.2. Wittenberg and Henry VIII: Doors Close

The decline of Lutheran influence in the Henrician Reformation and the shift toward a more Reformed model and theological mindset was neither immediate nor as early as many assume. Ryrie asserts, "In the early 1540s, however, it was the Lutheran party which appeared to have the upper hand within the evangelical movement: a dominance which was no less real for being extremely short-lived."[39] The lack of any further significant translations of Luther's works into English in the final years of Henry's reign provides evidence of Lutheranism's waning influence in the reformation in England as well.[40] There are a number of reasons for this decline. The issue

36. Doernberg, *Henry VIII and Luther*, 107.

37. MacCulloch, *Thomas Cranmer: A Life*, 161.

38. Tjernagel, *Henry VIII and the Lutherans*, 160–68.

39. Ryrie, "The Strange Death of Lutheran England," 77.

40. Euler, "Does Faith Translate?," 91.

of authority was resolved, for the most part, if not entirely, with the Act of Supremacy and other such acts. While resistance continued well into the Elizabethan years, with the passage of time, the concept of the monarch as the head of the English church gradually became the status quo. The marriage question became moot with the deaths of Catherine and Anne, whose deaths also allowed Spain to become more amenable to a possible alliance with England. The Schmalkaldic League's defeat at Mühlberg ended Henry's courtship of the German Lutheran princes on any significant scale.

There were other reasons why the English Reformation turned away from Lutheranism and toward Reformed Christianity, in part under Henry, but especially under Edward. In the renumbering of the Ten Commandments to make the prohibition of graven images a Commandment of its own, first explicitly employed in 1534 in Zurich and a few years later adopted in England for the *Bishops' Book* of 1537, we see the skepticism regarding images that had arisen among a growing number of English evangelicals and, it would seem, with Henry himself.[41] As the Archbishop of Canterbury, Thomas Cranmer continued to ponder the presence of Christ in the Lord's Supper, he became more and more inclined toward the Swiss view of Christ's presence in the sacrament, which was less abstract and thus easier to promulgate. The matter of Christ's presence in communion had been a focal point of Reformed polemics in England, and such a view of the sacrament had profound implications for other doctrines, as became evident in the Edwardian Reformation. The execution of Thomas Cromwell, who shared Luther's belief in the real presence, and whose reforms Luther had praised in a letter to the chief minister, also severely weakened Lutheranism's prospects in this regard.[42] The unified conception of a Christian church and state prevalent among many of the Reformed and the emphasis they placed upon Old Testament examples and precedents for defining the essence and role of a Christian king also fit well with Henry's view of himself. In addition to all of this, the doctrines of the Swiss were closer to those long held by the Lollards in England than those of the Lutherans.[43]

At the beginning of the Henrician Reformation, a considerable number of exiled evangelicals, at least those who played significant roles in the subsequent reformatory work that took place in England, found their way to Wittenberg at one point or another, far outnumbering those who visited for any length of time or studied in Zurich. Robert Barnes and William

---

41. Ryrie, *The Gospel and Henry VIII: Evangelicals in the Early English Reformation*, 231; Ryrie, "The Strange Death of Lutheran England," 82.

42. Ryrie, "The Strange Death of Lutheran England," 69; LW 50:137–38.

43. Ryrie, "The Strange Death of Lutheran England," 81.

Tyndale are but two examples. By the end of Henry's reign, however, the trend was clearly shifting.[44] Moreover, Heinrich Bullinger and others of the Reformed confession had been and were making concerted efforts to influence the course of England's religious developments as much as possible. They were extremely active, for instance, from 1536 to 1538.[45] Bullinger even hoped that the English Reformation would provide an opportunity to reconcile the Lutherans and the Reformed.[46] In turn, in the late years of the Henrician Reformation, English evangelicals with Reformed convictions were maintaining much closer ties to their coreligionists on the continent than their Lutheran counterparts.[47] For all these reasons and more, as James Pragman has noted, "The theology of the Augsburg Confession was reflected to some extent in some English formularies of the faith, but Henry and his government—in spite of pressures to the contrary—would remain their own theological masters."[48]

4.3. Hooper's Life up to the Controversy

Daniel Andersson observes, "John Hooper was a figure whose brief spell in the limelight of Edwardian and Marian religious controversy has seemed rather hard to understand: his personality was somewhat joyless and he had no very subtle theological mind. The paucity of documentary sources for the first fifty years of his life may reflect an absence of impact as much as the vagaries of the archives."[49] Whether Hooper was "somewhat joyless" is difficult to assess almost five hundred years after his death. The subtlety of his theological mind will be addressed in subsequent chapters. What is beyond dispute, however, is the veracity of Andersson's observation that there is a "paucity of documentary sources for the first fifty years of his life."

John Hooper was born in Somerset, most likely in 1495, although the exact year is uncertain. Historians assume his family was at least somewhat prosperous, as they were able to send their son to Oxford. He graduated from Merton College with a Bachelor of Arts in 1519.[50] Deibler explains, "That he was once a Cistercian monk, we learn from the sentence pronounced against

---

44. Tjernagel, *Henry VIII and the Lutherans*, 254.

45. Euler, *Couriers of the Gospel*, 57.

46. Ibid., 65.

47. Ryrie, "The Strange Death of Lutheran England," 75, 78.

48. Pragman, "Richard Taverner and the Augsburg Confession," 85.

49. Andersson, Review of *John Hooper: Tudor Bishop and Martyr*, 159.

50. The John Hooper mentioned in the register could be another John Hooper, but that is unlikely.

him in Queen Mary's reign."[51] He spent his monastic years at Cleeve Abbey in north Somerset.[52] It is believed he remained there until its dissolution by Henry VIII in 1536. He then spent sometime at Oxford again but left after a dispute with Dr. Richard Smith, who did not share Hooper's budding Protestant convictions. Hooper moved to London and lived as a courtier off "the kindness of my father," as he put it.[53] He wrote to Bullinger of his life as a courtier and the "impious worship and all manner of idolatry" with which he became accustomed through courtly life.[54] There, however, in the midst of all that impious worship and idolatry, he was exposed to the theology of Zwingli and Bullinger, which would change his life forever. He found a position as a steward for Sir Thomas Arundel, who shielded him from charges of heresy as a result of the Six Articles Act, the "whip of six strings," issued in 1539, which clearly renounced the theology that Hooper had embraced with increasing enthusiasm and conviction. Friends and even Bishop Stephen Gardiner tried to sway Hooper from his growing inclination toward the theology of the Swiss Reformation, but to no avail. As one historian remarks, "Gardiner found, as Cranmer discovered later, that once the mind of John Hooper was made up it was not swiftly unmade."[55] By the early 1540s Hooper was avowedly and by all accounts intractably Reformed.

As a result of the Act of Six Articles and the possibility of his prosecution for heresy in accord with it, Hooper fled to the continent in the hopes of finding a home in Zurich. He likely made one trip to Paris, returned, and then made a second trip from Paris for which Strassbourg was the notable landing point.[56] It was from Strassbourg that he wrote to Bullinger for the first time.[57] From his first letters to Bullinger would spring a long correspondence and close friendship between the English exile and Zurich's preeminent churchman. In Strassbourg Hooper also met his wife, Anne de Tscerlas. Together, after Hooper had made a brief return to England, the two moved to Zurich in early 1547. On the way they were married, most likely in Basle in late March, although no records of their marriage exist. They arrived in Zurich 29 March 1547.

51. Deibler Jr., "Bishop John Hooper," 267–68.

52. Sullivan, *John Hooper*, 13.

53. Quoted in Deibler, "Bishop John Hooper," 268.

54. Quoted in ibid.

55. Steinmetz, *Reformers in the Wings*, 102.

56. Some authors give, however, the impression that he made only one trip. This seems less likely, however.

57. Steinmetz presents it as one trip in *Reformers in the Wings*, 102. Deibler claims Hooper traveled to Paris, briefly returned to England, and, once again warned of imminent danger, then ventured to Strasbourg.

Ulrich Zwingli's reformation survived in Zurich largely because of the work of Heinrich Bullinger, who led the church there for four decades. A churchman of great ability whose presence and pastoral care contributed as much and probably even more than his theology, Bullinger held together and built upon what Zwingli had begun before his death on a battlefield near Kapel 11 October 1531. Moreover, through a regular and wide stream of letters Bullinger influenced reforming work well beyond his city's limits. As will be seen, his influence upon Protestantism in England has in the last few decades become increasingly apparent. While Bullinger was likely younger than Hooper, depending upon the year of Hooper's birth, he was every bit the mentor of the English exile. Hooper's theology bore the unmistakable imprint of Bullinger's, even if his pastoral discretion lacked some of the same. During Hooper's two-year sojourn in Zurich, the two men developed a close friendship, which would remain strong long after Hooper's departure from the city, with Bullinger even serving as godfather for Hooper's first child. In Zurich and through Bullinger, Hooper also became convinced of his principles for Christian worship, namely, that only that which was apostolic was to be observed. In the Vestment Controversy, his concern for apostolic simplicity, that is, what he considered to be apostolic simplicity, would be paramount. West writes, "The lessons Hooper learned in Zurich were not only theology from the pages of the text-book and from the clamour of the public disputation, but were also the working out of the theory in church practice. The lessons he learnt in Zurich were the very same lessons which Hooper in turn tried to teach the English Church."[58]

On 28 January 1547 Henry VIII died. A window was now open. What remained uncertain was who would benefit most from it. The evangelicals were determined to seize the opportunity. The Duke of Somerset, Edward Seymour, who held evangelical sympathies, served as the regent for Henry's heir, Edward VI, only ten years-old. The situation stayed precarious, though. Mary, next in line for the throne, remained a committed Roman Catholic, and what the young Edward's future would hold was far from certain. Hooper remained in Zurich for the time being, but by the end of the next year he was considering a return to his homeland. Finally, in January of 1549, he set out for England with his wife and infant daughter, with the apparent blessing and encouragement of Bullinger, convinced that he could better influence the course of reforming work in England there than from afar on the continent, hopeful of reshaping England's Church in the image of that which he had come to know and love in Zurich. He undoubtedly expected opposition, but little did he know that his life had but six hectic years

58. West, "John Hooper and the Origins of Puritanism," 346.

left. Foxe puts prophetic words in Hooper's mouth, striking, whether true or not, at the time of his departure. Supposedly, Bullinger warned Hooper not to forget his friends in Europe, and Hooper replied, "But the last news of all I shall not be able to write for there where I shall take most pains, there shall you hear of me burnt to ashes: and that shall be the last news, which I shall not be able to write unto you; but you shall hear it of me"—the stuff of good drama, but unlikely fact.[59] For his part, Bullinger encouraged Hooper, according to Foxe:

> Master Hooper, although we are sorry to part with your com-
> pany for our own cause, yet much greater causes we have to
> rejoice, both for your sake, and especially for the cause of
> Christ's true religion, that you shall now return, out of long
> banishment, into your native country again; where not only
> you may enjoy your own private liberty, but also the cause and
> state of Christ's church, by you, may fare the better; as we doubt
> not but it shall.[60]

The Hoopers had to travel an indirect route home because of the *Augsburg Interim* of Charles V. They arrived in Basle at the end of March 1549, making their way from there to Strasbourg. They stayed there until 2 April, when they sailed from the city. West includes an interesting account: "At Strasbourg Hooper found that Bucer was about to leave for an unknown destination-a refugee in the face of the Interim which the Emperor Charles V was forcing upon his empire. Although Hooper did not at that time know of Bucer's destination he soon discovered it, for Bucer too was on his way to England."[61] After some rough sailing they arrived in Cologne nine days later, and a week after that in Antwerp. Sir Philip Hoby, Edward VI's ambassador to the Netherlands, requested that Hooper visit Brussels, occupied by the Charles V's soldiers at the time.[62] His hopes to meet with the captive Elector of Saxony there were dashed, however, by the Spanish troops guarding him. He returned to Antwerp and from there set out for England. On 16 May 1549 the Hoopers landed on English soil and made their way to London. At one point on their journey, Anna, Hooper's wife, wrote to her family, only to receive bad news from the messenger, who found out that her father had died. Moreover, when her mother gave the letter to her brother to read, he "immediately threw it into the fire without reading it," so that, Hooper

59. Quoted in Deibler, "Bishop John Hooper," 276.
60. Quoted in Sullivan, *John Hooper*, 17.
61. West, "John Hooper and the Origins of Puritanism," 22.
62. Sullivan, *John Hooper*, 21.

explained to Bullinger, "the words of Christ are true, that the brother shall persecute the brother for the sake of the word of God."[63]

West writes of Hooper's initial reception in London: "His first experiences were scarcely encouraging. He carried a letter from Bullinger to Cranmer and delivered it to the Archbishop. The reception was cold. 'He did not vouchsafe a single word either respecting yourself or your most godly church,' wrote Hooper to Bullinger on May 31st."[64] From there, however, things improved quickly. Hooper's work in England began notably as the chaplain to the Duke of Somerset, whose later fall he would survive with limited lasting detriment. In his role as a preacher, he attacked Roman Catholicism and Lutheranism alike, insisting on a reform program in line with that of the Swiss. He preached often, usually at least once a day, but most of the time twice. His sermons were well attended and by all accounts not without effect. "Dr. Robert Smith, who was a particular critic of Hooper and other Protestants, declared sarcastically that Hooper was 'so admired by the people, that they held him for a prophet; nay, they looked upon him as some deity.'"[65] On 5 February 1550, Hooper was appointed to preach before Edward and the Council every Wednesday in Lent, a testament to his preaching ability and the growing esteem in which he was held among the evangelicals at court. He chose the Book of Jonah as his text. Edward was impressed with the sermons so much that he offered Hooper the bishopric of Gloucester. Hooper's acceptance of the promotion on the condition that he not wear the traditional and prescribed episcopal vestments famously sparked the Vestment Controversy with Ridley, who was to consecrate Hooper and objected to an exception being made for him.

During this period, Hooper also used his growing sway to push for the foundation of the Stranger Church in London. This too did not sit well with Ridley, as the congregation would be exempted from his episcopal oversight. Consisting of Swiss and Dutch Reformed Christians, Hooper hoped the Stranger Church would serve as an example of what English churches should begin to look like and of how they should operate. The king and others additionally hoped that it would help avoid "all sects of Anabaptists and suchlike," which they feared might arise as a result of the large numbers of exiles coming especially from the Low Countries and Germany.[66] While Cranmer and Ridley might have feared radicalism among those in the Stranger Church, Hooper was no friend of Anabaptists and sects. Cranmer himself dispensed

63. *Original Letters Relative to the English Reformation*, 63.

64. West, "John Hooper and the Origins of Puritanism," 23.

65. Sullivan, *John Hooper*, 25.

66. MacCulloch, *Thomas Cranmer*, 477.

him more than once to preach or teach against offshoots of the Radical Reformation which found their way to the island. MacCulloch writes, "One of the reasons for Hooper's enduring favour with the majority of Councillors was that he could be useful against Anabaptists, and he was sent off to Essex and Kent to help Lord Chancellor Rich pursue the campaign against them in the wake of Bocher's burning," so that "in this respect, Cranmer had no quarrel with the Bishop-elect of Gloucester."[67] Despite the reservations of Cranmer and Ridley, then, and with the approval of the king, the completion of the grant formalities for the Stranger Church came only one day after Hooper's confirmation as Bishop of Gloucester.[68]

4.4. Zurich's Theological Imprint upon Hooper

"England and Zurich were crucial for each other in the early years of the Reformation for a variety of reasons, both theological and practical. Were it not for the close relationship with Zurich, the Church of England and the culture of English Protestantism would have looked different upon the accession of Elizabeth I."[69] No single person in the Swiss Reformation was more active and responsible for the close relationship between the two than Heinrich Bullinger. Many English Protestants were naturally drawn to Zurich's theology and practice because of its iconoclasm and its denial of the real presence and all such doctrines they considered popish. In addition, Zwingli and his heirs' firm insistence upon the unity of the spiritual and sacred appealed greatly to evangelicals in England, especially some of the most prominent churchmen under Edward VI. This alone, however, does not account for the Zurich's success in serving as a model and in an advisory role for the Edwardian Reformation. Bullinger's skill as a pastor's pastor and religious diplomat—his ability to think long-term, counsel against actions that might create unnecessary obstacles, and suggest ways to work within the structures in place—played a prominent part in the relationship that developed and prospered between the two reformations. Indeed, it was at Hooper's suggestion that Bullinger dedicated the second volume of his *Decades* to King Edward VI, in which he stressed the role of a godly king in promoting the "hearing and following of God's Word" in his kingdom, lest calamity strike from its neglect.[70] Carrie Euler has carefully outlined and explained the significance of the correspondence between Zurich and

67. Ibid., 477–78.
68. Ibid., 477.
69. Euler, *Couriers of the Gospel*, 9.
70. Quoted in Deibler, "Bishop John Hooper," 217.

England, and especially between Bullinger and leading English Protestants, in her *Couriers of the Gospel: England and Zurich, 1531-1558*, quoted above. Diarmaid MacCulloch rightly concludes, "The reality is that in the time of Edward VI Calvin was not the towering international figure which he later became. For Elizabethan England, he was indeed the Reformation theologian par excellence; but when Edwardian evangelicals thought of Switzerland, it was primarily of Zurich and its presiding churchman Bullinger."[71] West notes, "The influence of Geneva on the later development of Puritanism is so marked that it is often forgotten that before this Geneva influence really began to make itself felt in England at the beginning of the reign of Elizabeth I there had been already a decade of Zurich influence working in the same direction."[72]

What is true of Edward's Reformation in general is even truer of John Hooper. Seventeen letters from Hooper to Bullinger survive, as well as one from Hooper's wife.[73] A good number more were certainly written. Bullinger regularly wrote to Hooper for information on the English Reformation and his own well-being. Most of these have been lost, especially those written during Hooper's imprisonment, when few letters were permitted to make their way to the accused heretic, for fear they might heighten his obstinacy.[74] When a letter did reach him as his martyrdom loomed ominously, Hooper was relieved. Bullinger counseled his friend with words that could well have been written by Flacius, "Therefore, seeing you have such a large promise, be strong in the Lord, fight a good fight, be faithful unto the end. Consider that Christ, the Son of God is your captain, and fighteth for you, and that all the prophets, apostles, and martyrs are your fellow-servants... Happy are we if we depart with in the Lord"[75] Hooper gratefully replied, "[I] am most thankful to you that in these most dangerous times you have not forgotten me."[76]

Perhaps no reformer in England bore the imprint of Zurich and specifically of Bullinger more than Hooper. This can be seen in his conception of worship and in his zealous devotion to the ministerial task, in his vocal denial of the real presence and his advocacy for church governance and practice modeled upon that which he encountered in Switzerland. This was perhaps evidenced most clearly in the Strangers' Church of which he

71. MacCulloch, *The Boy King*, 173–74.

72. West, "John Hooper and the Origins of Puritanism," 346.

73. Euler, *Couriers of the Gospel*, 80.

74. Sullivan, *John Hooper*, 51.

75. Quoted in Sullivan, *John Hooper*, 120.

76. Ibid.

was a sponsor.[77] MacCulloch explains regarding the tensions that fed into the Vestment Controversy: "Andrew Petegree has shown how this struggle was linked with the contemporary establishment of an institutional church community ('Strangers' Church') for the thousands of foreign evangelicals in London: led by theologians sympathizing with Zürich, it was intended by its supporters to provide models for further reformation in the Church of England."[78]

Edwin Clyde Deibler, Jr. outlines several important aspects of Zurich theology which shaped John Hooper's thinking and approach to reform work and parish ministry. They include the following: the sufficiency of Scripture, the sovereignty of God, the Lord's Supper, ecclesiology and state-church relations, and the sacrament of baptism. He attributes to Bullinger especially these additional formative teachings: hermeneutics, the place of preaching and experiential religion, the sovereignty of God, the ideas of the covenant, indifferent matters and the use of vestments, the place and use of the Sabbath, and the sacrament.[79] Each of these areas need not be examined in detail, but it is important to note that Bullinger's influence extended beyond vestments and church rites. Hooper had imbibed deeply the theology and practice of Zurich.

For practical purposes, in order to equip the reader to compare Hooper's assertions regarding vestments with those of his spiritual mentor, Bullinger, it serves well to review the Zurich theologian's doctrine and practice in that regard. First, however, it will prove helpful to survey Zwingli's teachings about and approach to state-church relations. Hooper's refusal to wear vestments presented more than a simply theological dilemma. It worked itself out through the machinations of the church-state structure of Edwardian England, as inherited and adapted from the Henrician Reformation. Hooper's convictions regarding the relationship between church and state are crucial for understanding why Hooper later supported Mary's accession to the throne, refused to stoke resistance to her reign and measures, and submitted to his martyrdom with obsequious dignity. Moreover, his assumptions regarding the relationship between a Christian king or magistrate and the church in his realm drove the appeals he made to Edward, the examples from Scripture he employed, and the measures he used to gage success for the Reformation in England.

---

77. Ibid., 117.

78. MacCulloch, *The Later Reformation in England*, 15; See Pettegree, *Foreign Protestant Communities in Sixteenth Century London*, chaps. 2–3.

79. Deibler, "Bishop John Hooper," iv.

Deibler explains, "Zwingli felt that all government should be founded on the word of God, that in states where this is true, Christians, obeying the laws, became the ideal citizens. They were under the law of men and under the law of God."[80] In this, he was not necessarily so different than Luther, who also taught that Christians made especially good citizens. Prompted by the gospel and their recognition of the divine establishment of governmental authority, Christians alone were able to offer external and internal obedience to the state, that is, the Christian recognizes that through the civil realm he or she serves his or her neighbor as a citizen of two kingdoms and not merely as one.[81] The chief difference between Luther and Zwingli was that Zwingli thought and taught that the church should be subordinated to a Christian government. Gregory J. Miller notes, "Zwingli was committed to a state-run church. The clergy are to be subject to external, human righteousness with the exception of the necessary freedom for the proclamation of the Word of God and 'so far as they [magistrates] do not order what is contrary to God. Even excommunication is by the magistrate. The minister is only to admonish."[82] Bullinger taught likewise. Deibler notes, "Bullinger teaches the same position in the *Second Helvetic Confession*: the care of religion belongs especially to the holy magistrate; he should hold the Bible in his hand and exercise care that nothing contrary to it is taught in his dominions; he should govern his people with good laws made according to the word of God."[83] While Luther taught obedience to the state outside of the *clausula Petri* or constitutional grounds, in the case of the lesser magistrate, Zwingli subordinated the Christian Church to a Christian government, such as existed in Zurich. Pastors became, in essence, agents of the state, not in the case of an emergency, as existed in Luther's approval of princes serving as *Notbischöfe*, which provided the foundation for a Lutheran state church, but as a scripturally established arrangement.

Zwingli's approach to the relationship between church and state obviously created tensions for Reformed theologians in England, where each monarch brought with him or her a new "Christian" government. This does not mean that Zwingli did not teach a right of revolution—he did allow that after much warning and with much care those whose duty it was to do so might deprive a ruler of his rule—but it did complicate matters of obedience in places like England.[84] Deibler explains how the tension implicit in

80. Ibid., 152.

81. Althaus, *The Ethics of Martin Luther*, 70.

82. Miller, "Hyldrych Zwingli (1484–1531)," 165.

83. Deibler, "Bishop John Hooper," 410.

84. Ibid., 155.

Zwingli's theology of church and state played out in the life and ministry of Hooper: "He recognized the need of instructing young King Edward and rejoiced when the monarch encouraged an advancing reformation. But he also recognized Roman Catholic Mary as his lawful queen and would not be party to the plot to keep her from the throne"—a truly fateful decision on his part, but one based upon the theology inherited and interpreted from Zwingli. Deibler concludes, "Hooper's Zwinglianism is nowhere more evident than in his views on the state-church relationship."[85] Like Luther, he grounded obedience to the ruling authorities in the honor and respect owed to parents. Even if the state commanded the Christian to do that which God forbade, the Christian had to accept the consequences of his disobedience and, while disobeying, not rebel.[86] Christians had to bear the cross out of faithfulness to God and his Word. While Flacius plumbed the Old Testament for examples of God's saints' resistance to the governing authorities, Hooper, from the opposite side of the spectrum, applied the "regulations set forth in the Old Testament for the management of the Jewish monarchy to the English monarchy of his own day."[87] Due to his high view of the role of the state in maintaining both external and internal obedience, civil and religious, Hooper took seriously the opportunities afforded him to serve King Edward VI and to preach in his presence. He emphasized the king's responsibility to care for his subjects both according to their physical and spiritual welfare. Hooper begged for the state to "put away not only civil but also theological evil."[88] Tragically for Hooper, Mary certainly thought she was doing just that when she ordered, among others, his own death as a heretic

Beyond the relationship between church and state, Hooper was heavily influenced by Zurich's practice with respect to adiaphora, or indifferent matters, and Bullinger's own teaching in that regard. The *Second Helvetic Confession*, strongly shaped by Bullinger, stated in Chapter XXII, "Of Religious and Ecclesiastical Meetings," that "everything is to be arranged for decorum, necessity, and godly decency, lest anything be lacking that is required for worship and the necessary works of the Church."[89] Moreover, "All luxurious attire, all pride, and everything unbecoming to Christian humility, discipline and modesty, are to be banished from the sanctuaries

---

85. Ibid., 389.
86. Ibid., 394.
87. Ibid., 395.
88. Ibid., 391.
89. Cochrane, *Reformed Confessions of the Sixteenth Century*, 289.

and places of prayer of Christians."[90] "Luxurious attire" can certainly be construed as referring to a number of the traditional vestments inherited from the medieval church. Moreover, the word "necessity" conveyed the Reformed insistence that only that which is biblical—sanctioned or prescribed in the Bible—ought to be employed in the worship life of the Christian community. The *First Helvetic Confession* summed up Bullinger's position well when it said of "chalices, priestly gowns for the mass, choir robes, cowls, tonsures, flags, candles, altars, gold and silver" that "these things we want to have banished far from our holy congregations."[91] Why? To one extent or another, they perverted the true religion and worship of God. This certainly has a different ring than the *Apology of the Augsburg Confession* when it insisted straightaway in its defense in Article XXIV (XII):

> At the outset it is again necessary, by the way of preface, to point out that we do not abolish the Mass but religiously retain and defend it. Among us the Mass is celebrated every Lord's day and on other festivals, when the sacrament is made available to those who wish to partake of it, after they have been examined and absolved. We also keep traditional liturgical forms, such as the order of readings, prayers, vestments, and other similar things.[92]

Deibler notes that in Bullinger's view "without piety and virtue among the worshipers there is no true ornamentation in the church."[93] Nonetheless, Bullinger did not argue for a strict rigidity across the spectrum of Reformed Christianity "for the churches have always used their liberty in such rites as being things indifferent."[94] This explains his hesitancy to hurry to Hooper's side in the vestment controversy. He recognized, first, that such a controversy might hinder the progress of reformation in Europe, and second, that every Reformed church need not be identical in its practice regarding vestments, etc. While Hooper might have expected Bullinger to back him up in the struggle over episcopal vestments, Bullinger had a long view of what was happening in England and exhibited the cautious, pastoral spirit that served him so well in Zurich.

90. Ibid.

91. Ibid., 109.

92. KW, *Apology of the Augsburg Confession* XXIV.1, 258.

93. Deibler, "Bishop John Hooper," 244.

94. Quoted in Deibler, "Bishop John Hooper," 248.

4.5. Edward VI and His Reform

In his groundbreaking work on King Edward VI, *The Boy King*, MacCulloch notes that "a negative image of Edwardian religion has prevailed since the early nineteenth century, the result of disapproval from both Roman Catholics and (within the Church of England itself) Anglo-Catholics."[95] He explains that one solution to the problem the Edwardian Reformation presents "the Church of England story" has been "simply to deny it any part."[96] This is most unfortunate, because it was during Edward's reign that steps were taken that would define later English Protestantism, steps so calculated and successful that Mary could not succeed in undoing them. While Elizabeth's approach to religion resembled her father's much more than Edward's, in the end, MacCulloch correctly assesses that "Elizabeth deliberately sought to take the spirit out of the Edwardian Church at the same time as she restored its husk."[97] Edward's reforms proved decisive and formative for the course of the reformation in England under Elizabeth. Few sixteen year-olds have left such an imprint.

Edward VI was watched carefully through his youth and great care was taken to ensure both his health and education. From early on "he was handed over to two of the best young humanists that Cambridge could provide—Richard Cox and John Cheke."[98] Edward proved himself a very capable student and began learning French already at nine years of age. Unfortunately the specifics of Edward VI's catechetical instruction are lacking. Jennifer Loach laments, "Given later events, it is unfortunate that we know so little about the prince's 'religious education.'"[99] We do know that all of his principle tutors later became vocal Protestants and both Cox and Cheke were Marian exiles on account of their convictions.

Henry VIII died 28 January 1547. Edward was then nine years old. In keeping with the 1536 Succession Act, Henry had appointed sixteen executors to form his son's Privy Council and carry out governance until Edward reached eighteen years of age. Edward Seymour, First Duke of Somerset, a man with obvious Protestant sympathies, became the young king's protector. Loach cautions, however, against reading too much into Somerset's religious policy. She writes, "Much of the religious change of this period—change that was sanctioned by the protector even if it was not initiated by him—should

---

95. MacCulloch, *The Boy King*, 105.

96. Ibid., 158.

97. Ibid., 194.

98. Loach, *Edward VI*, 11.

99. Ibid., 13.

be seen primarily as an attempt to consolidate the royal supremacy and to extend lay control over the Church, rather than as an effort to move the Church in a specifically Protestant direction."[100] While MacCulloch notes that "at such a distance of time, it is difficult now to disentangle sanctity from selfishness" in the motives of the *dramatis personae* of the Edwardian Reformation, he takes a more "positive" view of the "evangelical agendas of the leaders of the first Edwardian regime."[101]

The Edwardian Reformation was from early on influenced by a flood of Protestant exiles returning or immigrating to England. Loach notes:

> Archbishop Cranmer, very conscious of the lack of strong en-
> thusiasm amongst the English clergy for the changes that he
> personally desired, had early in the reign written to a number
> of important continental reformers, such as the Polish noble-
> man, John à Lasco, and the Germans, Martin Bucer, and Philip
> Melanchthon. He offered to pay their travelling expenses to
> England, and to accommodate them in his own household.[102]

The *Augsburg Interim* brought many to England, most prominently Martin Bucer. Persecution in the Low Countries added more. Some found their way into the Strangers' Church in London, one of several congregations planned to meet the need of religious immigrants. This all was a reflection of and a contributing factor to the international focus of Edward's reform. A goal among a number of its leaders was the arrival of England as both a head and haven for European Reformed Christianity. MacCulloch explains, "If there is any one respect in which the Edwardian Reformation was different in flavor from the latter Church of England, it was in the fervent Protestant internationalism it displayed," so that "there was a longing for England to stand at the centre of a renewed universal Church at a time of particular military and political crisis for the reformed movement."[103] Furthermore:

> Cranmer's dearest wish was to create a general council of re-
> formers which would outshine the false Council of Trent, and
> to draw up unifying doctrinal statements for the reformed uni-
> versal Church. I have argued elsewhere that it was only when
> the major continental reformers showed themselves to any im-
> mediate meeting that England was compelled to issue its own

---

100. Ibid., 47.
101. MacCulloch, *The Boy King*, 8, 223.
102. Loach, *Edward VI*, 117.
103. MacCulloch, *The Boy King*, 79.

doctrinal statement, the Forty-Two Articles, long-postponed but finally issued in 1553.[104]

After his return to England from Zurich, John Hooper served as Somerset's chaplain, a position of much influence. Yet, Somerset did not stay in power for long. Agrarian crises, Somerset's prolonged obsession with Scotland, and financial troubles that resulted from that and other factors left Somerset in a precarious situation in the second half of 1549. On 9 June 1549 the Edwardian Prayer Book, which had already won approval in Parliament, was introduced in the realm. Although the Prayer Book was a rather cautious reformulation of liturgics, unrest broke out in the southwest when the people of Sampford objected to the use of the book by their priest. Trouble spread quickly and in early July the rebels laid siege to Exeter. The siege lasted thirty-five days and suppression of the rebellion appeared anything but certain from the get-go. Thankfully for Somerset, Lord Grey succeeded in putting down the rebellion. The chaos in the west left its mark on Edward and his advisors, however, and there was a constant fear that something could spark a new uprising in the future. Scholars have debated for a long time the causes of the uprising—whether it was a strictly religious affair. It was almost certainly not a strictly religious affair. The Prayer Book appears to have been but one among a number of grievances against social and economic conditions in England. Religious differences simply exacerbated tensions between classes and within classes. In this case, anti-gentry sentiment coincided with religious conservatism, as Loach indicates.[105]

This rebellion, along with subsequent skirmishes that flared up throughout the rest of 1549, does make plain that there was no universal or unanimous desire for reform, that there were objections to reform dictated from above. Moreover, the instability of 1549 made Somerset's fall, if not inevitable, very likely—an unpromising prospect for the future of his chaplain, Hooper. Somerset had been "neither fast nor effective" in his response to the crises of 1549 and bursts of temper and uneven proclamations regarding the rebellions and the rebels—some of his statements seem to justify their actions—only brought him into further disfavor with the other councilors.[106] It must be said that Somerset's hesitancy likely sprang at least in part from his sympathy for the economic and social conditions in which many of the king's subjects found themselves. He had campaigned for reform for the sake of the common people. He was more in tune with the suffering of the English people than many politicians in his day. And so MacCulloch

104. Ibid., 99.
105. Loach, *Edward VI*, 83.
106. Ibid., 89.

wisely observes, "More charitably, we can see a leader of English high politics paying an extraordinary degree of respect to the concerns of the world of low politics; or at least that section of low politics which shared his own evangelical enthusiasm."[107] Nonetheless, the other councilors successfully ousted Somerset from power in early October. He continued to lose support within the city of London and throughout the country in the days to follow and eventually the young king also waned in his willingness to go to bat for his politically wounded protector. On 6 February 1550, Somerset finally gained release from the tower's long and inhospitable lodging. The king pardoned him twelve days later. On 10 April he regained his place in the Privy Council, but he was no longer in control of the government as he had been.

John Dudley, Northumberland, came to power next, although he did not assume the title of "Protector." The two personalities could hardly have been more different. Dudley talked less, displayed less, forced less, listened more, was more deferential to the young monarch. His religious convictions are less clear, but too much weight ought not be placed upon his later conversion to traditional Catholicism in the days leading to the scaffold. First, he stated in that conversion that he had indeed been a convinced Protestant earlier. Second, his conversion took place as the scaffold hung in the balance. He himself dated his Protestant convictions to the 1530s, which means that he had been an evangelical for quite some time before replacing Somerset. While many in the church were upset with his raiding of church coffers for the crown, he seems driven to have done so because the financial crisis, which was a partial cause for Somerset's undoing, was so pressing. In the end, while Northumberland's reign struck a new tone economically, implementing many policies which Mary's regime continued and built upon, in religious matters it was "more of the same," and there was "continuity, indeed an accelerated and more relentless pace of religious change."[108] MacCulloch observes, "The leaders of the Edwardian regimes set out to destroy one church and build another. That is the most important continuity between the ascendancies of Seymour and Dudley."[109]

1549 was by all accounts a disaster, but not insurmountable. Hooper surprisingly escaped Somerset's downfall for the most part unscathed. He could write to Bullinger of the "hope for better things" for Somerset, and more importantly, he expressed a hope that "God in his providence holds the ploughtail, and raises up in his Majesty's Council many more favourers of his Word, who defend the cause of Christ with vigour and courage."

107. MacCulloch, *The Boy King*, 51.

108. Ibid., 56.

109. Ibid., 57.

Moreover, he stated that Cranmer had become "now very friendly."[110] In the end, the Protestants had survived the setbacks of the difficult year and now pushed cautiously ahead, so that "winter 1550 was a time for consolidating the gains of 1549 and healing the wounds."[111] MacCulloch explains the challenges they faced: "The regime felt the need to work around three hostile constituencies: the Emperor, the majority of the lay political nation and those bishops who were not part of the inner circle."[112] One of the means and chief expressions of this desire to consolidate gains, then, was the re-shaping of the episcopate in England, which would change Hooper's life and ministry. Lindberg writes, "Catholic bishops were replaced by Protestants, some of whom, like John Hooper (1495-1555) at Gloucester, were proto-puritans and others, more radical Protestants, like John Knox."[113] Haigh calls Hooper "the most determined of the new bishops."[114]

The constant force in this and indeed throughout Edward's Reformation was Thomas Cranmer, the famous Archbishop of Canterbury. Lindberg writes, "The architect of English Protestantism was Henry's archbishop of Canterbury, Thomas Cranmer, whose Protestant orientation found significant expression under Edward."[115] He lists three main programs undertaken by Cranmer in these years: the revision of the Prayer Book, the Forty-Two Articles, which provided the basis for Elizabeth's later Thirty-Nine Articles, and the revision of canon law.[116] After years of service under Henry VIII, Edward VI's reign, therefore, allowed Cranmer to manifest a theological shift away from Lutheranism toward the Swiss Reformation. This is seen most clearly in his eucharistic theology and in his worship reforms. The liturgies of the Church of England now became less ambiguous in their Reformed inclination and emphasis. Moreover, Cranmer's *A defence of the true and Catholic doctrine of the sacrament of the body and blood of our savior Christ* set forth a view of the Lord's Supper stripped of its previous ambiguity. MacCulloch writes, "The *Defence* was Cranmer's second literary task behind the Ordinal in early 1550," a year which he notes was crucial for the consolidation of Protestant gains, "the publication of a semi-official explanation of the Eucharistic theology which lay at the heart of his Prayer

---

110. Quoted in MacCulloch, *Thomas Cranmer*, 453.

111. MacCulloch, *Thomas Cranmer*, 454.

112. MacCulloch, *The Boy King*, 61.

113. Lindberg, *The European Reformations*, 308.

114. Haigh, *English Reformations: Religion, Politics and Society under the Tudors*, 178.

115. Lindberg, *The European Reformations*, 307.

116. Ibid., 308.

Book." That semi-official explanation adopted the "classic expression of the *manducatio impiorum*," inconsistent with any real corporeal presence of Christ in the sacrament.[117] MacCulloch writes, "By the opening months of Edward's reign, it is virtually certain that the key formers of official opinion, Cranmer, Latimer, and Ridley, had abandoned belief in corporal presence in the eucharist, despite having maintained it in Lutheran fashion since the early 1530s."[118] Furthermore, "They came to regard the Lutheran view of Eucharistic presence as verging on the trivial and blasphemous."[119] The language of the real presence was "no longer acceptable, granted the new alignment with the reforms in Switzerland and South Germany."[120] Haigh puts things in perspective: "In 1548, when the first Prayer Book was finalized, almost all serious theological opinion in England supported a real presence; by 1551, when a new version was under consideration, this was no longer so, and transubstantiation was virtually a proscribed opinion."[121] Quick and substantial was the shift, then, from a Lutheran theological orientation regarding the sacrament, among other doctrines, to that of Zurich.

Understandably, given that it came before the shift Haigh notes, Hooper had been less than pleased with the Prayer Book of 1548. He described it to Bullinger as essentially a change in minor issues and "the name of the Mass itself," since that title was avoided.[122] West locates the unacceptability of the Prayer Book for those loyal to Zurich's theology and practice especially in the "the retention of the word 'mass,' the vestments, and the assumption of the existence of an altar. Moreover, "Hooper discovered also that the liberty of preaching was limited by the bishops, of whom by no means all were favourable towards the idea of reform in doctrine and practice."[123] The Prayer Book was never intended to be a final solution, however. Hooper, as will be seen in the Vestment Controversy, failed to appreciate the gradualism of Cranmer, Ridley, and others, although it was precisely this gradualism which allowed the Edwardian Reformation to accomplish as much as it did. Cranmer's *Defence* rested better with Hooper, particularly since, if the positions of the archbishop and Hooper on the sacrament were not identical at this point, they were indubitably drawing nearer, and that without Hooper's having changed at all. It is understandable, then, if Hooper felt emboldened

117. MacCulloch, *Thomas Cranmer*, 461.

118. MacCulloch, *The Boy King*, 67.

119. Ibid., 68.

120. Brooks, "Thomas Cranmner (1489–1556)," 246.

121. Haigh, *English Reformations*, 179.

122. MacCulloch, *Thomas Cranmer*, 462, 463.

123. West, "John Hooper and the Origins of Puritanism," 23.

by such shifts to speak plainly and act bluntly when it came time to address
the vestments to be used for his episcopal consecration, especially after Edward's expressed pleasure in his preaching and the theology he presented in
his sermons on Jonah.

This gradual, but not slow, theological shift expressed through and
guided by official publications demonstrates the extent to which Edward
VI's reformation was an official reformation, reformation from above.
MacCulloch writes that "the display of royal arms [in church interiors] an-
nounced an essential feature of the Edwardian Reformation: it was a revolution directed from above by the monarch, his council, and parliament in
Westminster. Those who ruled the realm took it upon themselves to decide
the form in which the European Reformation would be presented to the
people of England."[124] This does not mean, however, that there was no support among the common people. Preaching was especially important in winning popular support, especially in the populous and influential areas of the
county in southeast England. Nor was reformation forced ham-fisted upon
Edward's subjects without any discussion or with considerable persecution.
MacCulloch explains, "The Edwardian age began as one of glasnost, with
the abolition of the heresy laws and the lapse of censorship, and it remained
a period where there was an extraordinary degree of theological discussion, both formal and informal. The evangelical establishment constrained
conservative voices, but protests were not suppressed altogether even after the shift in power to the evangelicals in 1549."[125] Moreover, he rightly
echoes Petegree in observing, "Edward had burnt two Unitarians, but the
scale of Mary's burnings was, in Andrew Pettegree's words, 'now both intense and somewhat anachronistic', not simply by English but by European
standards."[126] Contrary to Jennifer Loach's argument that Edward was a lot
more the image of his father than scholars have recognized, Mary in this regard seems more akin to Henry than Edward. Moreover, Edward's religious
convictions seem much more clear and much more continental than those
of his father and the religious policy of his reign much more conscientious.
Hooper himself was "so impressed by Edward's learning and, no doubt, his
increasingly zealous Protestantism, that he declared the king to be 'such an
one for his age as the world had never seen,'" assuring Bullinger, "you have
never seen in the worked for these thousand years so much erudition united
with piety and sweetness of disposition."[127] Perhaps the principal key to the

---

124. MacCulloch, *The Boy King*, 163.

125. Ibid., 133.

126. Ibid., 179.

127. Sullivan, *John Hooper*, 37.

success of the evangelical program under Edward was the gradualism it adopted, which Hooper undermined with his objections to the retention, even temporarily, of things like vestments. It was such a gradualistic approach that indeed made it the better part of wisdom in Ridley's view to pull back the reins on John Hooper in the Vestment Controversy. This gradualism ensured that by the time any meaningful number of religious traditionalists felt it necessary to speak up, things had already proceeded too far to turn back the clock completely.

4.6. The Vestment Controversy

The Vestment Controversy broke out during an important time of refortification for evangelical leadership in England. MacCulloch writes of the "evangelical establishment" of Edward VI's regime in 1550, which had weathered a tumultuous 1549, that it "had seen off the political challenge from Catholics and was consolidating its power, its problems came as much from its own side as from conservative opposition."[128] It is no coincidence that John Hooper appears on the very next page. The Vestment Controversy would be the first of several internal struggles within the now ascendant Protestant establishment, of which Hooper had become a part. This establishment that appreciated his clear articulation of Reformed theology and practice in other contexts would in this case seek to muffle and muzzle it.

The Vestment Controversy took full flame, not when Hooper accepted promotion to Bishop of Gloucester, but when Ridley refused to consecrate him if granted an exemption from the prescribed vestments and rites. The issue at hand became whether or not the vestments were adiaphora and, if so, whether the state then had the right to legislate their use in the consecratory rites. The matter thus had a broader scope than vestments alone. Ridley stood in this case as the exemplar of the gradualism of the evangelical establishment led by Cranmer. Hooper challenged that approach through his insistence on the inappropriateness of the rite and vestments as currently construed in the official form of episcopal consecration. This was as much a debate over the path reform should take as the adornment reformers should wear.

Ridley, born into a leading family in Northumberland, was about five years younger than Hooper. Well-educated from childhood, he received his Master of Arts in 1525 at Pembroke College, Cambridge and then was ordained into the priesthood. He went on to study at the Sorbonne and returned to England in 1529. While a proctor at Cambridge a debate about

128. MacCulloch, *Thomas Cranmer*, 469.

papal supremacy broke out in which he opposed the teaching of Rome. He graduated in 1537 and was appointed to serve as a chaplain to Cranmer. In the early 1540s he began serving as one of the king's chaplains and became Master of Pembroke College. In 1547 he became Bishop of Rochester. In a move that would have certainly pleased Hooper, he had one of the altars in one of his churches removed and replaced with a communion table. He also assisted Cranmer in the composition of the Book of Common Prayer. On 1 April 1550 he was appointed Bishop of London, which included the now dissolved diocese of Westminster. Having weathered charges of heresy, Ridley learned the importance of a careful, measured approach to reform. Familiar with the inner machinations of those guiding evangelical policy, he was well-suited for such a prominent bishopric. Even more, as a seasoned veteran of the reform movement in England, Ridley saw in Hooper's refusal to wear the appointed vestments a threat on several fronts: the legitimacy of the king's legislation regarding adiaphora in religious matters; the authority of the church to establish ceremonies that served for good order within the church; and the gradualism that had succeeded in bringing England as far as it had come into Protestantism. Moreover, in the establishment Stranger Church he had already sensed a threat to his proper jurisdiction as a re-forming bishop as well as the possibility of the importation of heresies such as Anabaptism from the continent.

In this fear concerning the possible intrusion of Anabaptistic thought into English churches and the challenges Hooper's objections raised to the authority of the state in church practice and ceremony Ridley was hardly alone. The evangelical establishment as a whole feared the arrival of Ana-baptism on English shores and and the harm theological radicalism could have done by undermining the theological, ecclesiastical and political legiti-macy of Edwardian reform. This fear undermined the prospect of success for Hooper's arguments, since his arguments in this specific debate seemed to limit state power in ecclesiastical affairs, although in reality Hooper did not question the legitimacy of state oversight of the church. In this case, rather, he was concerned not so much with the role of the state as whether certain practices in use were indeed adiaphora as the evangelical establish-ment suggested. Newcombe argues, "Hooper's innate hostility toward both the authority of the church and the state is probably what cost him the argument in the end."[129] While Hooper certainly recognized the authority of both the church and the state in their proper realms, what was at stake here was their authority in the specific realm of adiaphora—indifferent cer-emonies and rites—and the defining of such things as adiaphora for the

129. Newcombe, *John Hooper*, 125.

individual. Hooper would show himself a dutiful servant of church and state throughout his life and, ultimately and indisputably, in his martyr's death, a fate he shared with his opponent in this debate. In this sphere of things allegedly indifferent, however, his conscience would not permit him to acknowledge the right of a king or bishop to introduce or preserve the use of vestments and rites inconsistent with his theology. In so doing, Hooper undermined the approach of Ridley and Cranmer while expressing theological views that were not so far distant from those of his opponents as one might assume. All involved wanted a reform of such rites and vestments. The question was when such reform should take place and whether its immediate undertaking was necessary or, as Ridley would argue, detrimental to the greater program of Edwardian reform and undermining of the authority of those overseeing and guiding that program.

Hooper fired his first shots in his sermons on Jonah during the Lenten season of 1550. On 3 March 1550, he objected in a sermon to the mention of saints in the oath of supremacy and the use of the vestments that were still being worn in the rite. These he called "rather the habit and vesture of Aaron and the gentiles, than of the ministers of Christ."[130] Cranmer, stung and incensed, attacked Hooper in Star Chamber a few days later. Sullivan writes, "[Cranmer] no doubt saw Hooper's words as being as much a challenge to his own authority, and the authority of the Church, as of oaths, vestments, and ceremonial."[131] He was summoned before the Council 15 March to defend his statements. Hooper, implacable, weathered Cranmer's initial campaign against him unscathed.

Hooper's nomination for the bishopric of Gloucester came after Cranmer's summons and charge that Hooper's statements bordered on if not constituted sedition. While Cranmer was unsettled by Hooper's words regarding vestments, this was a clear sign of the king's appreciation for Hooper's preaching. Hooper initially turned down the appointment, which shocked the king. Edward VI unsurprisingly asked Hooper to explain himself, since in rejecting the appointment he was disobeying the supreme head of the Church of England. The king seems to have accepted Hooper's explanation, that he objected to some aspects of the consecratory rite. Hooper, nevertheless, still had to explain himself to the Council to determine, as he put it, "whether I could justfully and lawfully decline the royal favour."[132] As Hunt rightly observes, those two words "justfully" and

---

130. Hooper, *Early Writings*, 478–79.

131. Sullivan, *John Hooper*, 45.

132. Quoted without citation in Hunt, *The Life and Times of John Hooper*, 118.

"lawfully" cut to the heart of the debate.[133] While the sovereign seems to have been satisfied with Hooper's defense of his actions, Hooper did not help his cause with the Council, Cranmer, and Ridley by the demands he set forth with regard to the consecratory rite after he reversed his initial decision not to serve as a bishop. He insisted there be ""no formal address as 'my lord', no shaving of his long beard, no episcopal white rochet or black chimere, no anointing," etc.[134] Expecting to get his way, Hooper then went on holiday to Somerset to see his father after years apart. Confident as he might have been, however, his refusal to wear the prescribed vestments "quickly inflated into a *cause célèbre*."[135] In the fight to follow there emerged on matters of adiaphora or indifference "sharp differences of opinion among people who, in the central matters of Christian doctrine, held remarkably similar theological positions."[136] In addition to the chief protaganists' many shared theological positions, they would also all be martyred under Edward's sister and successor, Mary Tudor.

Hooper won the debate regarding the oath. On 20 July, when Hooper again was summoned before the king and the Council, Edward VI, "in one of [his] first acts of teenage self-assertion in government," struck the clause about the saints from the rite with his own pen, a testimony to the Protestant convictions of the king.[137] Hooper, already confident, probably felt more emboldened than ever at this point. Yet the matter of the vestments would not prove so easy to resolve. Although Hooper won an initial compromise—according to which he would not be required to wear the prescribed vestments except when preaching at court and those who wanted to wear them could continue doing so—things soon deteriorated. Cranmer and Ridley refused to carry out Hooper's consecration unless he agreed to wear the appointed garments on the grounds that they were adiaphora and prescribed by the duly appointed authorities. Argue all he wanted, they refused to budge, and Ridley made plain that he would under no circumstances consecrate Hooper without the vestments rightly appointed by law by parliament. Ridley had bent the rules here and there for others, such as Robert Farrar and John Bradford, but he saw Hooper's demands as a direct challenge to the God-given authority of the church and the government.[138] Hooper had lost his momentum, and his continued outspokenness on other

133. Ibid., 119.

134. MacCulloch, *Thomas Cranmer*, 472.

135. Steinmetz, *Reformers in the Wings*, 103.

136. Ibid.

137. MacCulloch, *Thomas Cranmer*, 472.

138. Sullivan, *John Hooper*, 50.

matters, especially his controversial doctrine of divorce, only added fuel to the argument of Ridley and Cranmer that Hooper was undermining proper authority and order. This was a heavy charge, given the unrest of 1549 and the persistent fear through Edward's reign of insurrection and disorder.

In the controversy that ensued, most of the continental reformers in England and abroad sided with Hooper's opponents. These included Martin Bucer, Peter Martyr, and even Bullinger. Euler encapsulates Bullinger's involvement well when she writes, "Bullinger's involvement in the Edwardian vestment controversy (June 1550-April 1551) demonstrates simultaneously his reluctance to interfere directly in the affairs of the English church, his dislike of ceremonies not found in the Bible, and his pragmatic application of the doctrine of 'things indifferent.'"[139] Bullinger did not want to undermine his disciple, but he also did not want to derail the Reformation in England. Euler, after noting that Bullinger's letters to Hooper have been unfortunately lost, speculates that his advice to Hooper was the same as that of Bucer and Vermigli, who counseled a more moderate approach to reform. Such things "were *adiaphora*, not inherently evil or condemned by God and, therefore, could be tolerated for reasons of decorum and order."[140] Bullinger and Hooper thus disagreed on the indifferent character of the ceremonies and vestments under debate. This was not because Bullinger thought these things were desireable, but because Bullinger appreciated the benefit of a gradual report and the propriety of the state regulating such matters on the path to a more full reform. Even as Bullinger disagreed with Hooper's pace, then, and his objections to the consecratory vestments in this instance, Hooper nonetheless endeavored to bring the English church and its worship life in line with what he had experienced and what existed under the leadership of Bullinger in Zurich. Euler explains, "Bullinger, along with fellow Reformed theologians Martin Bucer and Peter Martyr Vermigli, supported the right of the king and his bishops to demand conformity to such indifferent ceremonies. It was only once the authority of the king and bishops had evaporated—once there was a Catholic queen in England and hundreds of her evangelical subjects had fled to the Continent, that the ambiguity inherent in the principle of *adiaphora* became a serious problem."[141] Steinmetz aptly summarizes the debate as follows:

> Nicholas Ridley, and those who shared his point of view, regarded these indifferent matters as theologically neutral, as a kind of no-man's-land between the fronts in which there could

139. Euler, *Couriers of the Gospel*, 189.

140. Ibid., 190.

141. Ibid., 202.

be legitimate differences of opinion without endangering the substance of the Christian faith. Hooper and those later Puritan divines who shared his convictions were thoroughly convinced that what is not commanded in Scripture ought not to be instituted in the church.[142]

While Hooper at first admitted that vestments did fall in the category of adiaphora, when pressed by Ridley with the argument that Romans 13 permitted the governing authorities to set standards with respect to their use, he backtracked and essentially rejected the indifferent quality of liturgical adornment and thus found himself at odds with Bullinger's opinion and counsel. As with the Adiaphoristic Controversy in Germany, then, Romans 13 played an important role in determining the place of the state over against the church in general and, more specifically, with regard to liturgical rites and vestments claimed as adiaphora.

On 30 July Hooper was called before the Council again to state his position. At this point Ridley had secretly managed to win the Council to his side outside of the framework of Hooper's official testimony.[143] It was reported to Bullinger by an observer that "many of the council members" at this point "were so convinced by Ridley's arguments 'that they would hardly listen to Hooper's defence, when he came to court shortly after.'"[144] Hooper was indignant. He crafted a written statement of his position which he submitted on 3 October, his "Notes." Ridley responded in writing as well. The Council eventually sided with Ridley and Hooper was put under house arrest, allowed to visit only his opponents or a select few bishops who were tasked with winning him over to Ridley's view. Hooper remained obdurate. On 27 January he was placed in the Fleet prison in London. This development led Hooper to reconsider his approach. He penned two letters of submission, the second accepted by the Council and Cranmer. In that second letter of 15 February 1551 he wrote, "In this matter I have begun so far to look with suspicion on my own judgment and opinion, that I have considered it more prudent and more becoming Christian humility, to stand and rely on the judgment of your clemency, or of those pious and learned men in the law of God whom you may nominate, than of myself alone."[145] Missing from the letter is any statement regarding vestments or confession of error in his teaching regarding them and other indifferent matters.

---

142. Steinmetz, *Reformers in the Wings*, 103.

143. Sullivan, *John Hooper*, 52.

144. Primus, *The Vestments Controversy*, 15.

145. Sullivan, *John Hooper*, 60.

Peace restored, at least superficially, between Hooper, Ridley, and Cranmer, John Hooper became Bishop John Hooper 8 March 1551. He was consecrated by Cranmer, assisted by Ridley, at Lambeth Palace, in the prescribed vestments. Sullivan notes that he was granted one exception, however: "As a man who, like other Continental reformers, viewed his distinctive long beard as a direct response to the tonsure with its Catholic connotations, he was excused the usual head shaving. He refused to 'become a pie,' as he mocking put it later."[146] For all the heat and light in the debate between the two important English bishops, Hooper and Ridley, in death they would die for the same cause, as protagonists of the same Protestant reform in England. Impending martyrdom brought definite reconciliation between the two men and each of the then imprisoned evangelicals would express their wish to each other that such rancor had never developed between them. Moreover, with the temporary divergence in opinion with Bullinger behind him, he set himself in his episcopal office upon the promotion of reform in line with Zurich's and maintained a friendly correspondence with Bullinger until his death under Queen Mary.

146. Ibid., 61.

Chapter 5 ———————————————————————————————————

Hooper's Case against Vestments

5.1. The Background and Nature of Hooper's Sermons on Jonah

ALTHOUGH HOOPER'S SERMONS ON Jonah before King Edward VI, at the king's invitation, had upset Cranmer, Hooper had them published with a dedicatory epistle in *An Oversight and Deliberation upon the Holy Prophet Jonah; Made and Uttered before the King's Majesty, and His Most Honourable Council.*[1] In the dedicatory epistle he set forth clearly his vision for English reform and the intention of the sermons. In what follows, the key themes and arguments of those seven sermons will be investigated, but here it is helpful to address the aforementioned epistle which introduces his sermons. There the core of his theology becomes clear and the influence of Zurich is manifest. Why Jonah? Hooper set forth the reason rather clearly: "The same evil vexes us at this present day. The ship of this commonwealth of England is tossed upside down, and the occasion thereof is imputed and laid unto Christ, and his holy word, though falsely; for Christ's nature is to appease and quiet all troubles and tempests with his presence."[2] Edward needed to steady the ship, but first he had to understand why it was sinking. Hooper planned to explain just that. While his sermons would spark controversy, Newcombe argues that few should have been surprised at what Hooper had to say. He writes:

> Not only were his theological prejudices well known and debated as he himself reported but his views on vestments and oaths had been published in *A declaration of the Ten Holy Commandments*. He made no secret of his intentions when he climbed

1. Hooper, *An Oversight and Deliberation upon the Holy Prophet Johan; Made and Uttered before the King's Majesty, and His Most Honourable Council*, 85–192.

2. Ibid., 112.

into the pulpit in Lent either. He immediately saw Cranmer's approach on 5 February as an opportunity to put forward his programme for the reform of the church at the highest level—whether Cranmer liked it or not.[3]

Hooper launched right into the chief purpose of kings and princes as heads of reformatory work. He wrote, "Among all other most noble and famous deeds of kings and princes, none is more godly, commendable, and profitable to the commonwealth, than to promote and set forth unto their subjects the pure and sincere religion of the eternal God, King of all kings, and Lord of all lords.[4] Throughout the sermons, Hooper advocated a top-down Reformation in keeping with this early assertion. The king was to serve as an example of penitence and faithfulness for his subjects and to see to it that godly bishops, priests, and teachers were appointed for the dioceses, parishes, and schools and universities of his realm. Edward was to complete his father's work, and this is key—Hooper insisted the English Reformation was far from complete. Henry had made "godly and virtuous beginnings," but it fell to Edward to "restore again the true ministry of the church."[5] And this was to be an iconoclastic task. He was to "take away all the monuments, tokens, and leavings of the papistry."[6] The king and his councilors were to take away the "feathers" of the papacy, which were "the altar, vestments, and such like as have appareled her."[7] The goal was nothing short of a "perfect and apostolic reformation," an emphasis throughout the sermons, so that England's church and ministry would be returned "to the primitive and perfect estate again" with it's "doctrine . . . catholic and godly in all things, nothing differing, but agreeing with the prophets and the apostles."[8] Though this was certainly a daunting task for a young king, Edward did not need to fear, Hooper assured him, for "if his religion in his youth be according to God's word, he has the favour and promises of God to bless, preserve and keep his majesty and his realm, though the devil and his members would say nay."[9] To this end, Hooper appealed to the example of Josiah and Joash.

The dangers facing the king's reformation were real and came from two very prominent foes, the devil and his antichrist. From the outset

---

3. Newcombe, *John Hooper*, 121.

4. Hooper, *An Oversight and Deliberation*, 85.

5. Ibid., 88.

6. Ibid.

7. Ibid., 90.

8. Ibid., 88, 91.

9. Ibid., 89.

Hooper set forth the devil's wiles for Edward and his godly magistrates and reformers. First, the devil strove to bring leaders to "utterly neglect the religion of the true God, as a thing foolish and of no estimation, or to provoke them cruelly to persecute it." The people of England were no strangers to such "violence and cruel tyranny of the antichrist" in the past.[10] Second, if this failed, Hooper insisted that the devil would "do the best he can to preserve a mixed and mingled religion." This was certainly how Hooper saw the state of things in the realm at the time, for clerical vestments were a glaring proof of the sorry, mingled state of affairs.[11] The fate of Edward VI's kingdom rested upon his relationship with the true religion of God, for, Hooper asked, "What king or prince of the world would suffer his statutes, laws and testament to be cut off and set on, at every man's liberty and pleasure? Should not the same glory, honour and majesty be given to the laws and testament of Christ, which is sealed with his precious blood?"[12] With the rebellions of the previous year still fresh in the memory of the king and his councilors, these words certainly left an impression, and later in the sermons Hooper would leave no doubt that the best way to avoid rebellion was to teach, admonish, and encourage the people of England with the pure word of God. In the epistle itself he reinforced this point, writing, "It is a foolish opinion, most gracious king, and unfit for a christian man to urge to the magistrates of God, that in case the doctrine of Christ and his holy sacraments should not be decked and set forth with these plausible and well liking ceremonies, (that is, to speak plainly, with papistical superstition,) sedition and tumults were to be feared." Rather, "doubtless if the pope's members would not deceive the people, but teach them God's word, the people would soon see the truth, and willingly leave as much as God and their king should command them."[13]

In short, what was needed to bring England back to God was reformation driven from above, focused upon the inculcation of what Hooper held to be the primitive and apostolic, cognizant of the threats posed by the trappings of the papacy, rooted in the Scriptures alone, modeled after the reigns of the godly Old Testament kings, brought about through leaders—in the court, in the pulpit, and at the lectern. Should Edward and his councilors cling to the word and the example of such kings, the reformation could only succeed. Should they allow any mixing or mingling of the new religion with the old, the true with the false, failure was inevitable. The stakes were clear

10. Ibid., 86.
11. Ibid., 85.
12. Ibid., 86.
13. Ibid., 89–90.

as well: salvation or damnation, first for the king and those he appointed to lead in the state and the church, and second for his subjects.

Having surveyed the epistle, then, it serves well at this point to look in more depth into some of the key themes of Hooper's sermons. It is important to note that the sermons sometimes wander and that each does not directly build on the other. Throughout the dedication and seven sermons, though, certain key themes and emphases become evident. A survey of Hooper's concern for apostolic, primitive simplicity in the church and its services will follow first. Attendant with this concern was his fear of and stern opposition toward what he deemed the traditions and ceremonies of men and the devil. Hooper pinned the failure to remove any and all of the same on current bishops and priests, and throughout his sermons, he vilified many of the bishops and priests of the land and used them as foils. Second, Hooper's use of the Old Testament, including his conception of Edward VI as a new Josiah, will be explored. Third, the relationship between obedience to the king and obedience to God in Hooper's thought deserves careful attention, as well as the role of the king in godly reform. It serves well to briefly outline here as well his utter detestation for rebellion and disorder in the land, which ultimately led him to support even Mary's accession to the throne. Fourth, consideration will be given to Hooper's treatment of the cross and affliction.

5.2. The Apostolic and Primitive

Hooper began the fifth sermon in the Jonah series with the following words: "Let the bishops and priests beware they go not about to try to please God with masses, diriges, pardons, rites, and ceremonies invented by men."[14] It is safe to say that in Hooper's view the apostolic and primitive were associated with liturgical, decorative, and architectural simplicity. Hooper wrote in "The Epistle Dedicatory" of his collection of sermons, in which he assigned to Edward VI the task of finishing what Henry had begun, "And a thousand times the rather shall your majesty restore again the true ministry of the church, in case you remove and take away all the monuments, tokens, and leavings of the papistry; for as long as any of them remain, there remains also an occasion of relapse unto the abolished

14. Hooper, "The Fifth Sermon upon Jonah," in *An Oversight and Deliberation upon the Holy Prophet Jonah; Made and Uttered before the King's Majesty, and His Most Honourable Council*, in *Writings of Dr. John Hooper, Bishop of Gloucester and Worcester, martyr, 1555*, 146. Hereafter I will refer to each sermon, as well as the "Epistle Dedicatory," according to their individual titles within this larger work, to help the reader gain a sense for connections or distinctions between the individual sermons on Jonah.

superstition of the antichrist."[15] Certainly a number of these "monuments, tokens, and leavings" were liturgical furnishings, practices, vestments, and customs which many Lutheran churches had retained, even Magdeburg. Nevertheless, in Hooper's opinion, such things, because there was no biblical prescriptive mandate for or descriptive mention of their use by the apostles, were irredeemable, inextricably tied to antichristian papal practice. What was truly "catholic and godly" was that "agreeing with the prophets and the apostles." Hooper declared himself "according to my bounden duty, ready at all times to make an answer, if anything shall be attempted to the contrary."[16] This goal was not unattainable, either, an ideal never realized in Christian worship or never to be realized until Christ's return and heaven's glory. Hooper maintained that Christian worship had once been perfect, and he makes plain when that was: in the apostolic period, as Hooper knew it through the Scriptures. He continued, "Help therefore, O ye bishops and priests, the proceedings of the king's majesty and his noble council, that all things may be brought to a perfect and apostolic reformation."[17] What did this perfect and apostolic reformation look like? It looked like what had been undertaken in Zurich. Zwingli and Bullinger's influence was evident in such seemingly innocuous statements as the his call for the English to "embrace only Christ and his doctrine, and worship God in spirit and in truth, as his word teaches."[18]

In connection with a concern for apostolic simplicity in demeanor and practice, a Zwinglian dichotomy between spirit and flesh pervaded Hooper's view of the place and purpose of the Lord's Supper in the Christian Church and its services. His appeal to simplicity was rooted in the notion that the spirit and flesh could, at least to some extent, be equated with the spiritual and material, so that material adornment, and indeed, even the real presence as taught by Lutherans, obfuscated the true nature of communion and misrepresented its role. He focused squarely on man's activity in the sacraments, not God's. He devoted a good deal of time to this activity of man in his sixth sermon. As an example, he noted that the Israelites ate the Paschal lamb standing, but that Christ ate it sitting, so that the emphasis now should now be on careful contemplation and solicitude on the part of its recipients. Hooper asserted in his sixth sermon that "we must therefore lift up our minds to heaven . . . and there by faith apprehend and receive the

15. Hooper, "Epistle Dedicatory," 88.

16. Ibid., 91.

17. Ibid., 88.

18. Hooper, "Third Sermon upon Jonah," 117.

body of Christ"?[19] Man, not God, then, had to bridge the gap between the spirit and the flesh, the spiritual and the material. This tension between the spiritual and the material also evidenced itself when he warned against false hope or ill-placed trust. He included in his list of things in which peope ought not place trust the bread and wine of the Lord's Supper. He wrote, "So do the true christians at this day; in beholding the mercy of God in Christ, they behold and wonder at the fond and false hope, help and trust, that men put in vanity, error, and forbidden help of the mass, water, bread, salt, bowing, candles, pardons and such like."[20] His list included a number of elements retained and held in high regard in many Lutheran territorial churches in Germany, both in Luther's day and well beyond it, things about which Flacius would have found little reason to raise objections. He rejected other practices retained in German Lutheranism when he wrote, "No scripture of God, neither doctor of the catholic faith, ever taught that Christ was to be honoured here on earth with candles and bowing of knees."[21] This is a fine example of Hooper's approach toward potentially indifferent practices. Hooper saw no explicit command in Scripture for the bowing of knees in Christian worship services and his rejection of the real presence ensured that he would accept no bowing of the knee in connection with the sacrament as a bowing before Jesus.

Ultimately, such practices were exactly the sort that convinced Hooper that the Lutheran Reformation and the Henrician Reformation, influenced by the Lutheran theology of several of its key theologians and spokesmen, were incomplete. Hooper was willing to admit no more of the two sacraments, baptism and the Lord's Supper, than that "both these teach and confirm no other thing than that the mercy of God saves the faithful and believers."[22] The bread was the body of Christ and the wine the blood of Christ only in so far as the bread and wine served as "seals" of God's promises and nothing was to be taught in that regard beyond the "plain and simple doctrine of the sacraments" unencumbered by the "malice of men" or superstition and papistry.[23] Like Zwingli, he insisted that the body of Christ can be in only one place, rejecting the notion of ubiquity, and warned that belief in the corporeal presence of Christ lends itself to idolatry, from which true reformation ought to free people.[24] Hooper argued, "If Christ were

19. Hooper, "The Sixth Sermon upon Jonah," 166.

20. Hooper, "The Fourth Sermon upon Jonah," 143.

21. Hooper, "The Fifth Sermon upon Jonah," 161.

22. Ibid., 155.

23. Ibid.

24. Ibid., 156.

here in the sacrament bodily and corporeally, he should every day suffer and shed his precious blood." Why? Hooper took the present tense as necessarily ongoing, answering, "Scripture saith, This is my body that is broken for you, and my blood that is shed for you."[25]

Hooper was unable, or perhaps unwilling to concede there could be any real presence of Christ in the sacrament unladen with all the sacrificial theology of Rome's transubstantiation. He thus devoted a great deal of his fifth sermon to his Zwinglian doctrine of the Lord's Supper, as well as the bulk of the sixth sermon. Hooper saw any vestige of a substantial presence of Christ in the sacrament as a failure to reform the church in a satisfactory or meaningful manner. While Flacius would lament the undoing of a reformation, Hooper bemoaned the failure to bring a reformation to full blossom. Flacius wanted an Elijah, or Elijahs, who would preserve God's remnant. Hooper wanted a Josiah to reform God's kingdom. He challenged the king and Council, therefore, "Gracious king, and my lords of the council, remember this doctrine of Jonah, and then you need not fear to reform this church of England unto the primitive state and apostolic doctrine."[26] In this way, he promised, the people of the land "would not take armour and weapons against the magistrates, but see help from God."[27]

Although Edward was by all accounts impressed, some in power clearly did not share Hooper's zeal. Even Edward must have recognized, though, as did a number of his councilors and bishops, that it would be imprudent to proceed too quickly or too slowly, in too wholesale or too haphazard a fashion. Yet this is what Hooper seemed to advocate in parts of his sermons. The caution of Edward and others flowed, not out of a lack of theological conviction or even disagreement with Hooper's basic sentiments, but rather for fear of rebellion—an understandable fear given the political climate and the tumult of the previous years. Hooper forthrightly rebuffed such a train of thought, though, and countered that rebellion should be feared, not on account of the prohibition of ceremonies which lacked apostolic simplicity, but rather because of their continued use. He wrote, "It is a foolish opinion, most gracious king, and unfit for a christian man to urge to the magistrates of God, that in case the doctrine of Christ and his holy sacraments should not be decked and set forth with these plausible and well liking ceremonies (that is, to speak plainly, with papistical superstition,) sedition and tumults were to be feared."[28]

25. Ibid., 157.
26. Hooper, "The Fourth Sermon upon Jonah," 144.
27. Ibid.
28. Hooper, "Epistle Dedicatory," 89–90.

Catechesis was Hooper's answer to the fear of tumult: "Doubtless if the pope's members would not deceive the people, but teach them God's word, the people would soon see the truth, and willingly leave as much as God should command them."[29] It was misleading and confusing to allow the old forms to remain while introducing new, or apostolic, doctrine. Such a reformation, as the Reformed would charge the Lutherans on the continent, was unfinished, and people were much more likely to act out of line with the scriptural doctrine of obedience to those in authority if they weren't properly grounded as clearly as possible in word and deed. It was the Scriptures, after all, which inculcated proper deference to duly constituted authority in Christian citizens. Hooper argued, "The bishops and priests disquiet the ship of this realm in two ways, one by neglecting their true duty, the other by a defence of a false and damnable superstition. In the primitive and apostolic church, the office of a bishop and priest was to teach in the congregation of the faithful the doctrine of the prophets and apostles, according to the commandment of Christ."[30] He echoed this theme again in the third sermon, writing of priests and bishops that "their office in the primitive and first church was to be preachers of God's word, and ministers of Christ's sacraments," on account of which he insisted university reform must go hand-in-hand with the reform of English pulpits. As in the parish, so in the university; those unwilling to serve in accord with the primitive example and without the traditional trappings were to be threatened and, if necessary, removed. In his fifth sermon, he reinforced this thought, "And this is the mark thou shouldest know a priest and bishop by; by his tongue, that soundeth the word of the Lord, and not by his cap or outward vesture." Hooper warned the king and his advisors not to let worldly sympathy get in their way in this regard. He counseled, "And beware of the ungodly pity wherewith all men for the most part are very much now-a-days cumbered, who will for pity rather let a fool or an evil man enjoy his benefice, than care that a thousand souls be brought to knowledge: this is no pity, but rather cruelty and destroying of the soul."[31] Rather, only he who "uses himself according to is vocation" should remain, whether they be bishops, priests, or other church workers.[32] Hooper was blunt: "In case they will not amend, into the sea with them! Put them out of their offices, and put better in."[33]

---

29. Ibid., 90.

30. Hooper, "The Second Sermon upon Jonah," 108.

31. Hooper, "The Third Sermon upon Jonah," 126.

32. Ibid.

33. Ibid.

Hooper did not hide the real danger to England that he perceived in allowing woeful neglect of the ministerial office by pastors and professors to continue. He alerted, "When godly kings and magistrates require and command a reformation of these evils, the ministry of the church is contemned with such false slanders, that the ignorant people will do more for the bishops and priests of Baal than for God, for God's word, or his anointed magistrate, as appeared last summer."[34] Unfit clergy were a constant destabilizing force, and none more so than the priest who held to the old traditions, whether doctrines, rites, vestments, or furnishings. Hooper wrote, "The bishops, priests, and others hinder this study and knowledge of God's law in princes and kings," undermining, not only the faith of those princes and kings in so doing, but of the entire land, so that those in power "persecute the truth and verity by ignorance, as the kings of Israel did who burned the writings of the prophets."[35] The king could spare no energy or care in examining those of his court and chapel, therefore, and what was true in the court and the parish was true in the household as well. Hooper counseled, "Even thus, as the king's majesty must do in his realm, so should every man do in his own household . . . he must diligently search whether there are any Jonahs within his house."[36]

It is helpful to observe again here that Hooper included liturgical practice and decorum within "the doctrine of the prophets and apostles" and his reference to the commandment of Christ once again rooted what he considered appropriate worship practices in a clear command from Jesus. Any addition to the ceremonies Christ has instituted, even ever so slight, was a step away from Christ and toward disorder, rather than an attempt to maintain order, as his opponents would argue. Hooper insisted, "Most gracious king and noble counsellors, as you have taken away the mass from the people, so take from them its feathers also, the altar, vestments, and such like as have apparelled her." Importantly, these feathers were not to be removed on strictly doctrinal grounds, that is, because they explicitly *taught* something, nor were they to be removed because they had not been put in place by the proper authorities—such practices continued under the auspices of the properly constituted church and state authorities of the realm—but rather because Christ had not commanded the use of such trappings and the Gospels did not mention their use. Hooper excluded any practice not endorsed by Christ in connection with preaching and the sacraments.

34. Hooper, "The Second Sermon upon Jonah," 109.
35. Hooper, "The Sixth Sermon upon Jonah," 175.
36. Hooper, "The Third Sermon upon Jonah," 127.

They were doctrinally unacceptable, but this was even though, in and of themselves, they might not have any inherently doctrinal connotation.

Here another difference between Hooper and Flacius becomes apparent. Whereas Flacius rejected the surplice because the emperor commanded it as part of a campaign of counter-reformation, Hooper objected to such vestments in and of themselves, because they were inconsistent with apostolic simplicity and lacked a divine mandate or clear New Testament precedent. He wrote in general terms, "No man should think any holiness to be in the external vestment, nor yet any hurt or condemnation in the meat; but the abuse of both displeases both." He then immediately trained his sights on priestly vesture: "As for the vestments of the priest in the ministry, I would wish the magistrate would remove them, for they either show or do not show virtue. If they show not, they use them in vain . . . . If he that wears them has the virtue, why does he show it to the world? If he has not the virtue, then he is a hypocrite, whom God hateth."[37] Hooper insisted, "Let the holy communion be decked with the holy ceremonies with which the high and wise priest Christ, decked and apparelled it first of all."[38] Hooper's rule was clear. Nothing was to be added to that which Christ had instituted, not only doctrinally, but liturgically as well, even if those liturgical additions were construed by some to serve to reinforce biblical doctrine. Hooper considered a break with the late antique and medieval necessary for a return to the apostolic.

Demanding a New Testament command or precedent for liturgical practice in English churches, Hooper countenanced no appeal to the Old Testament for liturgical precedents, whether with respect to altars, vestments, or other practices. While Reformed theology, like Lutheran theology, taught that the Old Testament Mosaic Law had been abrogated, Hooper also denied that any models or examples for New Testament worship forms could be drawn from Old Testament practices. He would have the English kings rule according to the model of the godly kings of Judah and Israel, but he would not have English clergy ministry according to the example of the priests of God's Old Testament people. In one of the most controversial lines of his sermons which earned him Cranmer's ire, Hooper exclaimed that there must be absolutely no place in Edward VI's kingdom for "the use of such vestments as obscure the ministry of Christ's church, and represent the form and fashion of the Aaronical ministry of the old law, abrogated and ended in Christ."[39] Nor was there any excuse for ministers who wished to

37. Hooper, "The Sixth Sermon upon Jonah," 176.
38. Hooper, "Epistle Dedicatory," 90.
39. Hooper, "The Seventh Sermon upon Jonah," 188.

persist in the same, for there were serious consequences for such liturgical obstinacy: "If they will not be desirous and glad to have, and to help the ministry of the church to the primitive and perfect estate again, the Lord proclaims vengeance towards them, and will not only require the loss of themselves, but also of all the people at their hands."[40] The practices of the church were perfect in Hooper's mind in so far as Christ prescribed and the apostles described them. Anything not so prescribed and described was corruption, and as stubborn Jonah threatened to sink the whole ship, so also stubborn priests who clung to superstition rites, clothing, and furniture threatened to sink the entire realm. The king therefore needed to act swiftly and deliberately in such instances. Hooper wrote, "If these threatenings will not amend them, then, gracious king, an you, my honourable lords of his high council, must do with them as the mariners did with Jonah."[41]

Altars particularly drew Hooper's ire in his fourth sermon. He insisted, "Seeing christians have no other sacrifices than these [namely, thanksgiving, benevolence, and the mortification of our bodies and death unto sin], which may and ought to be done without altars, then should there be no altars among christians." Moreover, "It was not without great wisdom and knowledge of God, that Christ, his apostles, and the primitive church were without altars for they knew that the use of altars was taken away."[42] He advised the king, "It were well then that it might please the magistrates to turn the altars into tables"—to alter the altars—"according to the first institution of Christ." Once again, it was not that Christ explicitly forbade altars, nor that we are told in the Gospels that there was no altar in the upper room, but rather because Christ did not command an altar and the Evangelists' record does not include one. The removal of the altars was especially important "to take away the false persuasion of the people which they have of the sacrifices to be done upon the altars."[43] Here Hooper, like Flacius, objected to a practice that brought with it doctrinal baggage, in this case, the notion of the sacrifice of the mass. While Flacius did not campaign against altars, and he certainly did not think it impossible for the altar to symbolize or remind the Christian of Christ's sacrifice for us, there was a shared concern in this regard, that adiaphora ought not lead the people back into papal superstition. Hooper continued, "For as long as the altars remain, the ignorant people, and the ignorant and evil-persuaded priest, will always dream

40. Hooper, "Epistle Dedicatory," 91.
41. Ibid.
42. Hooper, "The Fourth Sermon upon Jonah," 133.
43. Ibid.

of sacrifice."[44] The altars thus fall under Hooper's classification of "monuments and tokens of idolatry and superstition."[45] What mattered once again was the spiritual. "Prayer," Hooper argued, "said at the high altar" was no "better than that which is said at the choir," nor was that said at the choir better than that said "in the body of the church," or anywhere else for that matter.[46] After all, "The Lord hath no respect to the place, but unto the heart and faith of him that prayeth," whether he be in a cave of lions like Daniel, a clay-pit like Jeremiah, or upon a cross like the thief next to Jesus.[47] The altar served as nothing more than a boundary, then, "as though the veil and partition of the temple in the old law yet should remain in the church."[48] Everything, rather, was to be done as it was "in the primitive church," untainted by the doctrine and practice of the papacy and it abominations.[49] As has been noted, Hooper campaigned in this way against practices *allowed* in the Church of England, already a Protestant church body, and argued for the coercive removal of such practices, rather than, as did Flacius, against the reintroduction of practices by force through political means.

Hooper's call for liturgical reform and a Reformed theology of the sacraments reached a fevered pitch and he delivered a flurry of Old Testament examples in the second half of his seventh and final sermon in the series. Here Hooper conceded to the magistrates the ability to set certain days to eat fish, but only for economic reasons, to encourage the fisheries.[50] There, for all practical purposes, ended his willingness to countenance the retention of the special days, practices, vestments, and diets of the church under the papacy. He complained about crucifixes as "hangings of God's wounds, his flesh and his blood."[51] He listed a variety of things that needed to be abolished: "images; forbidding of marriage in Lent; the use of such vestments as obscure the ministry of Christ's church." This essentially embraced any and all of the mass vestments, because they "represent the form and fashion of the Aaronical ministry of the old law, abrogated and ended in Christ."[52] Here arises another difference between Hooper and Flacius. Flacius advocated for the preservation of Christian freedom in the face of the

---

44. Ibid.
45. Ibid.
46. Ibid., 136.
47. Ibid.
48. Ibid.
49. Ibid., 136–37.
50. Hooper, "The Seventh Sermon upon Jonah," 188.
51. Hooper, "The Third Sermon upon Jonah," 128.
52. Hooper, "The Seventh Sermon upon Jonah," 188.

restrictions and burdens of old papal and new imperial law. Hooper wanted the king to restrict the range of practices permitted within the churches of England. Flacius wanted pastors freed from imperial compulsion. Hooper wanted Edward to move pastors to adopt the theology and practice of the Swiss Reformation by means of it.[53] Citing the work of Jehoshaphat in removing idolatry and false religion from his Old Testament realm, Hooper essentially commanded his king, "All these things you must do, most gracious king, and you, my honourable lords of his high and wise council, if you will live in peace and quietness."[54] Edward simply had to "remove all these things, that are either the devil's or man's invention."[55] Such a course of action would not go without fruit. In addition to peace at home, Hooper promised, "If your majesty do these things . . . God shall make you a fear and terror to foreign and strange nations that know not the living God."[56]

5.3. The Old Testament

Hooper appealed throughout his writings to the Old Testament, both for precedent and illustrations. He paid particular attention to King Josiah. 2 Kings introduces Josiah to its readers in its twenty-second chapter: "Josiah was eight years old when he began to reign, and he reigned thirty-one years in Jerusalem. His mother's name was Jedidah the daughter of Adaiah of Bozkath. And he did what was right in the eyes of the Lord and walked in all the way of David his father, and he did not turn aside to the right or to the left."[57] The writer then details Josiah's restoration of the temple, which had been neglected and fallen into disrepair. Moreover, and most importantly, during Josiah's reign, a priest named Hilkiah rediscovered the Book of the Law. The king thus became aware of just how far the religion of his realm had strayed from the true religion of David. He tore his clothes when the book was read and set himself immediately upon a program of reform. He commanded his priests, "Go, inquire of the Lord for me, and for the people, and for all Judah, concerning the words of this book that has been found. For great is the wrath of the Lord that is kindled against us, because our fathers have not obeyed the words of this book, to do according to all that is written concerning us."[58] Josiah later read the Book of the Law to the people

53. Ibid., 190.
54. Ibid.
55. Ibid., 191.
56. Ibid.
57. 1 Kgs 22:1, 2 ESV.
58. 1 Kgs 22:13 ESV.

of his kingdom pledged himself to it, devoting every effort to the reform of the land. He broke altars and defiled high places, removed idols and burned chariots, removing any religious purity from his realm. He also restored the Passover and the temple services were brought in line with the commands of God, any additions of men cast aside.

It is understandable that Josiah came to mind, therefore, when Hooper considered the young king in whose presence he had been invited to preach. From the outset, Hooper's argumentation abounded with examples of Old Testament kings, both good and bad, godly and ungodly, and yet preeminent among them was Josiah. As Diarmaid MacCulloch has made clear, Hooper was hardly the only evangelical voice making comparisons or pointing to the example of Josiah—MacCulloch devotes one of the four parts that constitute his monograph on the Boy King to the theme—and yet Josiah did figure prominently in Hooper's sermons on Jonah.[59] After warning the king against "the diabolical sounds and speakings" of those who would doubt the ability of a young king to accomplish early and meaningful reform, Hooper wrote, "For those men's foolishness, or rather I should say their malice, is condemned by the word of God, which teaches how a king in his young age, with his wise and godly council, should abolish idolatry, and set forth the true and godly religion of the living God."[60] Certainly no king better exemplified this than Josiah, and so Hooper was quick to set forth Josiah's reforming work as the pattern for that which Edward VI ought to undertake. Hooper praised the young Old Testament king's destruction of the idols of his father and others in his realm, the link to his own iconoclasm obvious. He wrote, "Thus declares the notable and godly of Josiah, who followed the religion of father, not Amon the idolater, but of David, declining not to the right hand, neither to the left hand: and destroyed not only the images of his father, but also those of Jeroboam and of Solomon."[61] King Edward needed not go it alone, however. Rather, as Josiah was helped by his counselors in his reformation of religion, so also the English king was to surround himself with wise councilors of the true religion, and indeed he already had some such in his midst—hence, Hooper's invitation to preach. In addition, like Josiah, Edward needed godly bishops and priests, who neither defended error nor grew tired in upholding the truth. As Josiah commanded faithfulness from his priests, and removed those who refused the same, so Edward needed to take care to ensure the capability, orthodoxy, and zeal of the clergy in his realm.

59. MacCulloch, *The Boy King*, 57–104.

60. Hooper, "Epistle Dedicatory," 87.

61. Ibid.

Josiah was not the only king whose faithfulness and reforming zeal Edward should emulate. Joash also was a young king who was helped by his councilors in order to reform the religion of his land. His reign reinforced for Hooper the importance of "godly counsellors and virtuous priests." Hooper explained, "In case the princes, bishops, and priest, had not know it to be the commandment of God to have obeyed these two young and godly kings, they would not have consented unto his proceedings"[62] Contrary to the priests and bishops causing tumult in England through their stubborn adherence to the traditions of men, Hooper held up the example of the counselors and bishops who served Joash and other godly kings, He wrote, "The princes and counsellors moved no sedition; the bishops and the priests sought not for the defence of their doctrine, nor to mingle theirs with God's, but were content with the sole and only law of God."[63] Jehoshaphat also provided a positive example in this regard. Hooper wrote, "Jehoshaphat, before he could bring his commonwealth to any good point, restored good judges to the civil estate of his realm, and true teachers to the ecclesiastical state of the realm."[64] Here again Hooper's Zwinglian conception of the relationship between church and state is evident, as well as how at home he was within the arrangement achieved with Henry's Act of Supremacy, according to which the king operated as the head of both church and state, appointing leaders in both spheres. Hooper returned to Jehoshaphat in his final sermon on Jonah. He noted:

> First, he took away and removed idolatry from the people; secondly, he gave them true judges, whose godly conditions are written in the same book, (chap. xix.) who feared the Lord and accepted no persons in judgment, and they received no bribes nor rewards thirdly, he placed and appointed priests, not in one place, but in all cities of Judah; and not that they should play and pastime, and teach every thing but the law of God.[65]

Lest the king receive this as anything but a program for reform in England, Hooper added, "All these things must you do, most gracious king, and you, my honourable lords of his high and wise council, if you will live in peace and quietness."[66] He challenged the king and his councilors, "And first of all, because there is no man that sinneth not, look first unto yourselves, and then, with the king of Nineveh, and the nobles of his realm, repent ye, and

62. Ibid.

63. Ibid.

64. Hooper, "The Third Sermon upon Jonah," 128.

65. Hooper, "The Seventh Sermon upon Jonah," 190.

66. Ibid.

restore unto God that which is God's, and unto man that which is for the comfort of our subjects—good laws and diligent execution of the same."[67]

The Old Testament King Manasseh appeared as a warning in Hooper's preaching. He too began his reign in his youth, at twelve years of age, and yet his rule took the opposite tact of Josiah's. Manasseh was the son of the godly king Hezekiah, who serves as a model of repentance as repentance is described by Hooper. Manasseh failed to follow his father's example, though, and his unfaithfulness resulted in more than personal consequences. As a king, his sin and his toleration of sin in his realm became the undoing of his kingdom as well. 2 Kings 21 relates:

> And the Lord said by his servants the prophets, "Because Manasseh king of Judah has committed these abominations and has done things more evil than all that the Amorites did, who were before him, and has made Judah also to sin with his idols, therefore thus says the Lord, the God of Israel: Behold, I am bringing upon Jerusalem and Judah such disaster that the ears of everyone who hears of it will tingle. And I will stretch over Jerusalem the measuring line of Samaria, and the plumb line of the house of Ahab, and I will wipe Jerusalem as one wipes a dish, wiping it and turning it upside down. And I will forsake the remnant of my heritage and give them into the hand of their enemies, and they shall become a prey and a spoil to all their enemies, because they have done what is evil in my sight and have provoked me to anger, since the day their fathers came out of Egypt, even to this day."[68]

According to Hooper, this was the danger that faced England. Even the faithful were at risk. Edward VI's religious convictions, practices, and policies could bring God's judgment upon many more than the few in political power; it would shower down upon the whole land. Hooper wrote, "Manasseh, being twelve years old, was crowned king, and in his youth again established the idolatry that his father Hezekiah had abolished, and by his so doing heinously displeased the majesty of God, and at length was sorely afflicted and punished for so doing." In case the king might not draw the proper conclusion, Hooper added, "Behold the displeasure of God to a young king for a false religion."[69]

Jehoiachin was another king crowned young—at eight years of age. He too served as a cautionary example. Taken captive by the king of

67. Ibid.

68. 2 Kgs 21:10–15 ESV.

69. Hooper, "Epistle Dedicatory," 89.

Babylon for his failure to uphold true religion in the kingdom, his wickedness also resulted in the plundering of the sacred vessels of the temple as
well. Hooper warned, "This king ruled but three months and ten days,
before the Lord punished the false doctrine he maintained."[70] Hooper emphasized the lesson Edward VI must learn from such examples: "These
examples I doubt not, most godly king and virtuous counsellors, move
you to be careful of the true religion. The Lord hath strength and power
enough, seek ye him, and give no place to the infirm persuasions of the
flesh, for the Lord shall be with you."[71]

Not only Jewish kings served a paradigmatic role for Hooper, however.
The king of Nineveh also provided an example worthy of imitation. England
was threatened no less than Nineveh. Hooper wrote, "Further, the love I
bear unto the king's majesty and to this commonwealth of England, compels
me to speak; for I see the angry hand of God already stretched forth to punish us, if we awake not out of sin."[72] Hooper warned that the English must
neither "deny our sin with Cain" nor "extenuate and excuse it with Saul."[73]
Hooper stressed that the people of Nineveh did not take Jonah's message
to heart and repent until they saw the king's example, as well as that of the
priests and elders of the city.[74] Moreover, it was the king and the nobles who
led the religious reformation of the city: "In these persons first note, that
the king's officers, and the peers of the realm, are to cleanse their commonwealth from false religion by public and open proclamations."[75] The king of
Nineveh and his nobles were hardly the only Gentile kings to act in such a
way. Hooper cited the examples of Nebuchadnezzar, Darius, and Cyrus as
well.[76] He thus challenged King Edward, "And so, I doubt not, most gracious
king, but your highness will, according to your title and style, cleanse this
church of England to the purity and sincerity of God's word."[77]

At this point, Hooper launched into a long digression upon the
sacraments and idolatry, arguing that the two are connected—a supersti-
tious view of the sacraments and idolatry—through ignorance of God's
Word. He warned, "Ignorance . . . brings idolatry, idolatry brings eternal
damnation, eternal damnation comes not only to the ignorant, but also

70. Ibid.

71. Ibid.

72. Hooper, "The Third Sermon upon Jonah," 116.

73. Ibid.

74. Hooper, "The Fifth Sermon upon Jonah," 154.

75. Hooper, "The Sixth Sermon upon Jonah," 176–77.

76. Ibid., 177.

77. Ibid.

unto him that should in his vocation (or do his good will to remove) the ignorance."[78] There is, therefore, nothing better a king could do than to see to it that his people were well instructed in the Christian faith, free of idolatry, and penitent for their sins. Essential to this was the king's own continued instruction in the word and diligence in the instruction of the members of his court. Hooper counseled, "Your majesty shall do best to follow this godly king of the Ninevites, and embrace continually the word of the living God; and thus shall your grace be better able to do, in case your highness would have before you every Sunday one sermon, which should bring much knowledge and grace into your highness' court."[79] Nor should Edward put on airs when it came to repentance and his standing before God. Repentance knew neither king nor subject, but only sinners: "Of this we learn, that in faith and true repentance there is no diversity between the king and a mean subject: and thus shall it be at the latter judgment."[80] This was part of the problem with vestments, Hooper thought; they gave the impression of inequality before God. "Yet no man should think any holiness to be in the external vestment," He warned. Thus, King Edward was to cleanse his kingdom by the example of his own penitence, religious proclamations and the removal of vestments and idols, amendment of life, and trust in God's mercy.[81] In closing his sixth sermon, Hooper summed up his argument regarding the king of Nineveh: "Here princes may learn what proclamations they should make in setting forth religion, even such only as extend to the glory and mercy of God in Christ."[82]

Hooper concluded his seventh sermon with a litany of paradigmatic Old Testament kings. This only reinforced the fact that the Old Testament defined Hooper's conception of a godly ruler—one was a king in the type of Josiah and the godly rulers of Judah and Israel or no Christian king at all, a danger to the commonwealth and the church. It was with the godly kings of Israel and Judah in mind, after all, that he began the dedicatory epistle with a job description for a good king, delivered directly to Edward VI. He left no doubt about what was at the top of the list. He wrote, "Among all other most noble and famous deeds of kings and princes, none is more godly, commendable, and profitable to the commonwealth, than to promote and set forth unto their subjects the pure and sincere religion of the eternal

78. Hooper, "The Fifth Sermon upon Jonah," 156.

79. Hooper, "The Sixth Sermon upon Jonah," 175–76.

80. Ibid., 176.

81. Ibid., 177.

82. Ibid., 180.

God, King of all kings, and Lord of all lords."[83] He added elsewhere, "It is the office of the king's majesty, his council, and all his magistrates, to see that the true book of God, the holy Bible, be taught and received of his majesty's subjects, after the example of Moses, Joshua, David, Jehoshaphat, Hezekiah, and Josiah, the noble princes of God's people."[84] Moses and Joshua were included here because, though they were prophets and not kings, they were secular as well as spiritual leaders of God's people with responsibilities with respect to the civil and ceremonial law of Israel. Hooper also made plain that, should a king neglect this task, everything else would fail. Only if a king obeyed God "shall justice, peace, and concord reign."[85] Yet Hooper warned, this was no easy task. The devil did not rest and sought to undermine godly rule in one of two ways. First, he endeavored to bring about neglect of the Christian faith and right worship. Second, he stoked persecution. If both strategies failed, he did his best to make the religion of the land mixed or mingled, or "adulterated" as Flacius so often put it in his writings. Such mingled religion became a stew of God's truth and man's superstitions and inventions. To illustrate this and its disastrous results, Hooper used the example of Jehu. He wrote, "Jehu the king of the Israelites, when he had removed all gross and open idolatry; and with the sword had taken away all the idolatrous priests, 2 Kings x., is reproved of God nevertheless, because he walked not in the law of God with all his heart and left not the ways Jeroboam."[86] Jeroboam had also famously mingled the religion of his kingdom, the Northern Kingdom, and quite purposefully so. 1 Kings 12 recalls both Jeroboam's sin and motivation:

> And Jeroboam said in his heart, "Now the kingdom will turn back to the house of David. If this people go up to offer sacrifices in the temple of the Lord at Jerusalem, then the heart of this people will turn again to their lord, to Rehoboam king of Judah, and they will kill me and return to Rehoboam king of Judah." So the king took counsel and made two calves of gold. And he said to the people, "You have gone up to Jerusalem long enough. Behold your gods, O Israel, who brought you up out of the land of Egypt." [87]

An incomplete reformation was no reformation at all. God's wrath would not be stayed by half-measures.

83. Hooper, "Epistle Dedicatory," 85.
84. Hooper, "The Second Sermon upon Jonah," 106.
85. Hooper, "Epistle Dedicatory," 85.
86. Ibid., 85–86.
87. 1 Kgs 12:26–28 ESV.

While Hooper urged Edward VI to rule in the mold of an Old Testament king, employing the Old Testament in a different manner and yet in a meaningful way like Flacius, he did not make use of church history as extensively as Flacius. One reason is no doubt that the early church provides few examples of godly kings but many of a persecuted remnant, which was Flacius' focus. One might suspect that Hooper would have made use of post-Constantinian emperors, but that was not the case. Ultimately, Polycarp was one of perhaps a handful of early church figures to make his way into Hooper's sermons. Hooper used the saint's refusal to swear by Caesar as evidence that swearing by the saints should be removed from the rites of the Church of England. He wrote, "Polycarp rather suffered the flames of fire, than swear by Caesar's fortune."[88] Outside of a very few examples like these, the apostolic and primitive in Hooper's preaching served more as an idea than a well of examples, especially since Hooper's argument hinged on what the apostolic church *did not do* in its services. Whereas Flacius searched the New Testament and church history for examples of what the apostles and Christians of past ages did do, Hooper cited a lack of precedent for a practice in the New Testament or church history as part of his argument about what the church of his day should not do.

5.4. Church, State, and Obedience

Perhaps nowhere is a divergence between Flacius and Hooper so clear as in their conceptions of the relationship between church and state. While Flacius and the Magdeburgers defended the right of a lesser magistrate to come to the defense of his subjects in the Adiaphoristic Controversy, Hooper wanted nothing to do with disobedience or rebellion of any sort, as evidenced in his support of Queen Mary's succession to the English throne. This is significant because historians have associated Reformed theologians with resistance theories and Lutherans with near unconditional obedience of authority. In these two controversies over adiaphora, however, we see exactly the opposite at play. Hooper spoke to those in power and called for a reformation from above. Flacius called for a defense of the reformation from below—certainly not, to be sure, with a call to arms for every citizen, but rather through popularly constituted authority of the lesser magistrate. Hooper called King Edward to obedience, invited by the king to preach. He wanted him to serve as a Josiah. Flacius called for disobedience to the emperor, certainly without the emperor's

88. Hooper, "The Third Sermon upon Jonah," 124.

invitation or support. He wanted troublers of Israels, Elijahs to emerge from among Germany's Lutheran pastors.

Hooper set forth the proper relationship between church and state in his fifth sermon:

> It is not the office of the bishop to play the king and lord, nor the king's part to play the bishop. For the king's office is enough for a king, and the bishop's office enough for a bishop. Let them do they best they can, and study each of them in their office. But let the king take heed to be able to judge whether the bishop do true service to God in his vocation by the word of God: and let the bishop do the same; let him take heed whether the king or council command him to do any thing contrary to his vocation, which is to preach God's word; and in case he do, let him, with knowledge and soberness, admonish him, and bring him to a better mind.[89]

The king was not a bishop, and the bishop was not a king, but the king was obligated to judge the worthiness of a bishop, and, as Hooper counseled elsewhere, remove him should he fail to dispense it faithfully. The bishop was only to admonish, however, should the king err. There were no further steps to be taken. In all else he had to submit, as Hooper later did under Queen Mary.

While the king's laws were supreme in the realm, he was not without accountability. Just as he expected obedience from his subjects, so the King of kings expected the same from him. Hooper asked, "What king or prince of the world would suffer his statutes, laws and testament to be cut off and set on, at every man's liberty and pleasure? Should not the same glory, honour and majesty be given to the laws and testament of Christ which is sealed with his precious blood?"[90] For the king to rule well, and for the people to serve well as his subjects, it was imperative that all know the Father's will:

> It is the office and duty of every good child, that studiously labours to obey and follow his father's commandments before all things, to know perfectly the nature and conditions of his father's will. Whereof if he be ignorant, many times in the same things he judges best of, he most offends, and the things most pleasant and acceptable unto his father, he avoids and refuses as things most displeasant and unacceptable. Even so we, that are subjects and children of God the Father almighty, can do

---

89. Hooper, "The Fifth Sermon upon Jonah," 149.
90. Hooper, "Epistle Dedicatory," 86.

nothing gratefully and acceptably unto his Majesty, except we first know his good will and pleasure toward us.[91]

The king was to set the example for his subjects, first in learning the Father's will, and then in following it.

While the king was to exemplify justice and equity, England's greatest and capital city, London, was to play a special paradigmatic role as well. It was to be England's Jerusalem or Nineveh, the city from which repentance spread after the message was brought to it first. Hooper explained, "God has used, from the beginning of commonwealths, to be merciful unto the greatest cities, and hath sent most preachers of the truth to them, as is to be seen in these days what God hath showed to London."[92] London especially therefore needed powerful preachers and honest leaders. Otherwise, as would have happened with Nineveh except for their repentance, God's judgment would begin with the king and his greatest city as a sign and terror for others.

Hooper expressed a concern with more than religious righteousness in the land as well. He also advocated for social justice. He urged the king and godly magistrates to attend to two things especially: "First, that under the pretext and cloak of the law, to serve his affection or gain, he punish not the innocent . . . . Secondly, let the magistrate take heed he absolve not for gain, affection, good intention, or for any foolish and preposterous pity, him that God condemns."[93] Just as the king and those in authority were not to act without justice or on account of persons, Hooper, in keeping with his concern with the poor, throughout lamented that so many beneath the king and his court's authority acted for private advantage. He wrote:

> So shall his commonwealth and every other, if when the king and his council make laws to help and save the poor, he who steers at the hinder part of the ship behind the king's back, follows not that which he is bid to do, but that which he himself listeth, and which is for his own private advantage to do; and thus puts both the ship, the master, and all the mariners, in danger of drowning.[94]

Furthermore, he indicted all those who serve under the king and deceive him "by pilling and polling the poor and needy soldiers, so they decay and undo the whole commonweal," who "enrich themselves unjustly, to

91. Hooper, "The First Sermon upon Jonah," 93.

92. Ibid., 97.

93. Hooper, "The Third Sermon upon Jonah," 121.

94. Hooper, "The Fourth Sermon upon Jonah," 141–42.

the utter impoverishing and beggary of both the commonwealth and the heads thereof."[95]

Hooper made clear that the sad fact remained, however, that not all could be saved, no matter what measures were taken. Not every wrongdoer would repent, certainly not sincerely, and those who would not repent had to be cast off the ship. The king needed to employ God's law as a curb as a hedge to uphold social justice in the commonwealth and avoid the spread of backsliding. Hooper explained, "In these mariners the Holy Ghost teaches us two things: the one, how they would have saved the troubler of the ship; the other, that they could not save him." First, "the nature and condition of every godly magistrate . . . would have (if God and the law would) all men to be saved." Second, "we learn that no commonwealth can be quieted except the transgressors be punished," cast into the sea like Jonah.[96] The magistrate was to enforce not only the law of God, but also, peculiar to his office, the law of nature, that "he that sheddeth a man's blood, shall have his blood shed again."[97] As Romans 13 reminded Christian rulers, "The magistrate beareth not a sword in vain."[98] When the magistrate used that sword, God was at work. Hooper wrote that those condemned by the magistrates "should acknowledge that it is not the magistrate, that puts them to execution, but God, whose ministers they are." The magistrates had to "save such as God's word saveth, and condemn those that God's word condemneth," for "it is God that sendeth to hell, that hangeth for transgression."[99] Regarding rebellion sedition, and treason, Hooper explained that these especially "deserve the sword and the gallows."[100] Therefore, he urged, "Let the traitorous subject, the thief, the murder, and idle man say; 'The Lord brought me to the gallows; the Lord would I should trouble the commonwealth no longer.'"[101]

Besides rebellion and sedition, two other sins especially deserved punishment in Hooper's estimation. He wrote, "I humbly require all magistrates, both in peace and war, to punish chiefly these two vices,—adultery and blasphemy, in case they would have either victory in war, or quietness in peace."[102] Just as church discipline was to be severe and instill austerity and diligence, so also the state must leave little room for behaviors detri-

95. Hooper, "The Third Sermon upon Jonah," 122.

96. Ibid., 119.

97. Hooper, "The Third Sermon upon Jonah," 121.

98. Ibid.

99. Hooper, "The Fourth Sermon upon Jonah," 139.

100. Ibid.

101. Ibid., 140.

102. Hooper, "The Third Sermon upon Jonah," 123.

mental to the commonwealth. Hooper wrote, "The sloth and idleness, the impatience and rebellion of the people, must be punished and amended, or else they will cast the ship, the shipmaster, (that is the king and his council,) yea, and themselves also, into the sea, and bring his realm to desolation and utter destruction."[103] He called out the "fraud, guile, and covetousness of the lawyers, the sloth and idleness of the people.[104] According to Hooper, each person had to fulfill his vocation faithfully, to God's glory, and for the good of the kingdom. Jonah's affliction had come, after all, because of his neglect of his vocation."[105] The ship sailed best, Hooper observed, when "every man in his state and vocation does what he is commanded to do."[106] Hooper explained further, "Let no man, therefore, think he can do any thing acceptable unto the Lord, if he neglect the works necessarily appointed to his vocation."[107]

Although obedience to the king was paramount for a godly kingdom, the king, in turn, had clear spiritual and social obligations to his subjects. If he failed to fulfill his duties well, or even acted counter to them, Hooper wanted nothing to do with rebellion. Every subject owed obedience to his king, even as the king owed obedience to God. The king was to punish those who failed to furnish obedience to the throne. God would punish the king should he fail to do the same, Hooper claimed. Such a prohibition against rebellion, however, was not meant to excuse the king from faithful service to those under his care. It was in the king's own self-interest to rule well, after all: "For in case the magistrate does anything contrary unto God, doubtless he shall fall into two evils; first, into God's displeasure, and then what he does shall never prosper; as it is to be seen by the Israelites that warred before they were commanded by God. (Num. xiv)."[108] Faced with the enormity of the task before him as God's representative on earth and as one called to serve for the provision and protection of his servants, the godly magistrate or councilor should not even want the office he held. Out of respect for its seriousness and divine institution, and what could be said of the prophetic office could be said of the magisterial: "For that office has so may difficulties, labours, and dangers, that in case the man who is not well persuaded that he is come to it by the calling of God, he should never be able to endure the troubles annexed to the vocation." He

103. Ibid., 127.

104. Ibid.

105. Ibid., 113.

106. Hooper, "The Fifth Sermon upon Jonah," 146.

107. Ibid.

108. Ibid., 148–49.

continued, "Even so is the office of a good counsellor, or a good magistrate that in case he look not to come to his dignity and honour for ambition, pride, and private lucre, but comes when he is called of God; he shall find so many labours, and so much unquietness in his vocation, that were it not for God, he could be glad to leave it to another man."[109]

While the king was to take his task most seriously and serve not for himself but for his people, Hooper left no doubt about the divine institution of governing authorities, and because rulers were instituted by God, rebellion against them was nothing less than rebellion against God. If the seriousness of his office and the threat of divine punishment should not prove enough to keep a ruler honest, no rebellion would be enough either, and only more harm, spiritual and temporal, would result. Ultimately, what more could serve to motivate someone than the threat of hell? Hooper reminded those who hold office, with words spoken of clergy and the ruling elite, "I say this to every man of each of these degrees mentioned—the less they feel the danger of eternal damnation, the nearer they are unto eternal pain, and they have already one foot in hell, which shall never come again, but the whole body and soul shall follow, except they repent."[110] There was nothing more dangerous than spiritual complacency, a failure to keep one's salvation regularly in view: "For no man is farther from heaven, than he feareth not hell; and no man farther from grace than he that feeleth not the danger of sin; as we see no man is in a more dangerous disease, than he that knows not himself to be sick, as those men that have fallen into frenzy and madness."[111]

Hooper asked and then answered, "But what, according to the right judgment of the scripture pleases God? Obedience."[112] This meant obedience to God and to the king and magistrates. Rebellion was an unpardonable sin, at least when it came to temporal justice. It was a sin not only against the governing authorities and God, but also against the commonwealth, against one's neighbor and the good order that serves him best. Hooper asked:

> But I will suppose thee, though thief and robber of the king and of the commonwealth, to be king, and the king to be thy officer and receiver: wouldest thou thy officer should deceive thee? Or thou traitorous and false subject, if thou wert king and the king thy subject, wouldest thou be contented that thy subjects should conspire and imagine how to pluck thee out of thy realm. What

109. Ibid., 148.
110. Hooper, "The Fourth Sermon upon Jonah," 139.
111. Ibid.
112. Hooper, "The Fifth Sermon upon Jonah," 146.

> if my lord bishop and master parson were kings, think ye their majesties would be contented that their bishops and priests should whisper a tale of treason and sedition in auricular confession, or rather privy conventicles, to their subjects?[113]

Once again, disobedience jeopardized much more than the sovereignty of the king. It put the whole commonwealth at risk, imperiling the well-being of all the nation's subjects. Good, clear laws and obedience to the spirit and the letter of those laws was essential. Hooper illustrated this point with a lesson learned at sea in rough weather:

> The master of the ship, to conduct it the better, sat upon the main yard to see the seas aforehand, and cried to him that steered at the stern, upon which side he should steer the ship, best to avoid the danger of the sea. The wind blowing high, when the master cried a-larboard; and this once mistaking of the master's law, had almost cast us under water. Then thought I, it is not without cause that wise men compare a commonwealth to a ship, for the same thing loses or saves them both; for in case the master's officer in the ship obey not his law, the ship will be lost.[114]

Once again, the punishment for rebellion needed to be stern and its message unmistakable:

> Finally, I appeal to the consciences of the subjects of this realm which merit, for some deceit, falsehood, and deceiving the king, loss both of body and goods; some for preaching erroneous seditions and false doctrine, or for neglecting the preaching of the true doctrine, deserve most cruel punishment; some for false judgment merit the loss of their lives; the rest for rebellion, sedition, and treason, deserve the sword and the gallows."[115]

As the criminal suffers his punishment, he dare not wonder through whom it comes upon him. Hooper reminded the wrongdoer that he could say, "This I suffer worthily, and will the vengeance of God, because I have sinned against him, and the law of my commonwealth."[116] Similarly, "Those that are condemned by the magistrates should acknowledge that it is not the magistrate who puts them to execution, but God, whose ministers they are."[117] In

---

113. Hooper, "The Fourth Sermon upon Jonah," 140–41.

114. Ibid., 141.

115. Ibid., 140.

116. Ibid.

117. Ibid., 139.

other words, the transgressor failed to love God and his neighbor, whom he ultimately served through obedience to God in his vocation.

5.5. Affliction and the Cross

The theology of the cross ran throughout the writings of Flacius during the Adiaphoristic Controversy. Flacius framed the issue of adiaphora in the contest of God's faithful suffering, bearing their cross, for the sake Christ, who bore his cross for their salvation. Such a theme was almost completely absent in Hooper's writings, although the theme of affliction ran throughout. The differences rests herein: while Flacius focused especially on believers, especially the remnant, being afflicted on account of their faithfulness, Hooper treated affliction primarily as a consequence of the sin of the wayward. He warned of impending affliction for idolatry and superstition. He cautioned about distant affliction should Edward VI and his councilors not heed the Lord's examples and directives for governing a Christian land. Hooper did enunciate the fact that suffering could serve a salutary purpose for a Christian, but even then it was in the context of what Jonah suffered for trying to evade the Lord's call to Nineveh. He wrote, "But the cross of trouble is not unprofitable to the christian; it mortifies the flesh, so that in the afflicted dwelleth the Spirit of God; it exercises the faith, and proves obedience."[118] He quoted David, who after he was rebuked by Nathan and knew the consequences of his sin, accepted the Lord's chastisement as just. Once again, then, affliction, though salutary, was remedial, the result of sin and not a proof of faithfulness.[119] The difference between the believing and unbelieving in chastisement was not so much the cause, which was sin, but the result: "The evil are not amended by affliction, but indurated and hardened through their own malice and obstinacy, as Saul and Pharaoh; and their pains and torments here are the beginning of eternal pains."[120]

While Flacius admonished the persecuted again and again to steadfastness, Hooper called to all, "Amend, amend, amend!" Flacius certainly urged the Adiaphorists to amend, but doing so meant taking up the cross again, confessing in the face of persecution. Hooper's amendation was primarily moral, legal, and practical. Flacius' emphasis was upon theological confession, Hooper's upon ethical obedience; Flacius' upon the proclamation of the gospel, Hooper's the observance of the law. Flacius rooted the Christian's cross in the cross of Christ, in self-denial, in confession. Hooper instead

118. Hooper, "The Fifth Sermon upon Jonah," 152.
119. Ibid. 2 Sam 12.
120. Hooper, "The Fifth Sermon upon Jonah," 152.

located affliction in the Christian's moral correction and self-mortification. Flacius focused upon the affliction of believers, which is strictly speaking, the cross as Jesus speaks of it in the Gospels. Hooper focused on affliction in general, which for the believer brings ethical progress, but for the unbeliever only further deprivation.[121] The experience of the latter could only mirror that of Pharaoh.[122] This makes sense considering that the focus of his sermons was Jonah, whose affliction was self-inflicted through his disobedience to God's call and authority. Jonah was not a persecuted prophet like Elijah. He was a pouty prophet whose unwilling message God richly blessed for the amendment of life, and thus, salvation, of the people of Nineveh. He was like the priests and bishops of England, who called to preach to those threatened with damnation for their wicked deeds, refused to heed their calling and went their own way and were equally in need of amendment. Just as Jonah's personal salvation was as much at risk as those to whom he was to preach, so also the wayward priests and bishops faced the same hell from which they failed to deliver their people through biblical preaching. Hooper wrote, "The bishops and priests that have, either with false doctrine destroyed the church, or by negligence not built it with the true word of God, let them acknowledge their faults, amend them, and ask remission betimes, if they will not die in their sin."[123]

According to Hooper, any attempt by Christians to flee affliction in the end only amplified their suffering, deepened their obstinacy or lengthend the time of their purification. Hooper lamented that too often "we do not desire the Lord, to deliver us, to glorify and laud his holy name as Jonah did and David," citing the example of David's penitential fifty-first psalm. He complained, "From sickness and adversity we turn ourselves to all ungodliness and liberty of life; and where we were evil before trouble and sickness, we are worse after; therefore when God has wasted one rod upon us in punishment, he begins to make another more sharp than the first."[124]

Penitence, Hooper counseled, was the key when faced with the Lord's chastening hand: "Of this in the whole we learn that there is no danger so great, but we may escape, if with penitence we return unto the Lord and ask him for mercy."[125] Penance and amendment of life marked the core of Jonah's message and Ninevah's response. The example of the Ninevites was unambiguous: "First, they believed in the Lord; second, they fasted." Why

121. Hooper, "The Fourth Sermon upon Jonah," 131.

122. Ibid., 132.

123. Ibid., 135.

124. Ibid., 142.

125. Ibid., 145.

does Hooper mention both? "A man ignorant of God offends in two ways," Hooper asserted, "in body and in soul; and both these offences must be amended, if we will be reconciled unto God. By faith the mind is reconciled unto God, and by abstinence the body is kept in subjection, and the wantonness of concupiscence kept in obedience." Similarly, regarding the use of sackcloth, he noted, "It was the manner at that time so to do, and declared their repentance and amendment; and so I would it were now, that he who offends in apparel should remove the pride thereof, and go soberly."[126] Note that Flacius emphasized the self-denial worked by the cross placed upon the Christian by God for Christ's sake; Hooper emphasized the work of the Christian in checking his flesh through amendment of life and self-chosen self-mortification. What was true of Nineveh needed to be true of England if the ship of the commonwealth was to stay afloat. No miracle should be needed. Nineveh required no special sign. Rather, dull ears needed to be opened anew to the message of the Bible.[127] The Ninevites put the English to shame who would "defer and protract their amendment, and say that they will believe when the king comes to age."[128] There was no room for indifference. "If we hate not the evil we have committed, from the bottom of our hearts, we tarry still in death," Hooper wrote.[129]

Hooper insisted that there was mercy for sinners and strongly condemned those who would deny that fact, and yet for Hooper that mercy came with clear expectations.[130] "God will show mercy unto penitent and sorrowful sinners, yea, though all the world would say nay," and yet they were to be duly penitent and sorrowful, fully committed to sufficiently changing their wicked ways.[131] When Hooper spoke of Christ's saving task, it was seldom "sinners" Christ had come to rescue, but "penitent sinners." This might not seem much, but it is telling with respect to his view of the role of affliction. Affliction served to turn the impenitent to penitence. His was less a theology of the cross, therefore, that is, of suffering because one is a Christian, but of affliction, of suffering in order that one might become a Christian or be restored as a Christian.

126. Hooper, "The Sixth Sermon upon Jonah," 176.

127. Hooper, "The Fifth Sermon upon Jonah," 154.

128. Hooper, "The Sixth Sermon upon Jonah," 174.

129. Hooper, "The Seventh Sermon upon Jonah," 181.

130. Ibid., 182.

131. Ibid.

5.6. Bishop Hooper's "Notes" to the King's Council

Hooper's letter *contra usum vestium* appeared for a long time to have been lost, so that modern scholars were handicapped in their study of his arguments before the Council. The meat of Hooper's argument became available again through the happy discovery and publication of the "Bishop Hooper's 'Notes' to the King's Council," published in their original Latin in the *Journal of Theological Studies* in 1943.[132] The "Notes" represent the content of *contra usum vestium*, and by all accounts, they do so faithfully. As he "conjoins" the arguments of Hooper and Ridley, Primus demonstrates that the "Notes" correspond well with Ridley's responses, so that there is little reason to doubt the accuracy of their content and faithfulness to the basic argument of John Hooper.[133] As Hopf's historical introduction to the "Notes" states, "the essential parts of the 'Notes' are contained in the copy, and . . . only minor parts are left out."[134] In the "Notes" Hooper largely stated succinctly and in a more structured manner arguments he earlier made in his sermons on Jonah. Most important for consideration here are the four chief marks or conditions that Hooper argued had to be met for something to be truly indifferent and thus acceptable for usage in the church. It is likely that Hooper made a number of statements at the end of his "Notes" which were meant to anticipate the objections of his opponents. Ridley appears to have replied directly to a number of them, but his replies have not survived.

Hooper began his "Notes" with a succinct statement of the crux of his argument: "Nothing is to be used in the church unless it is seen to have the expressed word of God or is something in and of itself indifferent."[135] He then explained what made something in and of itself indifferent: "It profits nothing when it is performed or utilized and does no harm when it goes undone and is permitted to go by the wayside."[136] Hooper left no doubt how this general rule applied to the use of vestments in the church, and especially the vestments he objected to wearing. He finished his syllogism, "Personal and special vestments in the ministry do not have any command in the word of God, nor are they indifferent in and of themselves. There-

132. Hopf, "Bishop Hooper's 'Notes to the King's Council," 194–99. This work will be referenced as Hooper, "Notes." Quotations from the work will be my own admittedly free translation as the Latin of Hooper's "Notes" reads choppily sometimes. This dynamic translation is intended to help the reader get a sense for the basic meaning and flow of Hooper's arguments.

133. Primus, *The Vestments Controversy*, 16–34.

134. Hopf, "Notes," 195.

135. Ibid., 196.

136. Ibid.

fore they are not to be used."[137] Hooper claimed that the first part of his
argument required no testing or proof, and so he endeavored to give none.
He did, however, concede that he must explain the second part. He wrote,
"The second part I will show from nature and the properties of all things
indifferent, which must have these four conditions and qualities, or they are
not indifferent."[138] We will consider Hooper's four marks, or conditions, of
indifferent things and then his specific objections raised against vestments
in the final part of his "Notes," based upon these principles.

Hooper stated in the first mark, or condition:

> Indifferent things must have their origin and foundation in the
> word of God. For that which cannot be proven from the word
> of God is not of faith, and faith comes from hearing the word
> of God (Romans 10). What is not from faith is unable to be a
> sort of middle thing and indifferent, but as Scripture speaks,
> is truly sin (Romans 14), so that it is unable to please God
> and for that reason must be removed as a plant which has not
> been planted by the heavenly Father (Matthew 15), not to be
> supported by anyone.[139]

Hooper here restricted indifferent things to those which have their origin
and foundation in the word of God. This was critical. Not only did indifferent things not have to be unbiblical, but they had to be biblical—they had
have a basis in Scripture. This was quite different from the Lutheran position, which certainly required that a practice not be contrary to Scripture,
but not that it be scriptural, so to speak, in the sense of an explicit command
from Christ or the apostles. Primus notes that this first condition seems
to contradict Hooper's opening syllogism, which stated "that a thing to be
used in the church must have the authority of the express word of God *or*
be indifferent."[140] Primus argues, however, that a distinction must be made
between Hooper's "*expressum Dei verbum*," expressed word of God, of the
syllogism and his insistence that indifferent things have their "origin and
foundation in the word of God" in the first condition. It is perhaps best to
understand by "*originem suam et fundamentum*" the word *basis* in English.
Indifferent things are "not an independent realm but must also be subjected
to the norm of Scripture," Primus explains, so that "proof of indifference
must be established by means of the Word."[141] In other words, there had to

137. Ibid.
138. Ibid.
139. Ibid.
140. Primus, *The Vestments Controversy*, 19.
141. Ibid.

be a biblical basis or rationale for their use—not so much strict precedent, but clear "Biblical support."[142] If Primus is correct, then Hooper objected to vestments because the only support for vestments in the Scriptures was found in the Old Testament, where they were used to separate the Aaronic priests from the people. This was inconsistent with the New Testament and Reformation teaching of the priesthood of all believers, and thus was no scriptural support at all.

If Hooper's condition was intended as strictly as it seems at first glance, however, then vestments were inappropriate because Christ nowhere described or prescribed their use in the Christian Church. A later objection from Hooper seems to indicate that he expected a clear biblical mandate if vestments are to be considered indifferent, which is consistent with a reading of his first condition at face value, even though it seems to contradict his opening syllogism. There he insisted that his opponents could by no means demonstrate "why and when certain personal and peculiar vestments have been assigned by the command of the Lord to the ministry, for the adornment those who minister, the preservation of decorum, or to distinguish somehow one who ministers from the people as earlier took place in the ministry of the Aaronic priests." Even Primus concludes here, "Since the apostolic writings make no mention of the use of vestments in the primitive church, Hooper concludes that the prescribed apparel does not meet the first condition of things indifferent."[143] Primus furthermore observes, "Apparently, silence of the Word is not enough to support church use of things indifferent in Hooper's estimation. Positive origin and foundation must be demonstrated."[144]

With respect to the application of the first condition to vestments, however, it was not simply the fact that the apostles did not use them and Christ did not command them, but rather that in Hooper's view the apostles specifically rejected them—for instance, in Galatians and Hebrews—as remnants of the Old Testament priesthood, abrogated and abolished, made unnecessary and now even sinful, through the perfect priesthood of Christ.[145] Hooper wrote, "Paul in Galatians 2 where he rejects whatever things have been abrogated in Christ as contrary to the will of God. Likewise, Hebrews 7-10 clearly teaches that the Aaronic priesthood was abolished in the priesthood of Christ, together with its rites, vestments, reckonings, anointings,

142. Ibid., 20.
143. Ibid., 21.
144. Ibid.
145. Ibid., 23.

consecrations, and the like."[146] Primus notes, "He not only stated that the apostles did not use vestments. He established a Scriptural basis for the abandonment of distinction of dress in the apostolic church."[147] His opponents, he insisted, could make no such case. They provided, he contended, no such basis or foundation, for their cause.

In the second mark of indifference, Hooper argued:

> Even if something has its origin in Scripture, in order to be indifferent it should have neither an affirmation nor a prohibition, but be a free and open matter, left to conscience for use when it is seen to be useful and abandonment when it is not, so that whether such a thing is used or not it remains a matter of convenience or inconvenience, its use driven by conscience. We must always observe such things as are commanded by God, however. Likewise, we must always and necessarily shun and flee those things which are forbidden. This does not apply only to things commanded or forbidden by an expressed word of God, though, but also to all things regarding the divine will which may be clearly deduced from Scripture by collation and comparison [fol. 16 verso], as well as that which is implied to have the force and nature of divine commands, whether to command or forbid something, provided it is in accord with nature, the proportion of faith, and Scripture. An example of this is the baptism of infants, which does not have an expressed command, and yet through a collation of Scripture is seen to have equal force to an expressed command of God. Similarly we admit women to the Lord's Supper even though we do not have an expressed command in the word of God to do so.[148]

Here again it becomes apparent that Hooper considered vestments expressly forbidden. As such, they had to be shunned and fled. Yet Hooper was careful. Ridley and others had drawn connections between his stance and Anabaptism. As a result, Hooper took pains to note that he did not reject those things which lack a scriptural mandate and yet "may be clearly deduced from Scripture" and "have the force and nature of divine commands," such as infant baptism. This significantly restricted the number of adiaphora in the church. Hooper further restricted that number by making indifferent things a matter of conscience. While Ridley would argue that those in authority could regulate adiaphora, since they were adiaphora, Hooper insisted that

---

146. Hooper, "Notes," 198.

147. Primus, *The Vestments Controversy*, 22.

148. Hooper, "Notes," 196–97.

they must be "left to conscience" and their use "driven by conscience."[149] No doubt Hooper's opponents recognized that argument lent itself to a certain tyranny of the individual or of the weaker brother. One can understand why some would make comparisons to the arguments of the Anabaptists with respect to church practices and the role of the state in determining them. As we have already seen earlier in this study, however, Hooper certainly did not deny the king and the state a role in the governance of the church—indeed he encouraged the king's active involvement in his sermons Jonah—but he was unwavering in his insistence that for something to be an adiaphoron it must be "a free and open matter."[150] The state must not compel believers to observe something if it was indeed indifferent, and it ceased to be indifferent when instituted under compulsion. Hooper did, however, want the state to compel believers not to observe things that he did not consider indifferent. Here there is a distinction with the position of Flacius, who did not want the state compelling anything regarding the divine service, but insisted that such matters should be left to the free consent of the church. In England, however, Ridley emphasized the Christian freedom of the church to establish and regulate uniform rites, vestments, and ceremonies, while Hooper emphasized the Christian freedom of the individual to object to and reject such rites, vestment, and ceremonies. This was a clear challenge to the authority of the bishops and the greater church.

The second condition echoed the first in its insistence that Hooper's opponents had to offer a biblical basis for the practices they were defending. Once again, he demanded, not explicit precedent, but a *basis*, or rational. This is clear from the fact that he used the examples of the baptism of infants and the admission of women to the Lord's Supper. There was no explicit precedent in the Scriptures, so to speak, but there certainly was a basis. It was understood that infants were included in the command to baptize all nations and that the Lord's Supper was instituted for all disciples, man and woman alike. These practices could be "clearly deduced from Scripture by collation and comparison. They were "implied" and thus "have the force and nature of divine commands."[151] While his opponents could provide no basis for the use of vestments—their use was nowhere even implied—Hooper could provide a basis for their rejection, namely the New Testament's teaching that the Mosaic ceremonies had been abrogated in the person and work of Christ. At the end of his "Notes" Hooper supplied an interesting proof of that abrogation: "It is not lacking in its mystery that our Savior Jesus Christ

---

149. Ibid., 197.

150. Ibid., 196.

151. Ibid., 197.

hung naked on the cross . . . . . Christ truly, when He was sacrificing himself, put off all vestments, showing himself from that to be a priest in truth who needed nothing to amplify his work, whether with clothing or shadows."[152] Primus notes that Ridley did not disagree with Hooper on the matter of the abrogation of Mosaic ceremonial laws. Rather, quite understandably, Ridley's point of disagreement centered in whether "vestments are necessarily and exclusively marks of the Aaronic and/or Roman priesthood."[153] Hooper never addressed this issue; it was for him simply a given that vestments that distinguished the minister from the laity were Aaronic and Romish.

Hooper asserted in his third mark:

> Indifferent things must have a clear and obvious use recognized in the church, seen neither to be received through fraud nor introduced into the church by fraud or contrivance. Both the civil magistrate and the minister of the church should guard against this with the utmost attention. To both power has been given (as Paul says) for edification and not for destruction (1 Cor. 14), for the sake of the truth and not against it (2 Cor. 13). Neither one of them have the power to bring into the church things which do not serve for edification.[154]

Adiaphora had to be purposeful, their use clear. They had to serve for edification and the truth. Both secular and ecclesiastical leaders were charged to see to this. Ridley seized upon another possible contradiction in Hooper's argument here, however. Hooper had stated at the outset of his "Notes" that an adiaphoron provided no benefit or caused no detriment. In his preliminary syllogism he stated that an indifferent thing "profits nothing when it is performed or utilized and does no harm when it goes undone and is permitted to go by the wayside."[155] This does appear to be a contradiction. Primus argues, though, that "it is inconceivable . . . that a rational being, no matter how hot the controversy, could so obviously contradict himself in a document of comparatively small compass."[156] He argues that the contradiction is resolved through the comparison with the "in and of itself" in the opening syllogism: "Nothing is to be used in the church unless it is seen to have the expressed word of God or is *something in and of itself indifferent*, so that it profits nothing when it is performed or utilized and does no harm when it

152. Ibid., 199.

153. Primus, *The Vestments Controversy*, 25.

154. Hooper, "Notes," 197.

155. Ibid., 196.

156. Primus, *The Vestments Controversy*, 26.

goes undone and is permitted to go by the wayside."[157] An indifferent thing was thus to be employed in the service of an edifying thing. The edification, or usefulness, was not peculiar to the adiaphoron.

Hooper appealed to 1 Corinthians 14 and 2 Corinthians 13 to support his demand that indifferent things had to serve for edification and not destruction. In the former, Paul deals with the touchy issue of speaking in tongues in the Corinthian congregation, which had divided its members into haves and have-nots, those who could speak in tongues and those who could not. Paul insisted that unless someone interpreted what was spoken in tongues, those claiming the spiritual gift should remain silent, because their speaking did not serve for edification. This chapter appealed to Hooper on another level as well. Speaking in tongues without an interpreter, like vestments, disrupted and diminished the priesthood of all believers, threatening to introduce classes within the church, distinctions between the baptized inconsistent with the abolition of the Old Testament priesthood and its practices. 2 Corinthians 13 contains Paul's final warnings to the church in Corinth. The chapter itself bears little relevance for Hooper's argument. Hooper was rather focused on one specific verse from that chapter, verse 8, where Paul warned, "For we cannot do anything against the truth, but only for the truth."[158] Since Ridley could not, or at least would not, demonstrate the benefit of vestments in English churches, Hooper admitted no value in vestments for edification. Since the New Testament seemed to provide a basis for their rejection, he considered them harmful.

Fourth, and finally, Hooper set forth the fourth mark, or condition:

> Indifferent things must be instituted in the church freely, with apostolic and evangelical gentleness, without tyranny. They must not be established as though they were necessary or coerced. They must be free, such things as pertain to Christian freedom. Whatever is held to be indifferent in the ministry of the church ceases to be adiaphora if it at some point degenerates and falls into tyranny and servitude.[159]

This condition had the potential to raise the ire of the magistrates. Everything hinged on just who those were who had instituted adiaphora with tyranny. Everything indicates that Hooper here had in mind the papacy and earlier generations of princes and kings, from whom the vestments had been inherited, and not Edward VI, his father, or Thomas Cranmer, who were responsible for current practice in the church. The statement did play

---

157. Hooper, "Notes," 196.
158. 2 Cor 13:8 ESV.
159. Hooper, "Notes," 197.

into his opponents' hands, however, adding fuel to their arguments against him and raising possible concerns about Hooper's stance regarding the Act of Supremacy and the king's power in the Church of England. What is clear in the fourth condition, as in others, is that Hooper rejected any purported adiaphora instituted and regulated under coercion or compulsion. Indifferent things had to be free and the conscience supreme. This is what he meant when he referenced "such things as pertain to Christian freedom"—the Christian freedom, not of the church, but rather of the individual Christian's conscience, was paramount.[160] There was simply and absolutely no place for rules when it came to adiaphora, let alone repercussions should one reject them: "Whatever is held to be indifferent in the ministry of the church ceases to be adiaphora if it at some point degenerates and falls into tyranny and servitude."[161] Once again, Ridley questioned whether a practice, indifferent in and of itself, had to be cast away simply because it had been abused or coerced in the past. For Hooper, however, this alone was grounds to dismiss any such rite, vestment, or ceremony as tainted, papist, tyrannical, or harmful. For Hooper, it seems, once a practice had "at some point degenerates and falls into tyranny and servitude" it had to go.[162]

The "Notes" did not end with the fourth and final condition for adiaphora. Hooper included under the fourth condition a summary of the "Notes" and an indictment of his opponents' attempts to shift both the focus and the forum of the debate, making what should have been an ecclesiastical matter the subject of debate before civil authorities. He wrote, immediately after setting forth the fourth condition, "These are notes and signs by which they are able to discern indifferent things, so that nothing that fails to meet these four conditions may be considered indifferent. But now we come to this particular matter of disagreement, which hinges on the personal dress of the ministers of the church and the vesture assigned and allotted for those who minister."[163] Hooper insinuated that the only reason the debate had even found its way before the civil authorities was because his opponents could not find any convincing arguments to make within church leadership. He wrote, "I sincerely do not want the issue under debate to be shifted from the ecclesiastical-political to the civil as the adversaries irresponsibly do when it is they struggle to make the case in this cause's proper ecclesiastical forum, so that they instead solicit help and assistance from a civil forum

---

160. Ibid.
161. Ibid.
162. Ibid.
163. Ibid.

and from magistrates."[164] He repeated his charge that his opponents misrepresented and misdiagnosed the possibility and possible cause of rebellion. They, not he, advocated a practice that undermined obedience to civil authority, he argued. He minced no words regarding the wrongheadedness and deceptiveness of his opponents:

> They are trying to persuade the magistrates also of this, that if the liberty and power of using this pomp of vestments be taken from them, which they dream contributes to preserving utility, decorum, and order in the ministry, then there would immediately result from this contempt for the magistrates and the greatest diminution of their authority in civil administration and governance. O sons of this age, more prudent in your generation than the sons of light (Luke 16), who could just as easily persuade the magistrates that enemies were friends and friends enemies as you could that your superstition and blind church is able to serve, watch over, sustain, adorn and defend the dignity of the magistrates, who bear the charge of God himself here on earth, better than the perfect and illumined church of the apostles.[165]

Hooper would not be deterred. He was so confident of his cause that he volunteered to accept the most serious punishment possible should he fail to prove his case. He wrote, "I will not refuse to submit to that same punishment through which the new law aims to persuade through the fear of the prospect of death those who are unable to reject the old [religion] through righteous reasoning."[166] Surely no one involved, whether church or state officials, had any such punishment in mind, but Hooper did not hesitate to volunteer to accept capital punishment should he lose the debate on biblical grounds. He challenged his opponents, "Take up in your hands again the sacred volume of the Bible, which is your book as well as mine, your judgment and mine."[167] Hooper taught the Bible alone and would be judged by the Bible alone. In the end, he would eventually die for such a conviction, and even then the prospect of death would not move him.

As he closed his "Notes," Hooper judged vestments based upon his four conditions and, unsurprisingly, found them lacking the marks of indifferent things. He concluded that they "clearly seem to be among the Aaronic rites, ceremonies, priesthoods, types, and shadows abrogated by Christ," no

164. Ibid.
165. Ibid., 197–98.
166. Ibid., 198.
167. Ibid.

longer relevant through "his institution of a new and perfect ministry."[168] He again challenged his opponents to prove him wrong in this. The method for so doing remained unchanged: "From these books [of the Bible] they must show us why and when certain personal and peculiar vestments have been assigned by the command of the Lord to the ministry, for the adornment those who minister, the preservation of decorum, or to distinguish somehow one who ministers from the people as earlier took place in the ministry of the Aaronic priests."[169] He made no mystery about what they would find when they endeavor to make their case through careful study of the Scriptures: "The statutes, canons, and decrees of the apostles and evangelists make no mention of such a thing. Wherever and whenever this first property is lacking, which is required for indifferent things, then vestments must be excluded from the number of adiaphora."[170]

Hooper might well have been a very capable theologian, but in this instance he proved to be a poor tactician with respect to court and ecclesiastical politics. More likely, it simply was not in his nature to pay heed to such considerations when it came to matters of what he held to the truth of Scripture. He left himself no room for maneuver in the controversy, no path for possible retreat should things turn against him. His position was clear and he seemed unable to countenance any manner by which he could be persuaded. He concluded, "That which is prohibited by God can in no way be indifferent, as we demonstrated above" and insisted that this is the teaching of St. Paul.[171] Vestments were nothing other than holdovers from the "shadows of the Aaronic priesthood" and "the papistic priesthood."[172] As Christ hung naked on the cross, so ministers must go without the adornment of the Old Testament priests and the ministers of the Antichrist.[173] With some time in the Fleet prison in London, he would soften and compromise for his episcopal consecration. Afterward he labored tirelessly as a reforming bishop, eager to bring the doctrine and practice of the English churches under his oversight in line with those of Zurich.

168. Ibid.
169. Ibid.
170. Ibid.
171. Ibid.
172. Ibid.
173. Ibid., 199.

Chapter 6 ———————————————————————

Conclusion:
Comparisons and Contrasts

"One should now observe that there are three grounds for establishing adiaphora. The first is the general command of God that he wants to have everything in the church done in an orderly and proper fashion and to serve for edification, inasmuch as he is a God of order and not of disorder. The second is the free Christian desire of the church . . . . The third are the judicious, God-fearing people for whom the chuch is inclined to establish such adiaphora. This is what may be said about the establishment of adiaphora."[1]

"All things indifferent . . . must have these four conditions and qualities, or they are not indifferent. [1] Indifferent things must have their origin and foundation in the word of God . . . . [2] Even if something has its origin in Scripture, in order to be indifferent it should have neither an affirmation nor a prohibition, but be a free and open matter, left to conscience for use when it is seen to be useful and abandonment when it is not, so that whether such a thing is used or not it remains a matter of convenience or inconvenience, its use driven by conscience . . . . [3] Indifferent things must have a clear and obvious use recognized in the church, seen neither to be received through fraud nor introduced into the church by fraud or contrivance . . . . [4] Indifferent things must be instituted in the church freely, with apostolic and evangelical gentleness, without tyranny."[2]

1. Flacius, *Ein buch, von waren und falschen Mitteldingen,* Jiii v.
2. Hooper, "Notes," 196–98.

WHAT MAKES A COMPARATIVE study of Flacius' and Hooper's contro-versies over adiaphora especially fruitful is that these conflicts happened contemporaneously and over the same doctrinal topic. The Adiaphoristic Controversy in Germany lasted from 1548-1550, the Vestment Controversy in England 1550-1551. While Hooper could feasibly have become familiar with some of Flacius' writings on adiaphora and the English were certainly aware of the Interim Crisis in Germany, there seems to have been little demonstrable intellectual and theological cross-fertilization at this point. Verkamp speculates that Hooper might have become familiar with Flacius' writings during his return trip to England or through à Lasco, a religious refugee from Poland and superintendent of the Strangers' Church, but he is unable to establish anything certain and his argument is made only in passing.[3] As seen from the internal evidence of their writings themselves, there is no substantial consonance between the arguments of the two men. One does sometimes find similar language, but similar language does not require similar motivations or meanings. Both did deny that indifferent things could be compelled. Hooper, however, wanted the state to compel the church not to make use of things he did not consider adiaphora, even though many in the church, even in the heierarchy, did. Flacius wanted no state compulsion at all. Ultimately, both Flacius and Hooper developed their doctrines of adiaphora independently of each other and under the influence of different reformations. While both thought themselves faithful represen-tatives of the reformations and reformers who had so shaped them, both, interestingly, would also find themselves at odds, to one extent or another, with mentors. Flacius became an opponent of Melanchthon and Hooper acted against Bullinger's counsel to soften his approach for the time being. In addition, while they wrote and argued their cases at similar times, they wrote in different constitutional, political, social, and cultural contexts, and within different theological frameworks.

Hooper's controversy over adiaphora was likely inevitable. Vestments were simply intolerable in his view. He wanted a church that looked like that which he had encountered and grown to love in Zurich. In his view, vestments were inconsistent with apostolic simplicity and trappings of the superstitions of the papacy. Moreover, they were inconsistent with his doctrine of the Lord's Supper. In contrast, a fair examination of his life de-cisions and writings shows that Flacius' embroilment in polemics was not inevitable. Evidence suggests that Flacius could well have spent the rest of his life happily teaching in Wittenberg and remained largely untested in polemics had it not been for the *Augsburg Interim* and especially the

---

3. Verkamp, *The Indifferent Mean*, 71.

Leipzig Interim. Flacius' objections to a particular vestment, the surplice, which became symbolic for the whole imperial agenda of counter-reform, were conditioned by the situational factors surrounding the demand that that vestment be worn. Flacius was not personally very enamored with elaborate ceremonies or what some today might consider "high church" practices, but he did not object to them out of preference or because he did not find them in the New Testament. Had there been no imperial law regarding such a vestment or other liturgical rites, furnishings, and ceremonies, it is highly unlikely Flacius would have been bothered by a surplice in and of itself or many of the adiaphora he declared no longer indifferent in a state of confession. The exception to this would have been practices that inherently carried baggage from the papacy, that is, which might rekindle and or reignite what remained of the superstition and idolatry that Luther had worked to remove.

Flacius was no biblicist; he did not deny that practices not already present in the New Testament could be adopted. Rather, Flacius in this instance fought to ward off state intrusion into the affairs of the church and the reintroduction of some practices he held contrary to the gospel. Kolb, Arand, and Nestingen reinforce this point well in *The Lutheran Confessions: History and Theology of the Book of Concord*. They note, "Precisely this reinstating of long-discarded vestments elicited from Gallus and Flacius a stinging rebuke. Vestments are indeed adiapora, they observed: it is a neutral matter whether the pastor wears an academic robe or surplice or chasuble. The effect of such vestments on the congregation is not, however, a neutral matter, Flacius and Gallus argued."[4] Hooper, on the contrary, admitted no situation in which any ministerial vestment was acceptable within a truly Christian church or church body.[5] Flacius' *nihil est adiaphoron in statu confessionis et scandali*, that is, "nothing is an adiaphoron in a state of confession and offense," is conditional and contextual. Hooper's insistence that indifferent things have their *originem suam et fundamentum* in Scripture is not. Moreover, the official Lutheran doctrine of adiaphora, so influenced by Flacius' teaching, codified by the *Formula of Concord*, is also contextual.

Ultimately, Flacius objected to the use of some otherwise indifferent ceremonies, vestments, and rites as part of a program to reintroduce Catholicism and the papacy in Protestant Germany. He did so, not out of

---

4. Arand, Kolb, and Nestingen, *The Lutheran Confessions*, 201.

5. Olson, *Matthias Flacius and the Survival of Luther's Reform*, 160. Olson quotes an English description of the chorrock under dispute in Germany as the same vestment as the surplice in England: "[T]he chorrok which we commonlie call in English a surplesse." There is unfortunately no citation provided to explain where that English description originates.

an obsessive compulsion for liturgical precision, but rather in the midst of the single greatest challenge the Lutheran Church had ever faced politically, militarily, and theologically. Hooper, on the contrary, objected to any such ceremony, vestment, and rite that lacked a biblical basis and had been abused under the papacy as inherently inconsistent with Christian practice and sinful, and he wrote at a time when the future looked particularly promising for Reformed Christianity in England.

Adiaphora may be indifferent, but they do not exist in isolation. Politics, culture, theology, and personality played into these adiaphora debates and influenced what could and could not be considered adiaphora. Flacius operated under the auspices of a most hostile emperor, Charles V, in opposition to the aggressive recatholicization agenda of the same. He appealed to parish pastors and laymen. He advocated grassroots, bottom-up resistance spearheaded by lesser magistrates. Together with his colleagues in Magdeburg, although building off work earlier done by Luther and other Wittenberg colleagues, he set forth the first major formal statement of resistance theory in Protestantism.[6] Hooper, in contrast, had been invited to preach his sermons on Jonah by a king extremely friendly to his theological convictions and hopes for reform. There was no imminent threat of recatholicization on the horizon. The only hint of such a possibility in the future was Mary's continued survival and persistence in the old faith. Hooper lamented the ignorance and superstition of parish pastors and the laity and made appeals instead to the king, his councilors, and magistrates to aggressively pursue a program of reform, from the top down, through legislation and with punishment for those who would oppose reformatory measures. Hooper's doctrine of church and state had no place for those like Flacius in Germany, who would fail to submit to the governing authority in religious reform—he organized no rebellion when Mary undertook the Counter-Reformation in England and steadfastly distanced himself from those who countenanced such a path. Contrary to the traditional paradigm of the Lutheran Church's relationship to the state, Flacius relied on Magdeburg's city council for protection, support, and resistance to the old religion, an arrangement much more akin to the Reformed model of reformation. In contrast, Hooper endeavored to win over and then work through a prince, King Edward VI, for the implementation of religious reform, which aligns much more closely with the traditional pattern of Lutheran reform. This analysis of both men thus challenges traditional models and historiographical assumptions in important ways.

6. Ilić, *Theologian of Sin and Grace*, 93.

Flacius wrote and campaigned against the newly instituted "adiaphora" during a time of war. Magdeburg was under siege; the Schmalkaldic League had been defeated. Lutheranism appeared on the brink of collapse. Until Moritz decided to turn against the emperor, there was absolutely no prospect of a military defeat of Charles V. Magdeburg could not withstand its siege forever. In contrast, Hooper wrote during a time of peace. The uprisings of 1549 were certainly fresh in the minds of Edward VI and those in power, but the new king was rather solidly entrenched and there was no foreign threat at the time. Religious reform could spark hostility, but Henry VIII had weathered such storms fairly well, and there was good reason to assume that Edward VI would be able to do so as well. Evangelicals in England were optimistic, some more cautiously so than others, but optimistic nonetheless. Reform, and Reformed reform at that, was advancing apace, with Edward's approval. The chief concern was to make sure that it progressed neither too quickly, losing those it might otherwise bring along through gradualism, nor too slowly, opening a door for loud and seditious opposition from radicals or jeopardizing its eventual completion. Hooper certainly posed a threat to the former and in the minds of his opponents advocated the latter. At this time, Hooper, as well as Cranmer and Ridley, expected that completion to resemble what had taken place in Zurich. Geneva was largely off their theological radar. That is no doubt what stung his opponents so deeply about his polemics against vestments. They were all Reformed theologians—Cranmer had clearly joined that camp by this time. They all wanted for the most part the same things. Yet, that being the case, Hooper still caused a stir. He jeopardized the relationship between the church's leaders and the new king, between the bishops of England in general and the Reformed bishops holding preeminent seats of power in specific. Even having done so, though, he was promoted by a friendly king amenable to his theology and gracious about his stubborn demands.

Unlike Hooper, Flacius wrote, not as reformation advanced in Germany, but as Luther's Reformation was in retreat and a nascent Counter-Reformation steadily made gains through imperial military successes. Soldiers surrounded the gates of Magdeburg. Theologians undermined the foundations of Luther's reform. Flacius believed that through the concessions of Melanchthon, the Wittenbergers, and other Adiaphorists, the very heart and core of German Protestantism was at risk. Even the doctrine of justification, he held, was being adulterated, watered down into obscurity. While Hooper wanted to speed up the reform of England. Flacius labored desperately to stunt the gains of imperial counter-reform. Just as Hooper debated those who were, like him, Reformed in their theological convictions, some of Flacius' chief opponents were also Lutherans. Flacius, however, insisted that they had become so only in name, that they had forfeited the very essence of Lutheranism, by working with the emperor and drafting a compromise formula that reintroduced liturgical practices and doctrinal ambiguity under compulsion. This was not a debate over the pace of reform, but its very survival. Even his opponents recognized that the churches of the *Augsburg Confession* were in serious danger, although they took a different route, buying time through concessions in the hope that the political and military climate would change.

Hooper wrote under less pressing political situations and without any comparable looming threats to the English Reformation outside of those which had been in play internally since Henry's break with Rome. The utter lack of apocalypticism in his writings is perhaps evidence of this. While Bullinger's writings did bear apocalyptic themes in instances, especially when commenting on apocalyptical literature from the Bible, and although Hooper certainly recognized that the church found itself in the end times, in his sermons and his "Notes," he seldom sounded apocalyptical alarms or took up such themes. This stands in stark contrast to Flacius' pamphlets. The Last Day made almost no appearance in Hooper's Vestment Controversy polemics, while it hovered over nearly every page of Flacius' controversial writings. Hooper's enemies did not take on the personas of the protagan-ists of Revelation, and while Hooper occasionally mentioned the Antichrist, the Antichrist did not figure prominently in his sermons on Jonah and his "Notes." Flacius, on the other hand, consistently processed the events and threats of his day through an apocalyptic lens—this was a continuation and perhaps the final battle of an age-old war between Christ and Antichrist, God and the devil. While Hooper certainly framed his struggle as a response to an attack on Christ's Word, Flacius pictured his fight as a counter-attack against an assault on Christ himself. One does not get this sense in Hooper's writings. Hooper certainly believed in Christ's return, but he simply did not appeal to it like Flacius. While he did not paint his opponents in a favorable light and was clear that their arguments were unscriptural and did not serve for the benefit of Christ's churches, he did not depict them with such vigor and so bluntly as the age-old enemies of the Christian Church and Jesus Christ himself. An observation from a recent volume sheds some light on why this might be and how it relates to the theology of Zurich: "Our purpose is to examine how the leaders of the Reformation in Zurich looked to the past to make sense of their present and to give shape to a reformed Christian community. A community, they believed, that even in its imperfections was eschatological. The heavenly kingdom could in part be realized, awaiting its fulfillment at the end of time."[7]

7. Baschera, Gordon and Moser, *Following Zwingli*, 10.

The political and military instability in Germany also manifested itself in Flacius' use of outsiders in his writings, especially outsiders who posed a military threat to Germany like the Turks and the Spaniards, to which he likened his opponents. Hooper, on the other hand, did not compare his opponents to Turks, Mamluks, Jews, or Spaniards. His opponents were Englishmen, like him, involved in a skirmish over the path the reform of the English Church should take. He focused upon the priests and bishops within the church, who were undermining the progress of Protestant reform and clinging to the old religion. Such foes threatened the stability of England as a whole, and in Hooper's mind the vitality of the English state and the church were inseparable. While Flacius certainly recognized internal threats to the Lutheran Church—the Adiaphorists certainly qualify—he often projected even their opposition upon external forces like the Antichrist and the devil, and likened their hostility to that of external threats like the Turks and the Spaniards, the pope and the emperor. Interestingly, though, while he made appeals to German national sentiment, although a foreigner himself, he did not connect nearly as closely the survival and well-being of the German nation with that of the German Church, as Hooper did with things political and ecclesiastical in England. There was no German Church in Flacius' view. There was the true Church in Germany, the churches of the *Augsburg Confession*, constricted neither by national, temporal, ethnic boundaries. Contemporary threats to the Lutheran Church reflected for Flacius, not the ineffectual and unspiritual rule of a king to be remedied by a new, godly king, as so often happened in the Old Testament, but the handiwork of the devil himself, who utilized especially the yielding of theologians for his cause, and endeavored to accomplish nothing less than the silencing of the gospel and thus the death of the Christian Church. Such obstacles prefigured, not God's imminent judgment, which would last until king and people repented, but rather Christ's imminent return, at which time there would no longer be opportunity for repentance. It was because they threatened the vitality of the Christian Church and led souls to destruction, then, that Flacius could compare his enemies within the church to enemies without like Turks and Mamluks.

The different religious and political climates in which both men operated are also reflected in the illustrations and examples Flacius and Hooper employed as they made their respective cases. Flacius appealed more to the New Testament and especially the Apocrypha and church history than Hooper, which might be expected given his aptitude and acumen as a church historian, made famous through his later *Catalogus testium veritatis* and *Ecclesiastica Historia*. Both Flacius and Hooper made extensive use of the Old Testament, however, although they focused on radically different aspects of it. Hooper understandably focused upon the godly and ungodly kings of Judah and Israel, the former for encouragement and the latter for warning for the young monarch, Edward VI. He focused upon how Israel and Judah were ruled when they were ruled well. The remnant made little to no appearance in Hooper's writings, and yet the remnant permeated Flacius' pamphlets. While Flacius focused on how the faithful remained faithful, often under the tyranny of godless rule or in the depths of exile, Hooper focused upon the Old Testament pattern of suffering and afflic- tion as a consequence of sin. Those afflicted in Hooper's Old Testament accounts were usually the impenitent, those who had turned from the Lord and his ways and thus have come under his wrath. Hooper stressed the Old Testament pattern that the rule of a good king prospered, while the rule of a bad king brought every misfortune. Flacius, on the other hand, framed suffering as a result of Christian fortitude, as an attack on faith- ful preaching and teaching. In Flacius' OT references, the afflicted suffered most often, not because they had wandered, but because they had stood fast in the truth. They bore crosses and not God's wrath. The Lord disci- plined these faithful in love and does not punish them in anger. Moreover, Haberkern rightly observes that "according to a Lutheran theology of the cross, this suffering was an indelible mark of the true church and conferred soteriological benefits to the victims of persecution."[8]

Ultimately, Hooper wanted more Josiahs, Flacius more Elijahs. Hoop- er wanted a godly England, Flacius a Germany where the gospel could be preached. Flacius, unlike Hooper, made no appeal for an official, national, legislated orthodoxy in Germany. He wrote, after all, as the governing au- thorities had made obvious their failure to support and preserve evangelical preaching and teaching in their midst. Flacius sought not official policy, but grassroots steadfastness in the Word of God and Luther's teaching. Hooper, on the contrary, saw little hope for meaningful religious reform and fidelity among the laity apart from the guidance, example, and even legislation of the king. Hooper wanted the church regulated by a faithful king. Flacius wanted the church preserved through a steadfast remnant.

Throughout the flurry of publications issued from Magdeburg during the crisis sparked by the *Leipzig Interim*, Flacius articulated a clear theol- ogy of the cross, unmistakably marked by that of his mentor and teacher, Martin Luther. The Christian—and Christian theologians and pastors above all—not only had to be ready to suffer for the gospel, but needed to expect to suffer for the same. Like Christ, Christians had to suffer for

---

8. Haberkern, "Flacius' Human Face of Doctrine," 148.

the truth, even though they posed no real threat to the state, but instead served as the best citizens. In Flacius' mind, there could be no greater honor than to suffer so for Jesus. Suffering was inevitable in a fallen world. One might as well suffer for a good cause. Jesus' words from Mark 8 permeate his message: "If anyone would come after me, let him deny himself and take up his cross and follow me. For whoever would save his life will lose it, but whoever loses his life for my sake and the gospel's will save it."[9] On the contrary, the cross made few appearances in Hooper's writings, and when it did, there was seldom, if ever, a line connecting Christ's cross and the cross of the Christian. The doctrine of justification was evident, but not explicit. The age-old threat to the Christian Church was presented, not as an attack on justification by grace alone through faith alone, but on the Reformation *sola scriptura*. His struggle was for the primacy of the Scriptures, and the primitive, apostolic simplicity that should, in Hooper's expectation, flow from the same as a bulwark against superstition. Both men saw the bedrocks of Protestantism threatened, but in different ways, attacked from different sides, and with different risks.

Hooper and Flacius expressed their larger theological framework through the lens of adiaphora. Flacius proved himself a student of Luther and Melanchthon, even as he fell into disagreement with the latter. Hooper sought to emulate in England what he had imbibed of the approach and practice of the Swiss Reformation while in Zurich, even though his zeal surpassed Bullinger's pastoral counsel in this specific case. It is important to note that neither were radicals at this point in any meaningful sense. Hooper did seem to lack some of Bullinger's pastoral inclination toward gradualism and moderation, and yet he was working within the boundaries of the Church of England and not outside of them. Flacius was well inside the Lutheran mainstream that existed prior to the eruption of the Adiaphoristic Controversy, and, after the controversy, he remained within the confines of the larger structure of German Lutheranism, a prominent professor at Jena. Until the outbreak of the subsequent debate over original sin, he served as a respected scholar and spokesman for orthodox Lutheranism. After he accepted the call to Jena but before he began his work there, he was also called to teach at the University of Heidelberg at the invitation of the Elector of the Palatinate.[10] This was one of but several opportunities. His abilities were recognized and sought by more than the deposed Saxon elector, therefore. His reputation was noteworthy outside of his immediate confines. Hooper was outside the norm of the English Reformation when it came to his approach

---

9. Mark 8:34, 35 ESV.

10. Ilić, *Theologian of Sin and Grace*, 136.

to vestments, but this was more a matter of being out of step than out of the boundaries. Moreover, he was well within the mainstream when it came to his position regarding the Act of Supremacy and his willingness to submit the English throne, even unto death under Queen Mary.

Ultimately, Flacius objected to the purported adiaphora of the *Leipzig Interim* in order to preserve the foundations of the Lutheran Reformation as he understood them and had grown to cherish them while in Wittenberg, utilizing both Luther's doctrine and Melanchthon's methods, clearly analyzing his opponents' arguments and then carefully exposing their weaknesses. Hooper objected to the purported adiaphora of Cranmer, Ridley, and their gradualism because he was a product of Zurich's theology and practice, adopted though he was as an Englishman. Impressed with the success and thoroughness of the reformation in Zurich, he returned to England, with Bullinger's blessing, hoping to encourage reform along similar lines. His opponents were also concerned about adiaphora, but they sought to phase them out over time.

Hooper and Flacius both engaged in a fight over adiaphora, but with different aims. Flacius, who certainly taught the supremacy and doctrinal authority of Scripture alone in the church, fought for the survival of the doctrine of justification by grace through faith alone, a doctrine Hooper likewise accepted, although with different nuances and with application through different means. Hooper fought against those who shared his convictions regarding the doctrine of justification for the doctrinal authority of Scripture alone in the church, a conviction his opponents likewise shared, although with different applications in the realm of adiaphora. Two adopted sons thus struggled for the life of what they held to be the most foundational doctrines of Protestant reform—*sola scriptura* and *sola gratia* respectfully—on the battlefield of things indifferent, adiaphora. As they did so, they fought against vestments, ceremonies, and rites which they held to be inconsistent with true reformation, in Hooper's case, because they had no biblical basis and, in Flacius' case, because they were introduced unbiblically, that is, without good order and contrary to the will and consent of the faithful. While the two men differed on what constituted adiaphora, they shared a zeal for the truth and a love for the Christian Scriptures. In the quest for and defense of the truth, however, they looked to the Bible for different proofs, employed different examples, and emphasized different themes and teachings. For this reason, the two controversies were more dissimilar than similar and the divergence between the Lutheran influence on Henry VIII's reform, especially under Cromwell, and the Zwinglian inclinations of Edward VI's were clearly more pronounced than ever before. Flacius' stand on adiaphora rested on principle, Hooper's on precept. Flacius' objections were contextual, Hooper's unconditioned. Flacius saw the devil behind the chorrock, or surplice. Hooper just saw the surplice. The vestment was not part of a ploy. The vestment was in and of itself a problem. Therein rests the biggest different in their doctrines of adiaphora.

Bibliography

Primary Sources

Bekenntnis Unterricht und vermanung der Pfarrhern und Prediger der Christlichen Kirchen zu Magdeburgk. Magdeburg: Lotther, 1550.

Cargill Thompson, W. D. J. *The Political Thought of Martin Luther.* Edited by Philip Broadhead. Sussex, UK: Harvester, 1984.

Chemnitz, Martin. *Examination of the Council of Trent.* Vol. 2. Translated by Fred Kramer. St. Louis: Concordia, 1978.

Cochrane, Arthur C., ed. *Reformed Confessions of the Sixteenth Century.* Louisville: Westminster John Knox, 2003.

Christmas, H., ed. *Original Letters Relative to the English Reformation.* 2 vols. Cambridge: Cambridge University Press, 1856).

Confessio et Apologia Pastorum & reliquorum ministrorum Ecclesiae Magdeburgensis. Magdeburg: Lotther, 1550.

Flacius Illyricus, Matthias. *Bericht M. Fla. Jllyrici, Von etlichen Artikeln der Christlichen Lehr, und von seinem Leben, und enlich auch von den Adiaphorischen Handlungen, wider die falschen Geticht der Adiaphoristen.* Jena: Rebart, 1559.

———. *Breves Summae Religionis Iesu Christi, & Antichristi.* Magdeburg: Lotter, 1550.

———. *Clavis Scripturae Sacrae, seu de Sermone Sacrarum literarum.* Basel: Oporinus & Episcopius, 1567.

———. *Clavis Scripturae, seu de Sermone Sacrarum Literarum, plurimas generales Regulas continens. Altera Pars.* Basel, 1567.

———. *Ein buch, von waren und falschen Mitteldingen, Darin fast der gantze handel von Mitteldingen erkleret wird, widder die schedliche Rotte der Adiaphoristen. Item ein brieff des ehrwirdigen Herrn D. Joannis Epini superintendenten zu Hamburg, auch von diesem handel an Illyricum geschrieben.* Magdeburg: Rödinger, 1550.

———. *Eine Christliche vermanung zur bestendigkeit, inn der waren reinen Religion Jhesu Christi, unnd inn der Augsburgischen bekentnis. Geschrieben an die Meissnische Kirche, unnd andere, so das lautere Evangelium Jhesu Christi erkant haben.* Magdeburg: Lotter, 1550.

———. *Entschuldigung Matthiae Flacij Illyrici, geschrieben an die Universitet zu Wittemberg der Mittelding halben. Item sein brief an Philip. Melanthonem sampt etlichen andern schrifften dieselbige sach belangend. Verdeudscht.* Magdeburg: Rödinger, 1549.

―――. *Epistola S. Hulrici episcopi Augustani, circiter ante sexcentos et 50 annos, ad Pontificem Nicolaum primum, pro fefensone coniugii Sacerdotum, scripta, ex qua apparet, quam impudenter Papistae S. Patres jactent, cum et vita et doctrina cum S. Patribus plane ex Diametra pungent.* Magdeburg: Lotter, 1549

―――. *Ein geistlicher trost dieser betrübten Magdeburigschen Kerchen Christi, das sie diese Verfolgung umb Gottes worts, und keiner andern ursach halben, leidet.* Magdeburg: Lotter, 1551.

―――. *Qvod hoc tempore nulla penitus mutatio in religion sit in gratiam impiorum facienda. Contra quoddam scriptum incerti autoris* [Melanchton] *in quo suadetur mutatio piarum caeremoniarum in Papisticas per Hemannum Primatem.* Magdeburg: Lotter, 1549.

―――. *Eine schöne Historia von der standfaftigkeit des heiligen mans Basilij, beschrieben in der Tripartita Historia, und ander schöne Exampel mehr itzt zu dieser zeit sehr tröstlich und nützlich zu lesen.* Magdeburg: Rödinger, 1549.

―――. *Der Theologen bedencken, odder (wie es durch die ihren inn offentlichem Drück genennet wirdt) Beschluss des Landtages zu Leiptzig, so im December des 48. Jars, von wegen des Auspurgischen* [sic] *Interims gehalten ist. Welchs bedencken odder beschluss wir, so da widder geschrieben, das Leiptzgische Interim gennet haben. Mit einer Vorrede und Scholien, was und warumb jedes stück bisher fur unchristlich darin gestraffet ist.* Magdeburg: Lotter, 1550.

―――. *Ein vermanung zur bestendigkeit, in bekentnis der warheit, Creutz, und Gebett, in dieser betrübten zeit sehr nützlich und tröstlich.* Magdeburg: Lotter, 1549.

―――. *Vermanung Matth. Flacii Illyrici zur gedult und glauben zu Gott, im Creutz dieser verfolgung Geschrieben an die Kirche Christi zu Magdeburg.* Magdeburg: Rödinger, 1551.

Henetus, Theodor [Matthias Flacius Illyricus]. *Ein kurtzer bericht vom Jnterim. Durch Theodorum. Henetum allen frommen Christen.* Magdeburg: Lotter, 1548.

Henry VIII. *Assertio Septem Sacramentorum; or, Defence of the Seven Sacraments.* Re-edited by Louis O'Donovan. New York: Benziger Bros., 1908.

Hooper, John. *Early Writings.* Edited by S. Carr. Cambridge: Cambridge University Press, 1843.

―――. *Later Writings.* Edited by C. Nevinson. Cambridge: Cambridge University Press, 1852.

―――. *An Oversight and Deliberation upon the Holy Prophet Johan; Made and Uttered before the King's Majesty, and His Most Honourable Council.* In *Writings of Dr. John Hooper, Bishop of Gloucester and Worcester, martyr, 1555,* 85–192. London: Clowes, 1831.

Hopf, ed. "Bishop Hooper's 'Notes to the King's Council." *Journal of Theological Studies* 44 (1943) 194–99.

Kolb, Robert, and James A. Nestingen, eds. *Sources and Contexts of the Book of Concord.* Minneapolis: Fortress, 2001.

Kolb, Robert, and Timothy J. Wengert, eds. *The Book of Concord: The Confessions of the Evangelical Lutheran Church.* Minneapolis: Fortress, 2000.

Lasco , Johannes à. *Opera.* Edited by Abraham Kuyper. Amsterdam: Muller, 1866.

Luther Bibel, 1545.

Luther, Martin. *Luthers Works, American Edition.* 55 vols. Edited by Jaroslav Pelikan and Helmut T. Lehman. Philadelphia: Fortress and St. Louis: Concordia, 1955–1986.

More, Sir Thomas. *The Complete Works of St. Thomas More.* Vol. 5, *Responsio ad Lutherum.* Edited by John M. Headley. New Haven: Yale University Press, 1969.

Ridley, Nicholas. "Reply of Bishop Ridley to Bishop Hooper on the Vestment Controversy, 1550." In *The Writings of John Bradford: Letters, Treatises, Remains,* edited by Aubrey Townsend, 375–95. Cambridge: Parker Society, 1853.

———. *Treatises and Letters of Dr. Nicholas Ridley, Bishop of London, and Martyr, 1555.* London: Religious Tract Society, 1830.

———. *Works.* Edited by H. Christmas. Cambridge: Cambridge University Press, 1843.

Waremundus, Johannes [Matthias Flacius Illyricus]. *Ein gemeine protestation und Klagschrifft aller frommen Christen wieder das Jnterim und grausame verfolgung der wiedersacher des Evangelij.* Magdeburg: Lotter, 1548.

Secondary Sources

Althaus, Paul. *The Ethics of Martin Luther.* Translated by Robert C. Schultz. Philadelphia: Fortress, 1972.

Andersson, Daniel. Review of *John Hooper: Tudor Bishop and Martyr,* by D. G. Newcombe. *English Historical Review* 127, no. 524 (2012) 159–61.

Arand, Charles P., Robert Kolb, and James A. Nestingen. *The Lutheran Confessions: History and Theology of the Book of Concord.* Minneapolis: Fortress, 2011.

Bainton, Roland. *Here I Stand: A Life of Martin Luther.* Nashville: Abingdon–Cokesbury, 1950.

Baschera, Luca, Bruce Gordon and Christian Moser, eds. *Following Zwingli: Applying the Past in Reformation Zurich.* Burlington, VT: Ashgate, 2014.

Bente, F. "Historical Introductions to the Symbolical Books of the Evangelical Lutheran Church." In *Concordia Triglotta: The Symbolical Books of the Ev. Lutheran Church,* 1–256. St. Louis: Concordia, 1921.

Bernard, G. W. *The King's Reformation: Henry VIII and the Remaking off the English Church.* New Haven: Yale University Press, 2005.

Brecht, Martin. *Martin Luther: His Road to Reformation, 1483–1521.* Translated by James L. Schaaf. Minneapolis: Fortress, 1993.

Brecht, Martin. *Martin Luther: Shaping and Defining the Reformation, 1521–1532.* Translated by James L. Schaaf. Minneapolis: Fortress, 1994.

Brecht, Martin. *Martin Luther: The Preservation of the Church, 1532–1546.* Translated by James L. Schaaf. Minneapolis: Fortress, 1999.

Christman, Robert J. *Doctrinal Controversy and Lay Religiosity in Late Reformation Germany: The Case of Mansfeld.* Studies in Medieval and Reformation Traditions. Leiden: Brill, 2012.

———. "'Wir sindt nichts den eytel sunde': The Impact of Flacius' Theology of Original Sin on the German Territory of Mansfield." In *Matija Vlacic Ilirik (III): Proceedings of the Third International Conference on Matthias Flacius Illyricus, Labin, Coratia, 2010,* edited by Marina Miladinov and Luka Ilić, 106–21. Labin: Grad Labin, 2012.

Collinson, Patrick. *Birthpangs of Protestant England: Religion and Cultural Change in the Sixteenth and Seventeenth Centuries.* London: Macmillan, 1988.

Counsel, George Worall. *Some Account of the Life and Martyrdom of John Hooper, D.D.* Gloucester, 1840.

Davies, C. "'Poor Persecuted Little Flock' or 'Commonwealth of Christians': Edwardian Protestant Concepts of the Church." In *Protestantism and the National Church in Sixteenth Century England*, edited by Peter Lake and Maria Dowling, 78–102. London: Croon Helm, 1987.

Deibler, Edwin Clyde, Jr. "Bishop John Hooper, a Link Connecting the Reformation Thought of Ulrich Zwingli and the Zürich Tradition with the Earliest English Pietistic Puritanism." PhD diss., Temple University, 1970.

Dickens, A. G. "The Early Expansion of Protestantism in England, 1520–1558." *Archiv für Reformationsgeschichte* 78 (1987) 187–222.

Dingel, Irene. "Bekenntnis und Geschichte: Funktion und Entwicklung des reformatischen Bekenntnisses im 16. Jahrhundert." In *Dona Melanchthoniana: Festgabe für Heinz Scheible zum 70. Geburtstag*, edited by Johanna Loehr, 61–81. Stuttgart: Evangelische Friedrich Frommann, 2001.

———. *Concordia controversa: Die öffentlichen Diskussionen um das lutherische Konkordienwerk am Ende des 16. Jahrhunderts.* Göttingen: Gütersloher, 1996.

———. "The Culture of Conflict in the Controversies Leading to the Formula of Concord (1548–1560)." In *Lutheran Ecclesiastical Culture, 1550–1675*, edited by Robert Kolb, 15–64. Leiden: Brill, 2008.

———. "Flacius als Schüler Luthers und Melanchthons." In *Vestigia Pietatis: Studien zur Geschichte der Frömmigkeit in Thüringen und Sachsen*, edited by Gerhard Graf, Hans-Peter Hasse, and Ernst Koch, 77–93. Leipzig: Evangelische, 2000.

Dingel, Irene, ed. *Der Adiaphoristische Streit (1548–1560).* Controversia et Confessio. Theologische Kontroversen 1548–1577/1580: Kritische Auswahledition 2. Göttingen: Vandenhoeck & Ruprecht, 2010.

———. *Reaktionen auf das Augsburger Interim: Der Interimistische Streit (1548–1549).* [Controversia et Confessio. Theologische Kontroversen 1548–1577/1580: Kritische Auswahledition. Vol. 2]. Göttingen: Vandenhoeck & Ruprecht GmbH & Co., 2010.

Dingel, Irene, and Günther Wartenberg, eds. *Politik und Bekenntnis: Die Reaktionen auf das Interim von 1548.* Leipzig: Evangelische, 2006.

Doernberg, Erwin. *Henry VIII and Luther: An Account of their Personal Relations.* London: Barrie and Rockliff, 1961.

Duffy, Eamon. *Fires of Faith: Catholic England under Mary Tudor.* New Haven: Yale University Press, 2009.

———. *The Stripping of the Altars: Traditional Religion in England c. 1400–c.1580.* New Haven: Yale University Press, 1992.

Elton, G. R. *England under the Tudors.* 2nd ed. New York: Methuen, 1974.

———. *Reformation Europe 1517–1559.* 2nd ed. Malden, MA: Blackwell, 1999.

Estes, James M., ed. and trans. *Godly Magistrates and Church Order: Johannes Brenz and the Establishment of the Lutheran Territorial Church in Germany 1524–1559.* Toronto: Centre for Reformationand Renaissance Studies, 2001.

Euler, Carrie. *Couriers of the Gospel: England and Zurich (1531–1558).* Zurich: Theologischer Verlag Zurich, 2006.

———. "Does Faith Translate? Tudor Translations of Martin Luther and the Doctrine of Justification by Faith." *Archiv Für Reformationgeschichte* 101 (2010) 80–113.

Forde, Gerhard O. *On Being a Theologian of the Cross: Reflections on Luther's Heidelberg Disputation, 1518.* Grand Rapids: Eerdmans, 1997.

Friedeburg, Robert von. *Europa in der frühen Neuzeit.* Frankfurt: Fischer, 2012.

————. "In Defence of Patria: Resisting Magistrates and the Duties of Patriots in the Empire from the 1530s to the 1640s." *Sixteenth Century Journal* 32, no. 2 (2001) 357–82.

————. *Self-Defence and Religious Strife in Early Modern Europe: England and Germany, 1530–1680.* Burlington, VT: Ashgate, 2002.

————. *Widerstandsrecht und Konfessionskonflict: Gemeiner Mann und Notwehr im deustch brittischen Vergleich, 1530–1669.* Berlin: Dunker & Humblot GmbH, 1999.

Friedeburg, Robert von, ed. *Widerstandsrecht in der Frühen Neuzeit.* Berlin: Dunker & Humblot GmbH, 2001.

Genischen, Hans–Werner. *We Condemn: How Luther and 16th–Lutheranism Condemned False Doctrine.* Translated by Herbert J. A. Bouman. St. Louis: Concordia, 1967.

Gordon, Bruce. *The Swiss Reformation.* Manchester: Manchester University Press, 2002.

Greschat, Martin, ed. *Personlexikon Religion und Theologie.* Göttingen: Vandenhoeck & Ruprecht, 1998.

Gwyn, Peter. *The King's Cardinal: The Rise and Fall of Thomas Wolsey.* London: Barrie & Jenkins, 1990.

Haberkern, Phillip, "Flacius' Human Face of Doctrine: Sacred History Between Prosopography and Dogmatics." In *Matija Vlacic Ilirik (III): Proceedings of the Third International Conference on Matthias Flacius Illyricus, Labin, Coratia, 2010,* edited by Marina Miladinov and Luka Ilić, 140–65. Labin: Grad Labin, 2012.

Haigh, Christopher. *English Reformations: Religion, Politics, and Society under the Tudors.* Oxford: Clarendon, 1993.

Haug–Moritz, Gabriele. *Der Schmalkaldische Bund, 1530–1541/42.* Leinfelden–Echterdingen: DRW–Verlag Weinbrenner GmbH & Co., 2002.

Hendrix, Scott H. *Martin Luther: Visionary Reformer.* New Haven: Yale University Press, 2015.

Hopf, C., ed. "Bishop Hooper's 'Notes to the King's Council." *Journal of Theological Studies* 44 (1943) 194–99.

————. *Martin Bucer and the English Reformation.* Oxford: Blackwell, 1946.

Hunt, E.W. *The Life and Times of John Hooper (c. 1500–1555) Bishop of Gloucester.* Lewiston, NY: Mellen, 1992.

Ilić, Luka. "'Der Heilige Man und thewre held': Flacius' View of Luther." In *Matija Vlacic Ilirik (III): Proceedings of the Third International Conference on Matthias Flacius Illyricus, Labin, Coratia, 2010,* edited by Marina Miladinov and Luka Ilić, 294–315. Labin: Grad Labin, 2012.

————. *Theologian of Sin and Grace: The Process of Radicalization in the Theology of Matthias Flacius Illyricus.* Göttingen: Vandenhoeck & Ruprecht, 2014.

Jürgens, Henning P. "Der Konflict zwischen Matthias Flacius und Philipp Melanchthon in der Sicht des Johannes Cochläus: Die Schrift De Excusatione Philippi Melanchthonis, Adversus clamores Flacij Illyrici." In *Matija Vlacic Ilirik (III): Proceedings of the Third International Conference on Matthias Flacius Illyricus, Labin, Coratia, 2010,* edited by Marina Miladinov and Luka Ilić, 214–238. Labin: Grad Labin, 2012.

Kaufmann, Thomas. *Das Ende der Reformation.* Tübingen: Mohr/Siebeck, 2003.

————. *Konfession und Kultur.* Tübingen: Mohr/Siebeck, 2006.

————. "Matthias Flacius Illyricus. Lutherischer Theologe und Magdeburer Publizist." In *Mitteldeutsche Lebensbilder: Menschen im Zeitalter der Reformation,* edited by Werner Freitag, 177–200. Köln: Böhlau, 2004.

————. "'Our Lord God's Chancery' in Magdeburg and Its Fight against the Interim." *Church History* 73, no. 3 (September 2004) 566–82.

Kittelson, James M. *Luther the Reformer: The Story of the Man and His Career.* Minneapolis: Fortress, 1986.

Klann, R. "Article I. Original Sin." In *A Contemporary Look at the Formula of Concord,* edited by Wilbert Rosin and Robert Preus, 103–21. St. Louis: Concordia, 1978.

Knappen, M. M. *Tudor Protestantism.* Chicago: University of Chicago Press, 1939.

Kohnle, Armin. *Reichstag und Reformation.* Heidelberg: Verein für Reformationsgeschichte, 2001.

Kolb, Robert. *Bound Choice, Election, and Wittenberg Theological Method.* Grand Rapids: Eerdmans, 2005.

———. *The Christian Faith: A Lutheran Exposition.* St. Louis: Concordia, 1993.

———. *Martin Luther as Prophet, Teacher, and Hero: Images of the Reformer, 1520–1620.* Grand Rapids: Baker, 1999.

———. *Martin Luther: Confessor of the Faith.* Christian Theology in Context. Oxford: Oxford University Press, 2009.

Kolb, Robert, ed. *Lutheran Ecclesiastical Culture, 1550–1675.* Leiden: Brill, 2008.

Kolb, Robert, and Charles P. Arand. *The Genius of Luther's Theology: A Wittenberg Way of Thinking for the Contemporary Church.* Grand Rapids: Baker Academic, 2008.

Lake, Peter. *Anglicans and Puritans? Presbyterianism and English Conformist Thought.* Boston: Allen & Unwin, 1988

Lindberg, Carter. *The European Reformations.* 2nd ed. Malden, MA: Blackwell, 2010.

Lindberg, Carter, ed. *The Reformation Theologians: An Introduction to Theology in the Early Modern Period.* Oxford: Blackwell, 2002.

Litzenberger, Caroline. *The English Reformation and the Laity: Glouchestershire, 1540–1580.* Cambridge: Cambridge University Press, 1997.

Loach, Jennifer. *Edward VI.* New Haven: Yale University Press, 2002.

MacCulloch, Diarmaid. *The Boy King: Edward VI and thre Protestant Reformation.* Berkeley: University of California Press, 2002.

———. *The Later Reformation in England, 1547–1603.* 2nd ed. New York: Palgrave, 2001.

———. *The Reformation: A History.* New York: Penguin, 2005.

———. *Thomas Cranmer: A Life.* New Haven: Yale University Press, 1996.

Marquardt, Kurt. "Article X. Confession and Ceremonies." In *A Contemporary Look at the Formula of Concord,* edited by Wilbert Rosin and Robert D. Preus, 260–70. St. Louis: Concordia, 1978.

McCutcheon, R. R. "The Responsio ad Lutherum: Thomas More's Inchoate Dialogue with Heresy." *Sixteenth Century Journal* 22, no. 1 (1991) 77–90.

Meyer, John. *Studies in the Augsburg Confession.* Milwaukee: Northwestern, 1995.

Miller, Gregory J. "Hyldrych Zwingli (1484–1531)." In *The Reformation Theologians: An Introduction to Theology in the Early Modern Period,* edited by Carter Lindberg, 157–69. Malden, MA: Blackwell, 2002.

Moritz, Anja. *Interim und Apokalypse.* Tübingen: Mohr/Siebeck, 2009.

Nestingen, James A. *Martin Luther: A Life.* Minneapolis: Fortress, 2003.

Newcombe, D. G. *John Hooper: Tudor Bishop and Martyr.* Oxford: Davenant, 2009.

Noll, Mark. *Turning Points: Decisive Moments in the History of Christianity.* 3rd ed. Grand Rapids: Baker, 2012.

Oberman, Heiko A. *Luther: Man between God and the Devil.* New York: Image, 1992.

Olsen, V. Norskov. *The New Testament Logia on Divorce: A Study of their Interpretation from Milton to Erasmus.* Tübingen: Mohr, 1971.

Olson, Oliver K. *Matthias Flacius and the Survival of Luther's Reform.* Wiesbaden, Germany: Harrassowitz, 2002.

————. "Matthias Flacius (1520–1575)." In *The Reformation Theologians: An Introduction to the Early Modern Period*, edited by Carter Lindberg, 83–93. Oxford: Blackwell, 2002.

————. *Reclaiming the Lutheran Liturgical Heritage.* Minneapolis: Bronze Bow, 2007.

————. "Theology of Revolution: Magdeburg, 1550–1551." *Sixteenth Century Journal* 3, no. 1 (1972) 56–79.

O'Malley, John W. *Trent: What Happened at the Council.* Cambridge, MA: Belknap, 2013.

Ortmann, Volker. *Reformation und Einheit der Kirche: Martin Bucers Einigungsbemuhungen bei den Religionsgesprachen in Leipzig, Hagenau, Worms und Regensburg 1539–1541.* Mainz: Vandenhoeck & Ruprecht GmbH & Co., 2009.

Osten-Sacken, Vera von der. "Die kleine Herde der 7000—Die aufrechten Bekenner in M. Flacius' Illyricus konzeptionellen Beiträgen zur Neuformulierung der Kirchen-geschichtsschreibung aus protestantischer Sicht." In *Matija Vlacic Ilirik (III): Proceedings of the Third International Conference on Matthias Flacius Illyricus, Labin, Coratia, 2010*, edited by Marina Miladinov and Luka Ilić, 184–213. Labin: Grad Labin, 2012.

Paulson, Steven D. *Lutheran Theology.* New York: T. & T. Clark, 2011.

Pettegree, Andrew. *Brand Luther.* New York: Penguin, 2015.

————. *Europe in the Sixteenth Century.* Malden, MA: Blackwell, 2002.

————. *Foreign Protestant Communities in Sixteenth Century London.* Oxford: Clarendon, 1986.

Pragman, James H. "The Augsburg Confession in the English Reformation: Richard Taverner's Contribution." *Sixteenth Century Journal* 11, no. 3 (1980) 75–85.

Preger, Wilhelm. *Matthias Flacius Illyricus und seine Zeit.* 2 vols. Erlangen: Bläsing, 1859–1861.

Preus, Robert D., ed. *A Contemporary Look at the Formula of Concord.* St. Louis: Concordia, 1978.

Primus, John Henry. *The Vestments Controversy.* Amsterdam: Kampen, 1960.

Rabe, Horst. *Reichsbund und Interim: Die Verfassungs–und Religionspolitik Karls V. und der Reichstag von Augsburg 1547/1548.* Köln: Böhlau, 1971.

Rein, Nathan. *The Chancery of God: Protestant Print, Polemic and Propaganda against the Empire, Magdeburg 1546–1551.* Burlington, VT: Ashgate, 2008.

————. "Faith and Empire: Conflicting Visions of Religion in a Late Reformation Controversy—The Augsburg *Interim* and Its Opponents, 1548–1550." *Journal of the American Academy of Religion* 71, no. 1 (2003) 45–74.

Rex, Richard. "The Crisis of Obedience: God's Word and Henry's Reformation." *Historical Journal* 39, no. 4 (1996) 863–94.

————. "The English Campaign against Luther in the 1520s: The Alexander Prize Essay." *Transactions of the Royal Historical Society* 39 (1989) 85–106.

Ross, Don S. "The Role of John Hooper in the Religious Controversies of the Reign of Edward VI in England." PhD diss., University of Iowa, 1968.

Ryrie, Alec. *Being Protestant in Reformation Britain.* Oxford: Oxford University Press, 2013.

————. *The Gospel and Henry VIII: Evangelicals in the Early English Reformation.* Cambridge: Cambridge University Press, 2003.

————. "The Strange Death of Lutheran England." *Journal of Ecclesiastical History* 53, no. 1 (2002) 64–92.

Rupp, Gordon. *Studies in the Making of the English Protestant Tradition.* Cambridge: Cambridge University Press, 1947.

Scaer, David. *Getting Into the Story of Concord.* St. Louis: Concordia, 1977.

Schmauk, Theodore E., and C. Theodore Benze. *The Confessional Principle and the Confessions of the Lutheran Church.* St. Louis: Concordia, 2005.

Schorn-Schütte, Luise, ed. *Das Interim 1548/50.* Heidelberg: Verein für Reformationsgeschichte, 2005.

Shoenberger, Cynthia Grant. "The Development of the Lutheran Theory of Resistance: 1523–1530." *Sixteenth Century Journal* 8, no. 1 (1977) 61–76.

———. "Luther and the Justifiability of Resistance to Legitimate Authority." *Journal of the History of Ideas* 40, no. 1 (1979) 3–20.

Skidmore, Chris. *Edward VI: The Lost King of England.* New York: St. Martin's Griffin, 2007.

Skinner, Quentin. *The Age of Reformation.* Vol. 2 of *The Foundations of Modern Political Thought.* Cambridge: Cambridge University Press, 1978.

Spitz, Lewis W., and Wenzel Lohff. *Discord, Dialogue, and Concord: Studies in the Lutheran Reformation's Formula of Concord.* Philadelphia: Fortress, 1977.

Steinmetz, David C. *Luther in Context.* 2nd ed. Grand Rapids: Baker Academic, 2002.

———. *Reformers in the Wings: From Geiler von Kaysersberg to Theodore Beza.* 2nd ed. Oxford: Oxford University Press, 2001.

Sullivan, Pete. *John Hooper.* Faverdale, UK: Evangelical, 2004.

Tierney, Brian. *Liberty and Law: The Idea of Permissive Natural Law, 1100–1800.* Washington, DC: Catholic University of America Press, 2014.

Tjernagel, Neelak Serawlook. *Henry VIII and the Lutherans: A Study in Anglo-Lutheran Relations from 1521–1547.* Saint Louis: Concordia, 1965.

Trueman, Carl R. *Salvation and English Reformers, 1525–1556.* Oxford: Clarendon, 1994.

Verkamp, Bernard J. *The Indifferent Mean.* Detroit: Wayne State University Press, 1977.

Walther, C. F. W. *Law and Gospel: How to Read and Apply the Bible.* Translated by Christian C. Tiews. St. Louis: Concordia, 2010.

West, W. Morris S. "John Hooper and the Origins of Puritanism." *Baptist Quarterly* 15, no. 8 (1954) 346–68.

———. "John Hooper and the Origins of Puritanism." *Baptist Quarterly* 16, no. 1 (1955) 22–46.

———. "John Hooper and the Origins of Puritanism." *Baptist Quarterly* 16, no. 2 (1955) 67–88.

Whitford, David M. "Cura Religionis or Two Kingdoms: The Late Luther on Religion and the State in the Lectures on Genesis." *Church History* 73, no. 1 (2004) 41–62.

———. *Tyranny and Resistance: The Magdeburg Confession and the Lutheran Tradition.* St. Louis: Concordia, 2001.

Wilson, R. Paul. "John Hooper and the English Reform under Edward VI, 1547–1553." PhD diss., Queen's University of Kingston, 1994.

Wingren, Gustaf. *Luther on Vocation.* Evansville, IN: Ballast, 1994.

Wolgast, Eike. *Die Religionsfrage als Problem des Widerstandsrechts im 16. Jahrhundert.* Heidelberg: Carl Winter Universitätverlag, 1980.

———. *Die Wittenberg Theologie und die Politik der evangelischen Stände.* Heidelberg: Verein für Reformationsgeschichte, 1977.

Index

Printed in Great Britain
by Amazon